Worlds of Psychotic People

Is there any truth in the old idea that psychotic people have access to a world of meaning which remains locked to others?

Worlds of Psychotic People brings a fresh twenty-first century voice to the lives of those with serious psychological disorders, focusing on the way in which psychiatric patients experience their subjective worlds. Based on ethnographic research gathered at the psychiatric hospital of Saint Anthony's in the Netherlands over a period of five years, it seeks to describe from the perspective of the mental patient some of the fears and hopes that mark an individual's encounter with the reality of a clinical mental ward.

Balancing details from patient interviews and observation with the author's theoretical insights into clinical psychiatric practice, *Worlds of Psychotic People* considers such dilemmas as: how do psychotics struggle to express subjectivity in an atmosphere designed to restrain demonstrative emotion? How do they maintain personal integrity within a completely ordered regime? How do the distinctive symptoms displayed by many psychotic and schizophrenic patients – including disordered speech, the experiencing of words as physical sensations, and fear of touch – interact with the demands of standard therapeutic procedure? Introducing the concept of the psychotic patient as a wanderer through culture, creating a 'bricolage' reality from materials at hand, Els van Dongen aims to open up the often secretive exchanges that take place between therapists and patients, and to seek new meanings and interpretations from these for use within the therapeutic endeavour.

Els van Dongen is a highly respected authority on psychiatric illness and treatment. A senior staff member at the Medical Anthropology unit of the University of Amsterdam, she is co-editor of the book *Health for All, All in Health: European Experiences on Health Care for Migrants* (2000), the author of many books and articles about mental illness and editor of the journal *Medische Antropologie*.

Theory and Practice in Medical Anthropology and International Health

A series edited by Susan M. DiGiacomo, *University of Massachusetts, Amherst*

Worlds of Psychotic People

Wanderers, 'Bricoleurs'
and Strategists

Els van Dongen

Routledge
Taylor & Francis Group

LONDON AND NEW YORK

First published 1994 by Rozenberg Publishers
Rozengracht 176A, 1016 NK Amsterdam

First published in English 2004 by Routledge
2 Park Square, Milton Park, Abingdon, Oxon OX14 4RN

Simultaneously published in the USA and Canada
by Routledge
711 Third Avenue, New York, NY 10017

First issued in paperback 2013

Routledge is an imprint of the Taylor & Francis Group, an informa business

British Library Cataloguing in Publication Data
A catalogue record for this book is available from the
British Library

Library of Congress Cataloging in Publication Data
Dongen, Els van.
  Worlds of psychotic people: wanderers, 'bricoleurs' and
strategists / Els van Dongen.
      p. cm.
  Includes bibliographical references and index.
  1. Psychiatric hospital patients – Netherlands – Case studies.
  I. Title.
  RC450.N4D66 2004
  362.2'1'09492–dc21   2002068147

ISBN 0-415-30390-7
ISBN 978-0-415-65480-7 (Paperback)

Contents

Acknowledgements

Many intense experiences crowded the years that it took me to cover the subject matter of my book. It brought me into contact with people who displayed remarkable patience and persistent humor in dealing with a multitude of difficulties, and yet persevered to communicate with each other in most impressive ways.

Writing a book is seldom a solitary task. In this instance it reflects not only a synthesis of countless discussions held with individuals and groups from within and outside the subject area, but also the highly personalized accounts lived and retold by the individuals whose conversations constitute the core of this book. I want to thank all the assistants and patients whose substantial and concrete contributions I must humbly acknowledge. The warmth with which they received me as an outsider, the patience I was shown and their constructive criticism played a major role in the success of the research. For obvious reasons, I cannot name them.

I wish to express my sincere thanks to all my colleagues who offered suggestions and critiques during my fieldwork and writing, especially Arie de Ruijter and Beke Harms. The Netherlands Scientific Organization (NWO) must be mentioned. They financially supported the research and the translation of my work. Oswald Gibson, my editor, supported me and made my writings 'readable'; thank you, Ossie. I also thank Julene Knox, the editor at Routledge, for her support and understanding, and Susan DiGiacomo, the editor of the series for her patience and valuable comments.

When rewriting the book, I was tempted to eliminate references to some theoretical approaches that now seem outdated. However, on reflection I decided to retain them because they constitute the background – or, in anthropological terms, the context – of my work and that of therapists at the time of my fieldwork.

I would not have been able to complete this book without the enormous support from my family, and I dedicate it to them.

Els van Dongen

Chapter 1

Introduction

Fifty years ago the youngsters in our street played a somewhat dubious but exciting game. In a large house on the corner a crazy woman lived alone. She obviously preferred to keep to herself, she looked strange and she mumbled words that we did not understand – all of which terrified and enthralled us. Our constant taunting was meant to entice her from her house, and not even the intervention of parents had the power to stop us. The climax of the game was reached when she came out to protest at our constant pestering. Marbles and balls were abandoned on the sidewalk as we scattered behind trees in the gardens and listened to her with pounding hearts. Her angry words have faded into memory, but they never failed to enchant. We had come under the spell of the lunacy that dwelt on the corner of the block.

I remembered this children's game some years ago when the psychotic patients of Saint Anthony's, a psychiatric hospital in the Netherlands, played a similar game with me. They would challenge and tease me, and the climax was reached when I became 'furious' and said things that excited them, as they laughed and scattered to their rooms.

Curiosity about the world of insanity transcends all boundaries: for centuries philosophers, historians, psychotics, psychiatrists, anthropologists and psychologists have discussed and described it. Speculation about the realm of psychosis takes diverse forms, and a recurrent idea is that if only we could come to know it, we would gain an understanding of the basic and recondite processes of the human mind. Sometimes there is a spontaneous assumption that psychotic cognition and discourse possess a wealth of significance that far outstrips ordinary thought and speech. Psychotic people are thought to have access to a world of meaning that remains locked to others, even though this approach to the psychotic world order frequently amounts to no more than 'the old Platonic theme of inspired delirium' (Foucault 1966: 71). Mental aberration continues to fascinate, but there is a corresponding interest that has its origin in society's desire to control psychotics and obviate the dangers that they represent. From this perspective, psychosis has also been described and analyzed in many ways. Conventional wisdom holds that the more we know about psychosis, the better we can control and reduce its visible risings. The dual message of concern and interest emphasizes the ambiguous nature of society's response to people who are afflicted with psychosis. This combination of inherent attraction and expectation of heightened significance can confer on psychotics a feeling of being 'special'. Ultimately, though, the fear of losing control (and the consequent threat that this poses to society) conveys to mentally ill people a feeling that they are being excluded and pushed to the margins. We have come to deduce from this that we are supposed to be dealing with two different cultures, comprising this world and an 'other' world. Whatever its origin, fear has repeatedly provided the impetus for concerted efforts to control or expel psychosis.

A thumbnail review of Western thought on the subject reveals that developments such as positivism and rationalism may have helped to achieve better classifications, more effective manipulation and perhaps greater mastery over both 'reality' and the mentally disturbed. However, the way in which society deals with madness has shifted over the past decades from exclusion on moral grounds to exclusion on behavioral grounds. Current views emphasize the form or behavior in which the disorder is expressed. Where it takes an unacceptable form, it can constitute a societal taboo. Psychiatry, being embedded in a socio-cultural system, has changed accordingly. The focus has shifted from an interest in the symbolism of the psychotic world, to no-nonsense treatment of its behavioral aspects. Current developments in psychiatry (biomedicine, pharmaceutical aids, ever-increasing patient loads, austerity measures, etc.) create the potential danger that therapists will opt for short-term 'success' therapies, based on psycho-pharmaceutical drug treatments. In this scenario therapy is deemed to be a success if the patient can function adequately in society, not pose a threat or nuisance to others, and get by individually. Psychiatry has become an 'ego-psychiatry in our modern era of self-help' (Porter 1987). The individualization tendencies that have come to shape society are from the outset also noticeable in psychiatry. The assumption that psychotic people lack reality awareness and reality checks is important in psychiatry because it underscores the otherness mentioned above. To the extent that speech is able to reveal this, much of the existing research into discourse indicates that the experiences of psychotics serve to block normal interaction. The world comprising their experience is an obstacle, presenting a high threshold that must be overcome if there is to be meaningful interaction with psychotics. Taken together, these developments have led to an inadequate appreciation of the ways in which psychotic people experience and make sense of things.

It is remarkable that such a negation and undervaluation should be observed in a Dutch society that is purported to have a high threshold of tolerance for the eccentric and unusual. In spite of the 'creed of empathy' for psychotic people, this negation is found among therapists as well. Psychotic people and therapists often say remarkably similar things about individualism, justice and injustice, authority and dependency, common sense and madness. However, the different ways in which they use these concepts can be quite revealing, because it shows that they do not assign similar meanings to them.

During my research in a psychiatric hospital in the Netherlands, I became aware that the therapists had an image of psychotics as defective, bizarre and incomprehensible people, an image at odds with what I saw and heard as I moved among the patients and examined the sense of conversations between them and their caregivers. What I witnessed was marked by contradiction, ambivalence and paradox, certainly, but it also emerged that the picture being painted of psychotics was partly shaped by the training and theoretical paradigm of therapists and partly infused with personal interpretations and evaluations, i.e. what seemed to make 'sense' to the therapists. I noted that in the encounters between therapist and patient, each knew or recognized the other's concepts, but for various reasons (and not only because a patient lacked reality testing) the interpretations of these concepts could differ radically.

From an anthropological perspective the encounters seemed to be less a confrontation of two worlds and more a mixture of cultural, personal and professional interests, ideas, interpretations and assessments of a world shared by both patients and therapists. Placing itself in opposition to patients, the discipline of psychiatry called attention to the various ways in which one could live as a 'healthy human being' compared with the impossible dead end imposed by madness. As the authoritative discipline in mental health, psychiatry's tale of what constitutes reality is demanded, applauded and taken for granted by society. This tale is pushed center-stage to the degree that the discourses and the words of psychotic people fade into the background. However, as a cultural specialization psychiatry might well consider taking the words of psychotic people more seriously. Perhaps it would be different if the stories of psychotic people no longer needed to agree with or compete against expert discourse, if they were no longer viewed as *other world* stories. Psychotic people certainly transgress culturally imposed boundaries. By the same token, they lack a dimension other than their culture through which to reflect themselves accurately or give significance to their own or other situations: they may depart from the basic premise of 'ordinary' culture but cannot be said to create another culture. My view is that psychotic people neither abrogate the laws of cultural reality nor sever their ties with its formulations. Rather, they specifically and intentionally refer to society's values, norms, views, convictions and ideas and in so doing they call attention to the nature and the limitations of culture (see also Goffman 1961).

Psychotic people have always felt that in order to justify themselves and their way of life, they must repeatedly reinvent their story (Porter 1987). In therapeutic interaction, rapid and optimally efficient transformation of their words and behavior into more acceptable, 'healthier' forms makes it possible to interpret the behavior in a framework where 'the strong' speak about 'the weak', a framework in which the therapist's world order takes precedence over the patient's. However it has never been a discourse of 'the weak about the strong' (Richters 1991). I have observed that psychotic people feel this unequal power relation very keenly. This inevitably leads to problems in therapeutic interaction and results in frequent skirmishes between therapists and patients. To contribute to reflections on these matters and help to reconsider current approaches in dealing with psychotic people, I take constructions of reality as given form and content in the interactions between psychotic patients and therapists, and focus on the cultural aspects of those constructions. The book recounts interviews between psychotics and therapists and is complemented by the fieldwork, studies of patient files and hospital documents, as well as structured and unstructured conversations that I conducted with patients, therapists and nurses in Saint Anthony's psychiatric hospital in southern Netherlands.

Defining the problem

The underlying tenet of this book is that the discourses of psychotic people and the ways in which they articulate subjective meaning do not and cannot receive adequate attention in the current psychiatric hospital setting. This not only hampers healing, but in the process we also forfeit the opportunity to reflect on the negative aspects of our own culture. The perceived inattention to what psychotics are saying is not new in psychiatry. In the context of treatment, earlier attempts to accommodate the psychotic world have prompted a variety of approaches. Both phenomenological psychiatry, in which the focus is the life world of the patient, and anthropological psychiatry, where the focus is on the person as socio-cultural being, give primacy to the ill person rather than the illness itself. Not long ago (in the 1960s and 1970s), a psychiatric 'anti-movement' arose, which aimed its action and protest mostly at institutional psychiatry. An important basic element of 'anti-psychiatry' (which derived its tenets from critical sociology) was its positive appreciation of psychosis. It pointed to social factors as the origin of psychological problems, in stark contrast to the negative way that it was evaluated at the time in psychiatry. At present the debate on psychosis and schizophrenia is divided between those who favor the 'talking cure' and those who prefer to adjust the brain mechanically with a variety of neuro-chemical wrenches (Susan DiGiacomo, personal communication). A compromise would be to view psychosis as culturally defined illness, expressive of both a cultural-social and an organic condition (Estroff 1981).

However, many other approaches are possible. In the interaction between therapists and psychotic people the interpretation of psychotic experiences and its articulation is influenced by the views and values of a culturally determined specialization. Equally, it can be said that those experiences are often taken up into idiosyncratic interpretations of cultural images or even highly personal ideas and images. These begin to reveal the limits of what is possible in a culture, and what can still permissibly 'be said'. Limits and boundaries become very clear in the interactions between therapists and patients, along with the realization that the discourse must stay within a prescribed circle, if communication is to be sustained. Perhaps this is even more pronounced for therapists than for psychotic people, because the former are 'normal' and therefore expected to abide by the rules and norms of predictable behavior, whereas psychotics seem to have dispensed with the restrictions imposed by rules, authority and culture. Like everyone else they have no medium of expression other than that defined by culture, and therefore are expected to abide by the means provided. Owing to their condition, but also because of ostracism and societal character typing, they prefer (or have no option other than) to wander, and to tinker. They roam the world of values, norms, ideas and beliefs, looking for whatever is sufficiently useful to give expression to their musings. Like traveling 'bricoleurs' (Levi-Strauss 1962, 1996), they make specific and intentional use of whatever bits of knowledge or skills they may acquire in their wanderings. However, it will emerge as we progress that they do not act without strategy. It is not so much the uniqueness of wandering, *bricolage* and strategy that render psychotic people distinct from others; the salient feature that sets them apart is an excessive degree of pursuit. Since psychotic people draw on the same cultural course as 'normal' people, their stories display some peculiarities, but they certainly do not lack content. Common relation to this cultural source enables people to know and to understand one another. In order to gain access to these stories more readily, my study concentrates especially on cultural aspects of the interaction between psychotic people and their caregivers. Rather than relying on the deviational use of 'culture' as a means of describing and explaining the psychotic world, I try to show the place, significance and function of culture in the interaction between psychotic people and therapists.

This book reports on the experiential world of psychotic patients in Saint Anthony's hospital and what therapists and patients are actually saying to each other. At times the reader may find an oddity in these conversations, a strangeness that becomes more visible when one looks at the microscopy of *interactive* speech, rather than its structure or wider context in which the speech occurs. The notion is that a study of larger conversational wholes tends to confirm what is presupposed about psychotic people and their discourse more readily than a micro analysis can do. In debate with Jung, Freud once remarked that schemes inevitably triumphed over individual experience. But what can one learn from a 'microscopic study of interaction'?

It seems rather simple, perhaps: therapists and patients address each other in terms of different models. Therapists have thunderous firepower, psychotics introduce the static in the atmosphere; both make inappropriate moves and so create barriers to interaction. However, the scenario is even more complicated. At issue is a complex process of interaction, embedded in controversial, contradictory, paradoxical and ambiguous models and ideas from which both parties must be freed for the healing of the patient to commence. It is about a communicative process where both partners know which game is being played and in what way. At issue, finally, are the realities experienced and undergone by psychotic people, and the recurring question of whether these can be understood by the therapists, whose own definitions of experienced reality differ so radically from psychotics. Analyzing such underlying processes was far more troublesome than I anticipated, because there is no common ground between theoretical views on psychosis and psychotic language. Research findings (and researchers) appear to contradict each other, while similar concepts are used in contrasting ways. Often the views and ideas of therapists about what is possible, permitted or preferred, do not correspond. One soon realizes that it is a major task to unravel the cultural, professional and personal ideas of therapists and psychotic people. I would no sooner begin the process of reflection and interpretation than new events would crowd in and force me to reconsider: for example, when a patient was transferred, when a crisis arose, or patients told a revised version of their story, or after discussions with my resident hospital mentor. Matters kept cropping up to remind me that the 'complex, ongoing and subtle weave of culture' (Devisch 1993) would ensure that no dossier on the subject could ever be considered closed.

Research at Saint Anthony's

Saint Anthony's is a medium-sized psychiatric hospital comprising work units for clinical treatment, day treatment, alcoholism, sheltered housing, resocialization, nursing services (including intensive supervision), geriatric care (including day treatment for the elderly) and intramural training facilities. The ratio of hospital employees to patients is about two to one.

To comply with government requirements that mental health care should be positioned in the community to ensure close contact with an everyday environment, small-scale clinics have been built throughout the country. The official policy of decentralization and regional distribution has ensured that clinics have a measure of autonomy, notably on their treatment policy. Furthermore, the perspective on care and treatment of patients adopted by the individual hospital does not prescribe one model for all units in that hospital. This preference for diversity in approaches and perspectives regarding treatment is signified by the prefix 'stichting' (foundation) before the name of the hospital. Apart from its legal and organizational significance, this implies a sense of implementing new ideas. There is no rigidly uniform therapeutic framework to govern either daily practice or the individual staff members at individual clinics. Diversity and autonomy are considered to be an advantage because the capabilities of the individual workers can be used to optimize the quality of therapeutic processes. The national discussion on the quality of health care compels each hospital to formulate conditions and criteria that will ensure quality of care, and one of these conditions is the formulation of treatment policy.

Within Saint Anthony's the expressed aim of the therapeutic process is to be dynamic and tailored to each patient. The combination of a multidisciplinary approach and relative autonomy should, of course, be seen as commendable concern about made-to-measure care for each patient that can give recognition to the subjectively experienced problems that beset individuals. At the same time, it is inherently marked by internal disagreement, a lack of clarity regarding methods of treatment and a lack of transparency in the process of making decisions. The hospital's annual reports reflect friction between its various components on efforts to achieve diversity and optimization, daily practice in the separate clinics, and the external demands of society and government on mental health care. These frictions may not affect quality of care, but they certainly do nothing to remove the impression that compared with the efforts expended by staff members in caring for patients, too much time and effort is wasted on organizational matters. There was, for example, a clearly different approach between chronic care units and those for patients receiving short-term treatment. At this level, distinctive philosophies emerged in the treatment offered by the units, the capacity problems of a particular section, or the personal and organizational interests of individual therapists *vis-à-vis* the requirements of the clinics. Almost every transfer of a patient from a short-term unit to a unit for chronic patients meant that tensions became explicit and a veritable 'culture shock' was in store for the patient when confronted with a move from one 'regional culture' to another. This in turn meant that staff members had to spend time with patients compensating for this culture shock, time that could well have been spent otherwise.

Taken in the context of a decade of socio-economic developments, the institutional discourse has changed from an exchange of ideas on the philosophy of care and its nature to a discourse on productivity and its demands. This has been caused, among other things, by the increasing pressure of austerity measures on the psychiatric hospital, growing patient intakes, developments in the field of health care that have led to increasingly complex psychiatric problems, greater cooperation with other institutions, and the development of new forms of care such as 'outreaching' (care by hospital nurses and therapists in the patients' homes). The result of this change is that as the claims made on individual therapists intensify, specialization increases and the opportunity to adopt a holistic approach to patients must inevitably shrink.

The data for this book were compiled from fieldwork carried out between January 1991 and February 1993 among psychotic patients and therapeutic staff in Saint Anthony's psychiatric hospital[1] and from December 1988 to May 1989 in two units in the same hospital. Interim and post-research visits enabled me to complete and organize my information. In the period 1988–9 I was immersed in the daily life of two wards: one in the short-term treatment unit and the other in the unit for intensive supervision of chronic patients. I gained insight into the organization of the hospital and learned how daily life was arranged in the specific wards, and I observed the interaction between staff and patients, among staff, and among patients. I gathered life stories on tape, collected data about various activities in the facilities, attended staff meetings, observed the communication network of the facilities in as many different situations as possible and combined participant observation with interviewing staff members (mostly therapists) and patients. Occasionally I was allowed to be present during conversations between therapists and patients, and I attended a number of festive occasions in the hospital. In some cases I was able to sustain contact with therapists and long-term residents, and this continued beyond the formal fieldwork periods. The 26 patients participating in this inquiry were people diagnosed by their therapists in terms of DSM-III-R[2] for a disorder in which one or more aspects indicate disturbed reality testing. The choice was not arbitrary: 'reality testing' is a core concept in relation to experience and intersubjectivity, and the clients selected by the therapists were psychotic people. Between 1991 and 1993 I was able to record discussions between therapists and psychotic patients on tape (both audio and visual) and to read and receive information regarding case histories and life histories of this special group.

At the hospital there is no particular pattern per unit with respect to diagnosis, age and the number of admissions, and this is most evident in the units for short-term treatment. There is no policy in terms of which patients with similar disorders or profiles are placed together and consequently one finds psychotic patients in virtually every hospital ward. Multidisciplinary teams are deployed, comprising psychiatrists, psychologists, social workers, nurses, physiotherapists and creative therapists. Within the team there is specialization in both supervision and patient treatment, and each patient has both a general supervisor (a psychiatrist or psychologist) and a personal supervisor (a nurse). I spoke to patients about experiences and events that stood out for them and asked therapists to expand on their ideas concerning psychotic people. I was able to test my initial interpretation of each conversation transcript and compare it with the interpretations provided by therapists and patients and where necessary, I would revise or complement the transcripts. Sometimes therapists or patients joined me to view their videotapes and to comment on them. My understanding of the organization and structure of the hospital improved in discussions with the head of the treatment section and I was permitted to read a number of diaries in which patients jotted down their experiences during periods of florid psychosis. I visited hobby areas, coffee shops, foyers and living rooms, and took outings with some patients to get to know them better.

The basic data comprises 50 audiotaped conversations between psychotic patients and therapists, and some of the conversations were also recorded on videotape. Taping conversations is common practice in Dutch psychiatric institutions, and the recordings were all done in subsidiary clinics. They were not identical to the planned sessions conducted as part of specific therapies, but rather open-ended discussions dealing with situations that might arise in the life of a patient. Here I collected my data, established contact with patients and considered topics for further research. Moerman (1988: 7) says conversations provide 'the ingredients of interpretations, the components of meaning, the ones that are locally significant and locally occasioned'. Every conversation between a therapist and a patient could contain recurrent themes, and could thus become starting points for later conversations. The sequential organization, i.e. the successions of expression and turn taking (Sachs *et al.* 1974) revealed important activities – coordination, avoidance, accusation, restriction, etc. – and gave rise to closer study of the intentions and meanings in these activities. In this way the conversations between therapists and patients were the center of growing and increasingly diffuse circles, like stones thrown into a pond.

Since they were planned and conducted for my benefit, the conversations can be considered to have been artificial; this is inevitable in most hospital settings, and certainly in a psychiatric hospital. The advantage was that they were situated in the context of daily hospital life. Requirements for discretion were high and each participant had to be informed of the purpose of the research[3] and sign a declaration indicating that he/she was adequately informed and willing to participate. I never considered the possibility of approaching patients directly but even if I had it would have been difficult to gain access to them (cf Ten Have and Komter 1982). A number of therapists reported that they felt 'bothered' because my recorder gave them the unnerving feeling that 'somebody was looking over their shoulder'. Some patients were well aware of the recorder, which gave them an opportunity to perform. They would use it in a playful manner during the conversations or to try to outwit the therapists. Planned interviews were not unusual in the unit for short-term treatment. With one or two exceptions, the conversations differed little from those in which therapists spoke with their long-term patients.

From the outset I introduced myself to patients as an anthropologist. In the first fieldwork period this helped to ensure that I received information more readily, especially about relationships and conflicts, as someone who would not pass it on to fellow patients and staff members. In many ways my position gave me an advantage in that people talked more freely about their lives because I 'would not do anything with it', at least not within the hospital. In the multi-disciplinary health care teams there was a continuous exchange of information on patients and this discouraged some of them from expressing themselves fully during conversations. For others, my writing a book on the basis of their narratives meant a shot at eternity. As one patient put it: 'I'm glad we are on tape, because ... eh ... we both know it and we don't forget it, do we?' Here was a person to whom one could convey feelings or who listened when you complained about your stay in the hospital. To others, I was a novice to whom everything could be explained. People tried quite explicitly to strike a deal: 'I told you my story; now, will you get me a drink?'

The explicit posture of 'an anthropologist conducting research in a psychiatric setting' inevitably invited restrictions, and in practice my cooperation with the health professionals was mostly an 'uneasy alliance' (Skultans 1991). Initially the anthropologist can expect to encounter antagonism, skepticism, uneasiness or concerns rooted in methodological and theoretical approaches. These may surface as a question on how useful anthropology is in daily practice, or an invitation to suggest solutions to practical psychiatric problems. Since anthropology cannot claim to provide immediately applicable uses in a clinic setting I found humility to be the best attitude for someone who was obviously not engaged in applied research.

There was skepticism regarding the value of the conversations as well as their effect on patients. Sobering views were heard on the prospect of conversing with particular psychotic patients, especially on the danger of some possibly losing their grip on reality, if certain topics that could evoke strong emotions should be touched on. This meant that patients who in the opinion of the therapist might react in a negative way to greater tension were left out of the group. Hesitation by therapists to conduct more extended conversations with patients certainly had a practical basis as well, with the pressure of time in overcrowded units, meetings, reorganizations, and so on. Uneasiness could also arise when the inquiry extended to therapists, their expressions and conversation techniques, because I gave pride of place to *interaction* between them and psychotic people. A tape-recorder or video camera capturing the behavior of a therapist is indeed unusual, far more so than it is for a patient.

A factor that probably contributed to a feeling of uneasiness later was the top-down manner in which the second stint of fieldwork was introduced to therapists in the various units of the hospital. This consisted of appointments arranged by the secretariat with all the therapists attached to a unit. Accompanied by the head of the treatment council I was marched from door to door to explain what I had in mind. Eventually, I realized that my relations with the therapists were already more free and easy-going and that reservations voiced during the introduction were often minimized in direct contact. I came to surmise that perhaps the problem was not only the prospect of being an object of study, or concern for the patients or other utilitarian doubts, but also of an institutional and organizational nature.

Generally, cooperation with staff members and patients was positive. Staff members were knowledgeable about anthropology,[4] therapists found anthropology interesting,[5] and good relations with both therapists and patients were established in the first fieldwork period. These factors contributed to efficient gathering of the taped material, and offered many opportunities to work 'on the inside'. Important to this way of working was my 'therapist mentor', the head of the treatment council, whose answers to my questions helped to place matters in a broader perspective. We discussed fragments of conversations and related them to the framework of therapist and patient, and to psychiatric perspectives and institutional relations. I was initiated into psychiatric 'secrets', and we explored the relation between anthropology and psychiatry, opportunities for cooperation and limitations. We tried to arrive at a mutual picture of people and their desires, needs, joys and fears. This has certainly led in the present writing to an intertwining of my own thoughts and those of my mentor. Because I wanted to be receptive to the stories of psychotic people and how they experienced the world, I became involved in conflicts and differences of opinion between people, their inner struggle and suffering. I tried to maintain an appropriate distance, so that I could discover what was happening and why. Sometimes this entangled me in a duality similar to one that seems to imprison therapists: of nearness and distance, empathy and cynicism, credulity and disbelief; all of which made me more aware of being caught in my own culture. Fieldwork of this nature is deeply moving and the 'world of madness' has without doubt changed my personal and professional views.

Structure of the book

Chapter 1 introduces an anthropological perspective on the structural problems faced by caregivers and psychotics in a modern Dutch psychiatric hospital setting and the interactions required for the healing of the patient to commence.

In Chapter 2, I set this against the therapeutic perspectives in Saint Anthony's and focus on the concept of 'reality' and its different meanings in the hospital. An important issue in the hospital is discussed: the 'splitting' of psychotic people into healthy and unhealthy parts of the self. This split is related to the therapists' ideas of distance and involvement in the lives of the patients during clinical interactions.

The meanings of psychosis, explanations of illness and the expectations of the treatment of both therapists and patients, are set out in Chapter 3, as well as signs of madness that are picked up and interpreted by the patients and their social networks in the period prior to hospitalization. I suggest that ritualizing admission and treatment invites the risk of overlooking the subjective experiences of patients.

In Chapter 4, the distinction between long- and short-term wards in the hospital is linked to the splitting of patients' selves and this is in turn related to therapeutic views and control of patients by clinical narratives of hope and hopelessness, stories that are superficially confirmed and reinforced by the patients.

In Chapters 5 and 6, I deal with speech events between therapists and patients and describe how power relations are established and maintained and how the patients' narratives were transformed into the clinical canon of 'insight' and 'reality'. It is argued that the psychotic world is systematically concealed and revealed. I illustrate that the oddity of the conversations is a consequence of too prompt transformations of therapists according to their own agendas, and show the contradictions and paradoxes in the conversations.

In Chapters 7, 8 and 9, I offer a description of the meanings that psychotic people give to their lives and discuss what happened to them. It is shown that cultural systems provide a range of possibilities for making sense of experiences, lives and events. Presentations of self, relations with others, and experiences of life and death show that psychotic people live in irreconcilable and contradictory worlds, and often have no choice other than to 'tinker' with cultural material.

In Chapter 10 the 'costly discourses' of therapists and patients are discussed. Contradictions and paradoxes in speech events are summarized and explained, and alternative views to therapeutic interactions with psychotic people offered.

Chapter 2

The quest for reality and the work with culture

When psychiatrists and anthropologists explore psychosis

The presence of an anthropologist on the wards created more confusion than I had anticipated. One patient asked a mental health worker: 'What is an anthropologist? Somebody who studies monkeys?' I had assumed that he knew about me since he had discussed my research with his therapist and signed the agreement. His question, which brought to mind the practice of 'monkey gazing' in former 'madhouses' was a bit embarrassing and revealed some unexpected ethical and emotional issues.[1] Therapists were also puzzled by the 'anthropological content' of my research, because they observed that like the nurses I spent much of my time in the wards, and spoke at length to patients. This gave rise to debates about the different nature and methodologies of the two disciplines. One psychiatrist's criticism of anthropology was that it had no 'single consistent theory' and lacked 'the ability to predict human behavior'. His comment reflected current notions of validity and reliability, underpinned by an assumption that 'reality' is single layered, shared by everyone in a society, and capable of being studied and explained within a single frame. It highlights the difference between anthropology and psychiatry in approaching the ways that people perceive and deal with reality.

Therapeutic approaches of reality and interaction with psychotic patients

There have been rapid developments in recent years in specialist knowledge of psychotic disorders, especially in new medication and the technical refinement of diagnostics. Conventional wisdom has it that madness is silenced when mastery is obtained over it, despite the fact that it may rise again. Boyle (1990: 193–194) suggests schizophrenia as a concept for further research. It is an integral part of the legal system in three important respects. First, schizophrenia can be useful as a concept to explain criminal behavior. Second, it can be used to absolve people of responsibility. Third, diagnosis of the state of schizophrenia can be useful when involuntary detention or intervention by medical authorities is to be invoked. In short, it is a useful tool to inform 'decisions about the disposal of those to whom the term is applied' (Boyle 1990: 193).

Perhaps society has been seduced by the rapid developments in medicine and the promise held out by refined technology, and it may have fallen prey to its own high expectations concerning the expertise and mastery that can be attained by mental health practitioners. Health workers, therapists and psychiatrists at Saint Anthony's intimated to me that they often felt as if they were being slung to and fro between contradictory perspectives and ethical considerations. Psychotic patients became lost in the labyrinth of official assistance to the extent that they were eventually unable to cope with their experiences. Psychotic people in the Netherlands have not been cast adrift or left to fend for themselves. Nevertheless, many wind up wandering aimlessly from clinic to doctor, to consultation bureau, to sheltered dwelling, to the street, constantly looking for a story to tell, a story that can illuminate their struggle with society. The history of madness shows the ways in which psychotics are tolerated in a society and how their condition is given 'meaning' (for examples, see Foucault 1972; Porter 1987; Kramer 1990).

Tolerance is an essential element in trying to establish how normal or abnormal a person is and how that person's relationship to society ought to be structured. To understand the possible changes in the meaning given to the state of madness, it is important to realize that it is not defined exclusively by psychiatric norms that determine how the human mind should function. It is intrinsically related to complex expectations, values and norms that people apply to themselves and others; every society has its own characteristic constellation. Included in such constructions of normality and abnormality are the prohibitions implied by that society's norms and values. Each constellation specifies what are considered to be dreams, socially unacceptable fantasies, and impossible desires. Breaking a societal taboo or prohibition makes the psychotic patient doubly liable, for daring to cross a boundary and becoming a danger to others (Douglas 1966: 1.39). This sort of border crossing inevitably leads to exclusion (and later to subsequent rituals to undo the exclusion). At the same time, the psychotic can exhibit the attractive qualities of a clown or jester, precisely because society's norms and values are being flouted so openly.[2]

It seems that the element of enchantment has been removed from madness. Symptoms of psychosis and schizophrenia have come to be physically expressed and are no longer seen as symbolic manifestations of misery (cf Martínez-Hernáez 2000). The old fear of lunacy seems to have been replaced by a fear of psychotic illness. This seems to be a consequence of social processes promoting the idea that madness does not exist as a moral category. During the 1950s one of these social processes urged resistance to rationality and the narrow confines of reason, morality and decorum. Foucault (1972) argued that madness was detached from mental illness and that it would become part of the foundations of our culture. He stressed the clear distinction between the mentally ill and madness (*folie*), defining the latter as the relation of human beings with the *domain des interdits* or the domain of the forbidden (1972: 581) and *langage exclus* or excluded discourse (1972: 578). There has been a growth spurt in popular knowledge of psychotic conditions, generated via the media. Non-believers, followers of unusual religions, freethinkers, dissidents, prophets, seers, magicians – all of them are clearly visible in society, with television constantly parading such multicolored birds of paradise. For a significant number of people, madness and possession seem to have become tempting and desirable lifestyles. Social and scientific doubts regarding reason and rationality have led to an individualism in which anything, always, goes: nobody needs to appeal to an external standard of morality to justify their way of life (Richters 1991). This resonates with the social prohibition that nobody should be called a lunatic because of the way that he talks or acts, because decorum dictates against this kind of labeling. Even so, the number of people in psychiatric institutions in the Netherlands is growing and the majority are admitted for shorter periods. In solving the question of patient intake, the Dutch government seems to have been guided by changed norms of what constitutes abnormality. It applies certain criteria for psychiatric facilities and seeks to restrict the number of beds in psychiatric hospitals, replacing them by ambulant social care (Giel 1984: 244).[3] During the past decade the medical model has taken root in Dutch psychiatry and it is no longer necessary to refer to 'excluded discourse'.

Psycho-pharmaceutical developments and related scientific research, as well as the refinement of diagnostic techniques, have played a major role in this. The *Diagnostic and Statistical Manual of Mental Disorders* (DSM) used at Saint Anthony's and other Dutch institutions is an extensive system of classifications based on a view of psychopathology that is marked by well-defined disorders displaying specific symptoms. It is supposed to be value free[4] and the fact that legal agencies and insurance companies prescribe its use, as well as the creation of a number of associated diagnostic instruments, have combined to give psychiatry the veneer of being a 'high-tech' science, similar in many ways to biomedicine. The therapists at Saint Anthony's were at best ambivalent about the new classificatory system and many doubted its efficacy. They could not 'fit' patients into the categories and were concerned about the effect it would have on possible job applications later, if patients were 'labeled'. On balance the new DSM seemed 'more neutral' and they hoped that in future everyone 'would talk about the same illness'.

Dutch psychiatry has to deal with contradictory perspectives on the concept of illness (cf Pols 1984: 147–178), and competition among various branches of mental health care and social work. It is also marked by confusion about the effectiveness of these regimens and some profound social problems.[5] Even assuming that psychiatry should indicate which problems of life and behavior meet the criteria for dysfunction and abnormality, the formal system of classification cannot possibly be expected to offer every solution. Mental health workers at times have to make pronouncements on the abnormality of notions that remain publicly unexpressed. If they do, it begs the question of what the basis is for their assumptions. Mental health workers become unsure; after all, quite recently anti-psychiatry questioned the undiscerning way in which a society can perpetuate certain norms and values. When psychiatry evaluates problems in terms of its criteria, normative aspects of the concept of illness intrude. In terms of these normative aspects a person is seen as an autonomous, self-responsible individual capable of self-realization, whereas the disease concept would have it both ways. If people cannot be held responsible for their psychic disorders, it justifies patients taking a passive attitude and makes medical intervention seem more legitimate.

This is at odds with the *fin de siècle* psychiatric tenet that patients are co-responsible for what they make of their lives. The therapist must determine accurately whether or not the patient is able to influence a disorder and convince him that therapy is the road to improvement, even if the patient has been declared unfit (or considers himself unfit) to shoulder responsibility. In either case psychiatry is to an increasing extent forced to act as the social arbiter that must determine whether or not someone is ill, and if so, whether that person is eligible for certain social facilities (Pols 1984: 231). This constricts psychiatry, since governmental and insurance agencies want more control over the distribution of funds, care and treatment. The growing tendency to supervise brings the temptation to generalize psychiatric problems, to introduce stricter discipline and norms, and to play down uncertainties. Silence about scientific doubts and problems serves to mystify further the power of psychiatry, and perpetuates the mistaken feeling that psychiatry provides universally authoritative explanations: for example, the notion that psychosis is a medical problem that will be solved 'in time'.

Discussion of non-voluntary admission to psychiatric institutions (cf Pols 1984; Legemaate 1991) seems to turn on whether or not people with mental disorders present a danger to others or themselves. In considering the social processes that have an impact on the extent of tolerance shown towards psychotics and the social significance of madness, the only response appears to be that psychotic people 'present a threat'. In society (and in psychiatry as a part of society) there seem to be clear norms to diagnose 'madness' and decide what should be done about it. As the pertinent system of specialization, psychiatry has developed a highly complex and refined system of norms. However, the Dutch have characteristically developed a dual system, especially in relation to the approach and treatment of people with psychotic disorders.[6] The biomedical approach is oriented to 'technical' treatment and healing, whereas the humane–psychological approach is intent on healing through personal therapy. The latter approach emphasizes the subjective experiences of people, experience that refers to social relationships, values and norms, and to moral convictions.

The phenomenological approach adopted by Rümke (1948) is an example of this, emphasizing how the mentally ill person experiences his problem relative to himself and others. Kuiper (1980) describes this as 'hermeneutic psychiatry'. Views have changed regarding the professionalism of psychiatry in relation to social developments[7] and the humanistic–psychological approach is in retreat because of this. Kuiper (1989: 114), a Dutch psychiatrist who suffered from delusions and was treated in a mental hospital, writes in this context of 'the conspiracy against emotion in psychiatry'. The most important and influential assumption in psychiatry is that psychotic people are out of touch with reality. The description of a psychotic disorder given by the World Health Organization is 'a mental disorder in which impairment of mental functions has developed to a degree that interferes grossly with insight, ability to meet some ordinary demands of life or to maintain adequate contact with reality' (WHO 1978). Since 1978, 'psychotic' has become a descriptive term for people who suffer from delusions and hallucinations (WHO 1992). The classificatory manual (DSM-III-R) used in Saint Anthony's psychiatric hospital at the time of my fieldwork defined 'psychosis' as serious shortcomings in reality testing, conjoined with a tendency to create a new reality (cf Young 1988). Reality is closely related to psychosis in these descriptions and many noted psychiatrists have described the reality awareness 'shortcomings' of psychotic people. Freud (1924) defined psychosis as reality denial, a serious breach or conflict between the self and reality. He also spoke of loss of reality and regression, in which delusions and hallucinations were core symptoms. Lacan (1966) described a psychotic person as one who, by dint of rejecting the cultural order and its rules, has lost his position and will always be subordinate to others. Moyaert (1982a), a Belgian psychoanalyst, characterized psychotics as people 'whose world of meaning is poor and monotonous'.

Generally, when someone is assessed a distinction is made between reality awareness and impairment of reality testing (Frosch 1983: 313).[8] In theories about problems of identity, the libido, and repression and projection mechanisms, impairment is usually interpreted psychologically and often reductionistically because the content of psychosis is traced back to a single aspect, such as sexuality. Reality is defined as having an inner and an outer world (Frosch 1983: 277). The outer world consists of objective, material phenomena and the conventional social representations of these phenomena. The inner world consists of perceptions and mental functions such as fantasy, memory, recollections, impulses and feelings. Disturbances in reality testing are described as an impairment of the capacity to evaluate 'in the proper manner' phenomena in both the outer and inner world (Freeman 1973; Frosch 1983).[9] What this amounts to is that reality as experienced by psychotic people is not credible, true or real to other people. Assessing the extent to which someone's reality awareness and reality testing may be impaired raises the question of which reality should predominate. The psychiatric view leaves no room for doubt: the correct criterion is considered to be the reality of conventional social knowledge (Frosch 1983: 335). Although it accepts that reality is constructed, psychiatry does not see its own specialty as belonging to the surrounding culture. It assumes that society is based on general views as to what is true, possible, real and credible and does not (at least not openly) question the truth thereof.[10] Since these views are far from being unequivocal, one can speculate as to whether psychiatric discourses are still bound to a specific view of culture (Richters 1991: 468). Accordingly, it is difficult to determine whether anyone's evaluation of reality is correct. From the psychotic person's perspective his own views and perceptions are as valuable, and every bit as much part of reality, as the experiences of others. Apart from the question of whether or not they refer to a reality, the features of delusions and hallucinations are notably similar to the social–cultural order of society (Van Dongen 1991a). It is not clear how this relates to cognitive impairments. Delusions tend to be presented systematically and supported with consistent arguments – hence the term 'systematic delusions' (Schilder 1933: 11). The personal value and reality of extraordinary experience is expressed in an 'idiom of distress' (Nichter 1981) which is in turn based on an 'idiom of culture'. In this sense, psychoses may be seen as homologous to social norms and values (Devereux 1954) to which people can give widely divergent forms. Presumably not all psychotic people have a tendency to function poorly in reality testing. Some are able to keep functioning socially (Jacobsen 1967; Kooy 1992), their delusions and hallucinations notwithstanding.

Research findings on reality testing are quite varied and it is difficult to judge with any degree of accuracy whether or not a person is in touch with reality. It is doubtful that reality testing can be maintained as a core concept in future, partly because of a noticeable shift in psychiatry from individualizing perspectives to system–theoretical approaches. In the latter, signification is no longer viewed as a private category but rather seen as a process of cooperative creation, a process that involves everyone.[11] Reality is the result of this creative process, and the truth of the interaction. In this view the psychotic person is not an individual with disorders in his reality testing but rather a part of a 'problem-determined system' (Hoffman 1988; Anderson et al. 1986). This therapeutic 'system' comprises all those who may be intent on a specific problem, or who are alarmed by someone's behavior (Goolishian and Winderman 1988: 135). The psychiatrist becomes a manager who must ensure that conversations among all those who participate in the system continue until the problem is no longer experienced as a problem (Goolishian and Winderman 1988: 135). In the case of psychotic people this may imply that in the course of the conversation a new reality is constructed, a reality that is acceptable to each of the participants. A system-oriented therapy aims at solution of the 'problem-determined system' rather than solving a problem. The significance of relationships is placed at center stage because they are no longer understood as an instrument to gain insight into intrapsychical processes, but seen as the final goal. This demands that there should be consensus among those involved, and it also means that the traditional concept of reality testing loses its usefulness. Where reality arises in the interaction of equals the conserving and consolidating functions have disappeared,[12] because of an awareness that the meanings and definitions of reality are flexible. This latter approach promises to be a counterbalance to psychiatry's tradition of interpreting symptoms on an individual level.[13]

It is open to conjecture whether a problem-determined system can be replaced with a new reality and problem-free system simply by way of debate. Can the problem in the system be solved and is it in fact always desirable to 'solve problems'? The Dutch philosopher Oosterhuis (1993) suggests that instead of problem solving there could be places for people to 'speak of meaning'. People should be able to pose questions about the meaning of existence without being embarrassed; a psychiatric clinic could be such a space. The open-ended, continuous discourse of the system–theoretical approach makes it difficult for people to offer a definition of themselves and others: 'In denying the ontological status of the "I", one risks to destroy its semiotic value, and thus its ethical value' (Rosseel 1990: 29). After all, this system–theoretical approach states that reality is a domain that is constantly rearranged in interaction with others. If this is the case, it cannot possibly provide answers to the universally persistent questions of psychotics: Who am I? What is the meaning of my life? Why me? Why does the world close its doors on me? What must I do?

Psychiatry features many studies of psychotic discourse and interaction with psychotic people that are characterized by quantitative research, laboratory analyses, theoretical interpretations and clinical descriptions. By describing and categorizing the differences between 'normal' discourse and psychotic articulation, researchers construct a 'medical model' in terms of which psychotic people can be classified. These studies focus primarily on diagnostic refinement.[14] Pressed by medicalization processes (Fahrenbort 1991), they respond to the demand for scientific quantification.[15] Many studies which according to Van Hoorde (1986) should be characterized as 'statistiatry' (statistical psychiatry), have rightly or wrongly influenced current dealings with psychotic people.

One of the most extensively researched features of psychotic speech is its lack of any narrative competence or comprehensibility. It is vitally important to be able to understand what patients say, since a patient's story helps to determine diagnosis of the malady and the choice of therapy. One of the shifts that evidently occurred in psychiatric research during the 1970s was that laboratory studies made way for the linguistic competence studies. An advantage of the latter is that quantification can still play an important role, but it uses the natural language of psychotic people rather than artificial test data. Psycholinguistics holds that speech disorders should be investigated in terms of linguistic variables and the study of rules and regulations in using language (Rochester and Martin 1979). Linguistic studies of speech disorder can help to lend objectivity to the diagnostic process and in particular the definition of speech disorder (Hotchkiss and Harvey 1986: 158). This may well be the case but psycholinguistic research has also yielded contradictory results.[16] In dealing with psychotic people it is best to avoid ambiguity and complex situations.[17] It is fair to say that in response to these communication problems, more attention is being given to therapist training.

In psychoanalytic literature the meaning of psychotic speech has been clarified in terms of case descriptions.[18] A separation came about between experience as an individual matter, and experience as a 'signpost of points of tension, generated by the structure of society' (Richters 1991: 389). Research results into the lack of narrative competence and comprehensibility amongst psychotics address the problems of discourse, not those of therapists.[19] The introduction of discourse analysis heralds a new phase in the study of psychotic speech. Gradually, the language used by psychotic people in interaction with others is receiving more attention and researchers are showing that non-psychotic discussion parties play an important part in the discourse.[20] Studies indicate that there is room for considerable nuance in current assumptions about dealing with psychotic people, and in the severity of the psychotic defect.

As with psycholinguistics, discourse analysis is primarily interested in unfolding everyday rules and strategies by which people can clarify what they mean (Chaika 1981). Recently, interaction analysis has been added to the study of psychiatric conversations (Gale 1991) and psychotic discourse (Van Bijsterveld 1987). Such inquiry is focused on the process of interaction since it investigates 'the interactions of *both* therapist and client, considering systemic concepts, developing behaviorally focused micro-theory and in addition, [it] bear[s] relevance to clinicians' (Gale 1991: 100). The emphasis shifts from interpretations that ascribe deficiency to people, to interpretations that focus on problems in interaction. A focus on more competent therapists may also imply a gradual regeneration of interest in the humane–psychological approach in psychiatry, but it is taking a long time to develop. Traditionally, interest in cognitive disorders in psychosis has been greater than interest in subjective experiences, although there have been exceptions. Van den Bosch (1993) relates cognitive processes to the subjectivity of schizophrenics, while others (e.g. Kaplan 1964) have presented the autobiographical material of psychotic people together with comments by psychiatrists. Psychiatric literature still lacks a clear stance on the relationship of person to culture, and the tensions arising from it. Since a stated objective of psychiatry is more competent therapists (cf Gale 1991; Van Haaster 1991) attention is also given to the discourse problems of psychotic people, placing these at the center of the interaction between therapists and patients. It would indicate that the reality constructions and decisional norms of both parties should be studied. To this end, I concentrate on the acts performed during discourse,[21] acts to which meaning is ascribed by all the partners in the discussion – therapists, nurses, psychotic people and anthropologist.

A starting point of interaction approaches is that people activate their world by giving it meaning (cf Ten Have 1987), and that they do so by way of certain practices, with the presumption of shared knowledge. Interaction analysis seeks insight into the links people make between knowledge and the concrete situation in which they find themselves. Meaning in this sense is the outcome of interactive processes. I examine what happens in the public disclosure called conversation (Ten Have 1987: 14), how psychotic people talk about their disorder, how therapists try to initiate conversation and the differing interpretations that the therapists and patients arrive at. In this, I direct my attention to what Tyler (1978) describes as 'the said'. It is not the goal of this book to examine the means that people use in their conversations (the 'interactional organization' as it is termed in interaction analysis). Suffice it to say that the latter approach can help to trace subjective experiences in the expositions of therapists and psychotic people, and to see how culture as a manipulative system of meanings and symbols continues to assert itself.

The work of culture and the work with culture

Anthropology and psychosis

'The work of culture' is the process whereby symbolic forms existing on the cultural level come to be 'created and recreated through the minds of people' (Obeyesekere 1990). I add another process, 'the work with culture', which is the process of manipulation, bricolage and non-conventional use of symbolic forms.

Rather than viewing the presentations of psychotic patients as signs of a disorder, I examine them as cultural forms expressing severe misery and distress. The stories of psychotic people derive from something deep and fundamental. Kirmayer (1993: 173) says they contain metaphors, myths and archetypal images that emerge from interactions between the person and society. Healing may mean 'to create con-substantiality between [bodily] experience and myth' (Kirmayer 1993: 184). However, in the Saint Anthony's psychiatric system the psychotic's domain was considered to be 'unreal'. The system had produced conditions wherein this world should and did remain private and closed off. Yet it remained an essential part of the life worlds of psychotic patients and often emerged during therapy and in conversations with therapists or nurses. The focus should therefore be on psychotic patients as the 'makers' of that world, and by extension as creators and recreators of cultural patterns.

Interpretations of the feelings, emotions, life world and subjectivity of psychotic and other people are paramount in this study. The basic premise is that people are formed by cultural practice and that the meaning of these practices includes ways of understanding and dealing with things, people and institutions[22] (cf Garfinkel 1967; Geertz 1973; Rabinow and Sullivan 1979). According to Kleinman (1988), an understanding of how people see their life world is necessary for interaction and cooperation. It may seem that these elements are present in interaction since therapists and patients live in the same culture and have the same goal (i.e. to heal the patient). However, their constructions of reality differ in important respects and their intersubjectivity and cooperation are, in part, mere appearance. To distinguish between the world of the therapist and that of the psychotic patient, I focused on 'models'. Geertz (1973) has refined this as a distinction between models *for* and models *of*. In psychiatric practice, the models of therapists and nurses may be understood as models *for* reality, because they are required to make how psychotic people relate to others understandable and they present an appropriate set of behaviors for social intercourse. Models of psychotic patients may be understood as models *of* reality, because they are used explicitly to give meaning to the social and psychological reality in which people have to live. The distinction is not infallible, since the models used by health workers are also ways to give meaning, but the psychotic models are manipulations of a psychiatric symbolic system, which uses the metaphor 'brain disease'. Nevertheless it is the health worker models that most often function as the blueprint that shapes clinical interactions and the psychiatric ideas of normal social behavior.

My primary aim was to outline the models as understood and interpreted by therapists and psychotic people to construct their reality. The question was how in their interaction these reality constructions relate to each other. It addresses the key concepts and meanings (embedded in the norms) that therapists and patients apply to a psychotic disorder and to life as a psychotic person.[23] Traditional psychological approaches explain the reasons for human action in terms of universal needs, desires and motives, while cultural theories view human action as the direct result of cultural constructions. However, I wanted to show that while human action is based on cultural constructions, these constructions do not automatically explain it. If we want to know why therapists and psychotics do what they do in their interactions, bringing out leading constructions of 'psychiatry' or of 'society' does not go far enough. These constructions are transformed into personal representations, and where actions occur in accordance with these representations, the subsequent interaction creates new reality constructions (cf Sperber 1985).

The new realities are not mental constructs fashioned from models in a rational way. Human miseries like psychosis and schizophrenia are first and foremost shaped by emotions. The difference is that psychiatry considers emotions as the internal characteristics of an individual, while anthropology sees emotion referring to situations, relations and moral positions. In the anthropological view psychosis could be caused by personal instability or blocked mental powers, but also by social instabilities that hinder or block mental and emotional development (cf Richters 1991). Emotions can be viewed as culturally constructed opinions; aspects of 'meaning' systems that people use to understand their situation (Shweder and Levine 1984). Levy (1984) shows how 'emotion talk' is used to inform others about the relationship between the individual and his social context. Lutz (1987) studied the Ifaluk of Micronesia and showed that people could live in many different emotional situations, operating on an extended emotional idiom that was not directed internally but rather used to express relationships with others. This idiom of the Ifaluk is fundamentally directed at the 'moral' level.

Because treatment in psychiatry targets the coping behavior of psychotics and uses medical treatment to change the way a person is biopsychologically organized, there is little space left in the therapy for the above approach to emotions. Psychotic patients will wander in ambivalent spaces between the self and the other, and the self and culture. The effect can be an incessant battle between the psychotic's own desires, feelings, thoughts and beliefs, and the views, norms and values of society. The strain of the effort that is required to deal with the contradictions, inconsistencies and tensions that may arise in relations between self and culture in order to create the 'illusion of wholeness' (Ewing 1990) creates a continual disturbance.[24] I suggest that when subjectivity is understood in this way it can help to trace the origin of the interaction problems experienced between therapists and psychotic people, because it is on the basis of this subjectivity that they adopt positions to speak about things.[25] But they do not do this in a non-committal way.

Interactions between therapists and psychotic people can best be understood in terms of human problems, transactions, transformations, power relations, roles, sources and strategies. Culture is a system that also manipulates the strictures which people can impose in order to stereotype, ostracize, penalize and restrict (Richters 1991). These strictures contribute to the process of stabilization and continuity in a society, but can also lead to a concealment of those aspects that lead to cultural malady. Culture, then, is inherently paradoxical and the paradox permeates to every level of human interaction. Therapists and psychotic people can try to achieve their objectives via numerous strategies but precisely because culture is at once manipulative and paradoxical, the interactive balance of power keeps shifting (cf Davis 1988). Yet it is doubtful that such interactive shifts are strong enough to lead in time to more equal and democratic communication between therapists and patients, or to a critical review of our norms and values.

There is a complex relationship between interaction and culture as 'source' and basis for manipulative strategies on the one hand, and social action and processes both psychic and physiological on the other. Much of culture plays a role in interaction without becoming a theme of discussion, and earlier literature illustrated that interactions between therapists and patients represented only part of that which happens around, within and to psychotic people in a psychiatric hospital. That which remains unsaid is as important precisely because knowledge is not thematized (Habermas 1988). Assumptions can generate communication, but they need not be taken up explicitly into the interaction, and can be left outside it. In the psychiatric hospital the distinction between the 'normal' and 'psychotic' worlds is quite explicit. The world of psychotic people is considered to be a *personal* world of significations. What people say from within this world or about it can produce effects that therapists are not always able to relate to conventional meanings. In such cases, to quote the therapists, the symbols of the psychotic world essentially fail to correspond with everyday symbolic meanings (cf Moyaert 1982a). For my purpose the distinction between a personal and a cultural world of meaning is not helpful, since it places the psychotic world 'outside' of culture. As noted the symbols used by psychotic people are not unique but stem from culture and derive their meaning from both the motivations and history of individuals (Obeyesekere 1990), and the broader social context.

This realization is crucial in understanding the world and the language of psychotic people. Everything patients say during conversation sessions can be meaningful, but psychiatry is selective in what it regards as significant. Symbols in psychotic speech are interpreted in terms of the biological needs and the psychological drives of people, which in turn influence their behavior.[26] Such explanations are based in traditional motivation theory, which states that biological needs and psychological drives determine behavior. Human needs such as the desire for success, belonging and being appreciated produce motivation for behavior. Theoretically, needs and drives are channeled within culture. People internalize dominant values, norms and the like, via certain models. These influence the needs and drives and in part, they guide behavior.[27] People's needs are largely shaped by culture, but tracing why psychotic people say what they say and do what they do takes more than just examining what they learned and how things went wrong. We must coax out the ways in which their choices and goals are being influenced and guided and examine how well the models serve to cope with the inconsistencies, changes, ambiguities and injustices that psychotic people encounter in society and their own lives. Studying the cognitive representations of cultural knowledge can help clarify how the choices and goals of people are influenced and guided. This confirms the position of culture as both a 'regulating principle' and a goal (D'Andrade 1984, 1992; Holland and Skinner 1987, 1992; Quinn 1987, 1992; Strauss 1992).

Attempting to chart the relationship between therapists and psychotic people by examining discourse is not in itself adequate because the conversations can provide only random indications, like snapshots. The story on both sides remains incomplete until it is related to other speech events. Segments of speech formed in the conversation must be joined to others, to things said (or left unsaid), to a personal history as contained in diaries, letters, or patient files. They can also be related to that which people consider appropriate, necessary or possible. The permutations are virtually unlimited and are similar to those of an organism in its environment.[28] The contextualizing (con-textere = to intertwine, to connect) of conversations should be aimed at describing and analyzing how experiences and interaction with the environment are organized. The question becomes: What exactly belongs to the context? One might endlessly continue to add phenomena. Psychiatry is familiar with a comparable process: the concept of substitution as used in psychoanalysis, i.e. that a symbol can be transformed almost endlessly into other symbols. Usually this is done on the basis of isomorphic characteristics, and subdivided into various levels of symbolizing. The difficulty of substitution is that the symbol may become so remote as to seem arbitrary: doubt arises whether it still relates to an experience.[29] This is, *mutatis mutandis*, true of 'context' as well.

One possible way of limiting the context to phenomena deemed relevant by psychotic people might be to start from the perspective they take on events and situations. However, since the context of conversations between psychotics and therapists can keep changing as the activities in the talks change, with people alternately concealing and revealing, adding new themes and changing the context, the process can be extended indefinitely. In moments of concealment it is usually the history or the emotion of the patient that provides the immediate context. The discussion partners may at times seek to establish a relationship or achieve a breakthrough in the conversation, and at others they ensure that they keep their distance. The context changes as tactics shift and the process becomes even more complicated because in the conversation the protagonists successfully appeal to alternative frameworks. To narrow down the shifting context, we seek 'contextualization cues' (Gumperz 1982a, 1992) as offered by the discussion partners. Gumperz cites the examples of intonation, emphasis, pauses and hesitations that produce certain effects and indicate the significance of a given culturally shaped theme in a certain episode of the conversation.

It is common practice in psychiatry to 'contextualize' the speech and narratives of psychotic people. Analysis of the reality constructions in the interaction of psychotic people and therapists is also a form of contextualizing. The meaning of life as a psychotic person may dwell in the relation between texts produced in the hospital and their social–cultural dimensions. For this reason I prefer to 'over-contextualize' (Basso 1992: 253) by relating the texts to important themes in the conversation, as indicated by the participants. This is done by way of contextualizing cues, like pauses and minute elaboration, in the hope of gaining access to an implicit socio-cultural experiential world (Ochs 1992; Sherzer 1987).[30] Apart from portraying some aspects of how psychotics see themselves and their relationship to the world, it helps to reveal the special way in which models can be used as personal goals. These models of reality are related to important experiences in their lives and so constitute a system of beliefs that can clarify seemingly impenetrable behavior.

What is the relation between normality and abnormality in a cultural tradition? How do people look upon the narratives of psychotics? Studies in ethnopsychiatry show that psychiatric systems are the incorporations (Csordas 1990) of concerns with and the restrictions imposed on normal and abnormal persons in relation to others in a society (cf Devereux 1980; Obeyesekere 1985). This perception is not based on observations and measurements tested in terms of an absolute standard of normality; rather, confirmation arises in comparison with diffuse models of health and mental illness (Devereux 1980). The opposition is based, then, in the concept of the person. In psychiatry, the person is clearly distinguished from others and the social context, and the definition resembles Geertz's (1973: 48): 'The Western conception of the person as a bounded, unique, more or less integrated motivational and cognitive universe, a dynamic center of awareness, emotion, judgment, and action organized into a distinctive whole and set contrastively both against other such wholes and against a social and natural background.'

Dumont (1970) notes that each person is conceived of as an incarnation of abstract humanity, capable of undertaking personal projects (Shweder and Bourne 1984: 192). This implies a stable 'core character', whereas a swathe of anthropological research points to the contrary (cf Shweder and Levine 1984). In various reports about the concept of the person, there is a tendency not to separate the person from the social context (Shweder and Bourne 1984: 167). Another element in the equation is the struggle that psychiatry wages against its own dualistic nature. There have been recurrent shifts, from an emphasis on biomedical, natural–scientific approaches to a humane–scientific perspective, and vice versa. But the humane–scientific perspective also splits into two. The pathos of empathy is awakened by the 'law' of professional distance. The discourse of psychiatry may be viewed as a moral discourse, even when therapists themselves say that they do not want to 'be moral'. Therapists may try to persuade psychotics to accept a therapeutic myth, but 'myth cannot be reached by persuasion; persuasion belongs to a different area in which the criteria of the technical resilience of judgments have their force' (Kolakowski, cited in Kirmayer 1993: 181). The stories of patients are forbidden narratives, forbidden because they fall outside the 'proper professional' standards (Church 1995).

Drawing a distinction between the physical world and the mental world can obscure our understanding of the psychotic life-world. While the psyche is the object of therapy, the same body which is a source of suffering for psychotic people is also fundamental to their experience, assuming enormous proportions. Bodies – 'the existential beginnings of the experience of perceiving in all its indeterminacy and richness' (Csordas 1990: 9) – reveal a flood of sensations that evoke anxiety, pleasure, fear, disgust, sadness or joy. Madness is a total experience that flows from the body to the social world and vice versa.

A resurgence of 'the subjective' in social science, i.e. as found in anthropology, is at the core of change. Anthropologists have used their 'selves', and their experiences of distress and suffering as data to oppose medical, psychiatric and 'others' views' (Church 1996; DiGiacomo 1987; Murphy 1987). These are powerful voices that counter professional discourse on disorder, and the work is important in resisting and reversing the process of depersonalization that accompanies an alien and alienating medical discourse. They also challenge the usual anthropological view and make regeneration possible. If psychiatry shares its constructions of and presuppositions about psychic disorders with the beliefs of the society of which psychiatry is a part (cf Gaines 1992), and the diagnosis of 'madness' is a process that starts in the community and ultimately comes to its formal conclusion in a psychiatric clinic, it is important to have an approach that enables people to be active agents. This offers alternatives (Frank 1995) to the authorative ways of expression.

Illness itself does not lead to critical autobiography. It needs cultural authorization, which until recently has been lacking. Frank (1994) has referred to the subjective narratives of illness and suffering as an 'orphan genre'. The situation is changing, but many stories still disappear behind professional discourse. With the conclusion that in psychiatry therapists and patients lack a 'shared myth' and that patients must invent their own myths (Kirmayer 1993; Good 1994), the idea that psychotic patients will have to 'wander', 'tinker' and employ strategies to survive emerges. The mythical thought of psychotic patients appears to be a form of *bricolage* (a tinker's artifact). It 'builds up structures by fitting together events, or rather the remains of events' (Lévi-Strauss 1962, 1996: 22). Because their narratives are forbidden, psychotic people have to travel through time and space, through history and future, collecting 'events' or the remnants of events to give meaning to their experiences and their suffering. This act of dwelling is an act of total experience for the person: body, life, and being-in-the-world. But the authorized therapeutic myth has a power beyond those *bricolages*. It 'creates its means and results in the form of events, thanks to the structures which it is constantly elaborating and which are its hypotheses and theories' (Lévi-Strauss

1962, 1996: 22). There does not seem to be a midway between the two, for in Saint Anthony's psychotic patients are split into a 'healthy' part and a 'sick' part. Therapists 'work' with the first. The 'sick' part, the psychotic world, is tamed, eliminated or forgotten in psychiatric practice, but it remains the source from which patients derive meaning in their lives.

The personal experience and the life-world of psychotic people are subjective and may seem 'unknowable', but by making use of the stories which therapists and psychotic people tell about themselves, about each other and to each other, it is possible to offer an account of their 'lived' world. Frequently recurring conversational themes and the positions adopted by therapists and patients relative to each other and their illness come to symbolize the suffering of psychotic people. Therapy and narrativization are efforts to 'find an image around which a narrative can take shape'; the communication can be viewed as 'a process of locating suffering in history' (Good 1994: 128). It is sad to witness that the struggle of psychotic people to find meaning often fails, because psychiatry cannot meaningfully symbolize their suffering (cf Good 1994: 130). Just like patients, the therapists and researchers are in a sense caught in their culture, the 'reservoir of knowledge from which they can draw interpretations' (Habermas 1988). For therapists and patients culture is a shared well, yet they do not draw the same water from it.

I try to show how in their reflections and conversations psychotic people, more clearly than therapists, arrive at *bricolage* intent on regaining wholeness in their experiences of inner fragmentation. To compare psychotic people with 'bricoleurs' occasions a reference to 'the mytho-poetical nature of bricolage' (Lévi-Strauss 1962, 1996: 17): in the sense of its unforeseen results. The elements that psychotics draw on are combinations possibly restricted by the fact that they derive from a language 'where they already possess a sense which sets a limit on their freedom of maneuver' (Lévi-Strauss 1996: 19). Often, others can only guess at the meaning, because the structure is so reorganized that its resemblance to the original is vague. The bricoleur gives an account of his world by the choices he makes and, as Lévi-Strauss argues, 'speaks not only with things, but also through the medium of things'. I link elements of the (subjective) understanding and use of models by therapists and patients, with actions. As the various contexts unravel, I show how they are mutually related, obstruct one another, or lead to paradoxes and contradictions. For example: empathy towards and distance from patients is both encouraged and discouraged by how psychotic people are (theoretically) split into healthy and unhealthy parts. This irreconcilable world reveals the struggle of patients to live and to survive, and the damaging aspects of culture. Although the interactions may seem odd because they are frozen by inscription, there is an intricate and at times very delicate choreography in an interaction. The restrictions imposed by the discussion partners and freedoms which they grant each other are at the heart of this interplay. One of the restrictions in the dialogue is, for instance, that not everything the patient says is considered equally worthwhile for the therapeutic process (cf Ten Have 1987: 164). The analysis will make clear that 'worthwhile' should be understood in terms of valid and true rather than in terms of utility. Sometimes patients learn to look upon their problems as invalidity that requires a prosthesis or permanent medication and learned techniques to avoid stress, or as a reversible psychic malfunction. Self-evident views and actions are made into a problem and subjectivized.[31]

In the microcosm of the interactions, the expressions and behavior of the patients are continually tested for abnormality by the therapists. At the same time both groups must create the room needed to tackle the patients' problems. Encounters between therapists and patients are 'focused interactions' (Goffman 1963b); that is to say, they are occasions where people meet expressly to discuss a shared problem. To be able to talk about the problem it is assumed that a measure of agreement should be achieved between the partners. Agreement implies an acknowledgement of validity and an essential openness to criticism of each other's utterances (Habermas 1988). Often it is very difficult for therapists and patients to reach this kind of agreement. I show that it requires the specific features of a psychiatric institution and the rules of psychiatric consultation, the rules of asymmetry, firmly anchored presuppositions, power, ethics, morals and truth: all of which are in turn linked to specific situations.[32]

Communication between therapist and psychotic person is, as I shall show, a conversation about each other's truths, with a sizeable risk of dissent. Dissent and conflict confirm and strengthen the discussion partners' presuppositions, and reduce the space for subjective experiences. The analysis shows that communication consists of 'simple repairs; leaving controversial truth claims aside and out of consideration, the consequence of which is that the common ground of shared convictions shrinks; the transition to superficial discourse with uncertain results and the effects of new problems arising; break-down in communication and finally a shift to strategic action' (Habermas 1988: 84). If the intention is to analyze the conversations between therapists and psychotic people, relatively few persons can be involved in the research. The approach is individually oriented and remains as close as possible to the texts of people. Although it is not the only way to investigate the role of culture in a person's existence, this type of analysis can yield subtle interpretations when attempting to approach the life of psychotic people from an internal perspective, in spite of incompletely articulated experiences.

The aim of the analysis is an interpretation which, via the surface of discourses between psychotic people and others including therapists, describes and explicates the 'depths' of human subjectivity. My aim is neither therapeutic nor 'monkey gazing'. What I mean to do is to is to give voice to 'excluded discourse'. As Frank (1995: 15) has said: 'Illness can teach us all how to live a saner, healthier life. Illness is a threat to life, but it also witnesses what is worth living.'

Chapter 3

Shaping the context of speech events

Models of therapists and patients

Prior to admission and during hospitalization, the experiences of psychotic patients at Saint Anthony's psychiatric hospital often led to a 'battle for reality'; a struggle between patients and therapists about conflicting explanations of illness and constructions of reality. Psychotic people, family members, neighbors and therapists frequently attached widely differing meanings to the signs of distress that accompanied the onset of psychosis. Because this conflict rarely emerged in the conversations, I met the groups separately so that therapists and patients could talk freely about their interaction, without endangering any delicately balanced relationships.

How psychosis is explained

Before admission to a psychiatric hospital there is an inexorable transition in which psychotic people feel as if they are being pushed to the margins of society, and experiencing social death. Everyday thoughts and feelings tend to become hindrances and with this disintegration, order collapses. Well before the full onset of psychosis, telltale signs[1] have intruded, including hallucination, depression, hyper-reaction and feelings of remoteness. Since these symptoms are not initially interpreted as a problem, they are rationalized and often dismissed. The trigger can be conflict or tragic events such as the loss of a partner, losing a job or failing at school, and the crisis is often blamed on tension:

> I was a tiler, and worked much too hard, slaving away, working overtime, achieving; that piled on the tension. When it happened to me I ran to the library to see if there were still people who could understand me.

The metaphor of a steam engine, well known in the Netherlands, is frequently used by psychotic patients to express distress (Nichter 1981),[2] without connecting it immediately to madness or mental illness. As accumulated stressful situations merge to elevate the distress, the first signs of approaching psychosis are dismissed as 'blowing off steam', and 'reducing the pressure'. This is also an attempt to transform it into a less frightening emotional problem, and my case studies indicated that it led to problems being neglected until a crisis point was reached. Until then, the stressed person was described as 'quiet', 'remote', having 'strange notions' or 'something wrong in the head'. Rationalizing or denying pre-psychotic and psychotic phenomena conforms to the norms, values and beliefs regarding the individual, as well as notions and assessments of madness in current Dutch society. The process of denial and rationalization indicate that irrationality and vulnerability are 'forbidden' territory. Not only is there an initial denial of the seriousness of psychotic thought patterns and behavior, but there is also a tendency to tolerate its growth for as long as possible. In Dutch culture, privacy is highly valued and the individual has a great deal of latitude. Intimate feelings are often not expressed and many topics are avoided, even in the familiar social settings of family, work environment or neighborhood. Neighbors may be willing to take action if someone is experiencing psychological problems, but seldom before it reaches an advanced stage.[3]

An example: Mrs Jansen lived with her daughter in an intolerable situation, a *folie à deux*, and it took several years before help was sought or given. Mrs Jansen claimed that she and her daughter were terrorized by magicians who prowled around the house. They were out to get the daughter, especially if she wanted to undertake something by herself. Mrs Jansen used pills and injections to counter the illnesses that the magicians induced in her daughter, although the daughter reportedly began to develop doubts about these 'magicians' and resisted the treatment. Their quarrels and fights were clearly audible in the neighborhood. The family doctor and their relatives were aware of the events, but found it impossible to act until it had escalated to the point where neighbors called in the police. The daughter had hit the mother on the head, and was taken away. After the municipal health service (GG and GD) interceded, the daughter was admitted to a psychiatric clinic. As long as Mrs Jansen successfully projected a public image of being 'normal', albeit over-concerned about her daughter, no one seemed in a hurry to act. Evidently the idiom of distress must be very powerful to prompt any sort of response. This reflects views about privacy and personal space, as well as widely held notions of competence and autonomy. The effect is that people strive for as long as possible to present a semblance of normal behavior to the world. Often it is not only the problem that is hidden: when the person is also made invisible, like Mrs Jansen hiding her daughter, the situation becomes almost impenetrable. Patients at Saint Anthony's often hid themselves, retreated to their rooms or remained indoors. A patient (Joanna) said:

> I sort of thought, well, I want to do this myself. I had this before, when I wanted to get married and I solved that myself, so I will be all right this time, too. I am not going to bother them [the relatives] with this.

Making the problem 'invisible' means that others remain unaware of it or hold back because of the high threshold before intervention. However, if the invisibility is exaggerated and there are other signs of concerted action to escape detection, the situation can become sufficiently powerful to provoke outside agency. This is what happened with Joanna, who was admitted to a short-term ward at the psychiatric hospital for the first time after being compelled by a court order. She arrived there in a condition of serious neglect: full of fear, feeling extremely vulnerable and believing that the world had turned against her. A short synopsis of her life revealed why. Her mother had committed suicide; her father sent his children to church every day to pray for the salvation of their mother's soul; her own marriage had gone sour; and her daughter never lived with her because she moved continually between rented rooms. In the end, Joanna's only wish was to have a place of her own. When an inheritance enabled her to buy a flat she tried to order her life, but her income was insufficient to cover the costs. Turning her home into a literal fortress, she barricaded herself inside and would let nobody in. Joanna was eventually declared bankrupt and placed under legal restraint. From the moment she was evicted by the police and had to move to another flat, the war was on:

> I felt myself mentally invaded. To me it seemed that they were trying to break me. There was a big conspiracy against me.

The relationship with the new landlord soon degenerated:

> I had no trust any more. When they cleared me out of the flat I felt like a Jew being deported. They pestered me.

Patient histories in this book reveal recurrent conflict and evidently (besides relationships with family members) the lives of psychotic people are dominated by their relationships with the outside world. The social network to which they have instrumental and emotional recourse tends to be limited and weak[4] and their capacity to resolve conflict with authority figures (such as a work supervisor) is inadequate. More often than not, an attempt to reverse the process of social isolation and rejection will fail, leading to feelings of powerlessness, helplessness, hurt, inadequacy, anger and fear. According to Joanna:

> I wasn't allowed a thing. My landlord permitted nothing. I was not supposed to pay rent; I was not supposed to do anything. I just eh had nothing at all. Well, once in a while N. [the caretaker] would drop by and her little office, that was close to me there too, around the corner and I could have a quick cup of coffee, yes, and other than that eh I did nothing else when I was awake, usually around noon, then – and if I went out, I went to B. [the pub], starting on beer immediately and around about five I would go the Hema [a department store], to get a warm meal yes, and after that back to B. and at night eh I came back to that flat.

To express their distressed state of mind people intentionally cross the socially accepted and determined limits of communication and behavioral norms:[5]

You see the whole world was against me. I went out with my hair in a mess and unwashed, because I thought: Let the whole world see what they have done to me. But they didn't really look. There are lots of strange people walking around.

If this step did not succeed, another boundary had been crossed. Joanna's therapist told me:

She sat in her open house day and night. The dossier mentioned a woman lying behind the window frame, suicidal tendencies.

Eventually her behavior led to admission to the psychiatric ward. These intentional forms of expression, however, always seemed to operate in two directions. They were ways of hiding emotional and social problems, in order not to be forced to speak of them, or to escape them. On the other hand, they were also ways of expressing the person's condition. People revealed themselves through such behavior and it made sense because it enabled others to take over and make the decisions. The kind of idiom used by people to express their state of mind is obliquely related to an appreciation of skills such as the ability to cope, responsibility, competence and self-control. The choice of idiom is related to society's ideas of what a mentally healthy person should be capable of. It comprises behavioral forms such as self-neglect, alcoholism, vagrancy, aggression, exhibitionism or suicidal tendencies that do not resonate with society's image of nurturing or respect for one's own life, physical body and privacy, or that of others. The choice of a specific idiom is not random: it depends on the social circumstances of people and the changes that occur in them. For example, people often behaved out of character. When the problems manifested and the psychotic disorder began to take form, most of the patients lived with their parents or a partner.[6] It was estimated that almost half of them began to wander about, while the balance lived on the street or became very reclusive. Quite suddenly, a woman who had been a hard-working housewife and caring mother turned slovenly. Joanna, who had wished so strongly for her own home, neglected not only herself but her new flat as well, leading to conflicts in her personal network. Loners like Joanna gradually slid into extreme self-neglect, possibly in combination with attempted suicide. In Dutch society, vagrancy is associated with failure, drugs, alcoholism or psychological problems, but a wandering psychotic is highly visible in public[7] because exhibitionism, loud behavior, or total neglect call attention to the person, in addition to the usual vagrancy and begging. Psychotics also stand out because compared with wandering alcoholics they tend to be 'loners'; people who neither seek nor desire contact and make this clear by their body language. They also tend to return home, albeit at irregular hours. Wandering is a way of expressing dissatisfaction and malaise, and it has sufficient communicative power to be recognized by others, to be understood, and to trigger a response. One therapist recalled:

> He was wandering through the city, badly catatonic. He was very disheveled and neglected. Expelled everywhere; people abused him.

Another remarked:

> You could see him degenerate, drinking, wandering. For years he was in a psychotic world, so that absolute degeneration followed. At that point we stepped in.

In the Netherlands 'we' usually means parents, the police, municipal health service or social workers or a combination of the above. Sometimes wandering is seen as a way to avoid the reactions of others to the psychotic disorder (Baasher *et al.* 1983), to avoid conflict at home, or to escape from expectations and emotional pressure (Giel *et al.* 1974). As I see it, however, this interpretation has an individualizing effect and it too readily assumes that the psychotic person is a *homo calculus*. To wander or to retreat is both functional and significant in making it clear to others that something is seriously wrong, and it also attempts to clarify very decisive pointers in a person's life. Christian:

> I was sitting at the table writing something shortly after my final exams, and then I went outside and the world had suddenly changed. After that I went completely crazy. I went wandering everywhere, I went to Rotterdam, then to Amsterdam, but I kept running into the same world, just like it was back home. It drove me mad. Everywhere everything was different . . . They were all things that went against my principles. There were a lot of automobiles and they all drove very fast. And then again they drove slower, pulling out on purpose when I came by . . . I see people saying that I am crazy . . . Those things . . . It seemed as if the whole world was against me . . . I felt threatened.

The above excerpt illustrates that the functional objective of this kind of idiom can differ from psychiatrists' expectations. The intention underlying the wandering had moved it to another plane: here, wandering was a kind of test, checking to see if the world had really changed. It sought an answer to the question: 'Who is crazy, them or me?' Wandering, like licentiousness or neglect, could also signify an act of opposition on the part of psychotic people. Bert took a stance against society with its rules and regulations. To him wandering constituted freedom, as passages from his diary clearly showed:

> When I am on the street and I get the urge again, I know that there is a way out . . . The weight is heavy, it burdens me. I really have to shake off this madness, otherwise I will go crazy. A child knows that, but I am no longer a child. I smell, taste and I myself can see now, and that is my great freedom. So, in the years I still have to live, I must throw myself into

everything that is invisible and visible. Feeling good and knowing that you are an angel who lets nothing disturb him. That is really your true self. But, too bad, I am not alone in this world and I have to fit in with the world as it is, a world where everybody is in a hurry. I'm not, I have time and a life of my own. That is my fortune . . . stepping into a life without restrictions. That is the bliss that has been given to us, is it not? And we need not lose heart, much better to get out of the mire.

Sometimes wandering can provide a meaningful context for one's own identity, the lived experience of being-in-the-world, or of an earlier existence:

I've always been an outdoor person . . . I live in the times of *The Painted Bird*[8] really . . . That's about a little boy, really. A little boy of eight, whom the Germans, eh eh, the father and the mother, too, were taken by the Germans. And they wander to Poland. And there they really . . . in my feeling I am very much like that little boy of eight years . . . I simply had to. I had to follow that route . . . Final year of the HBS[9] and all that, and after that I started roaming . . . I studied mathematics and for the rest I moved around . . . That makes me the kind that does not die in bed, I will die in the street.

How patients experience hospital admission

When a patient voluntarily consults a physician it is usually in connection with a complaint, coupled with a request for healing. Psychotic people usually do not directly express complaints and they are, as a rule, admitted to the psychiatric hospital by parents, an agency such as RIAGG (regional ambulatory psychiatric services), or on account of a court order. Since others filed the complaint, the psychiatrist examines the patient to determine if the complaint is justified. To expedite this, people are placed in the admission unit of the hospital, often in a closed ward, where the conditions reinforce feelings of helplessness, vulnerability and incompetence. This is especially true of people who are admitted on the basis of a court order or after having been taken into police custody. Joanna:

I didn't know there was a court order for me. I mean eh . . . I eh . . . Well, I have eh . . . at the . . . M.-avenue early March, eh doctor H came by. And I had a short talk with him and he was sent by the court, and he eh . . . probably eh . . . he has probably passed it on and after that eh . . . the prosecutor and doctor H eh . . . Mr D, my lawyer eh at first anyway. And those two people from the homebuilders association, the caretaker and a social worker, too, of the housing association, about eight people were there that morning. And then eh . . . it was decided that I would be taken into the hospital here. And about a week later, eh . . . a Monday morning, the caretaker and the social worker came back and they called a taxi for me and they brought me here.

Maybe everything was said before, but I don't really recall that now. I mean, it was only when I got to D [a ward] that I really discovered that there was a court warrant for me, what that meant . . . When I got to D I noticed that eh that I had lots more restrictions that for instance if eh . . . C came on her own, voluntary-like and eh . . . I found out that there was a court warrant for me because I was only allowed three-quarters of an hour eh . . . or some-times I could go an afternoon. But eh . . . yes, I simply noticed that for me there were a lot more . . . and that's when I really understood that I was really there by warrant of the court.

Besides their freedom and initiative being restricted, people experienced this kind of admission as if it were an external event and they were dazed bystanders. Once inside the hospital, they felt as if they had arrived on an island with but one category of patients: people with psychotic disorders. There was a certain image attached to a psychiatric hospital, and to have to see and hear 'those people' induced fear. Joanna:

I was still very much afraid to have to stay with all those people and so I have arranged beforehand with R: if it doesn't work I want to go back to the consultation room.

The feeling was one of alienation. Marie:

I spent two weeks at D. That was a closed ward. I didn't belong there, you know. All those men and women walking around, screaming and crying. I only spent two weeks there, thank God.

New arrivals expressed feelings of compassion and pity for others in the hospital, and a fear of becoming 'like that':

I can remember that I sat here at the table for the first time. Inside, I was laughing at all of them. They were all little children eating their little sand-wich. I had this inside. Those people who lived like that and talked like that and so on. They really pulled me down with them, you know? To that black hole.

Admission to a psychiatric hospital could be compared to a form of culture shock. People were confronted directly with others whom they considered crazy, and realized that for the time being they had to live with them and spend a large portion of the day in their company. They had to adjust their behavior to the ward and to the hospital rules. It was also a shock to note that other people were 'that way' and that every thought and deed prior to one's own illness was clearly not as self-evident as hitherto assumed. People did not arrive on just any island; in fact, they found themselves on a therapeutic island (Van Haaster 1991: 18).

Among other things it meant that the task and role divisions of patients and staff were quite clear, sometimes stated in a written contract. Psychiatric treatment was the basis of this contractual relationship. Although the hospital tried to conclude written agreements with all psychotics, this could not work where patient admission had been involuntary or patients may have been totally confused about the events. Caregivers outside the realm of the patient decided on the construction of the problem, the proposed treatment and its desired effect. The psychotic person's interaction and freedom of movement were restricted, and predictably there was frequent resistance in this initial period. A patient recalled:

> In the beginning I fought admission tooth and nail. Later on I worked out that I should do something to be able to return to the community and to lead a normal life.

Resistance was fueled not only by the involuntary admission and fear of hospitalization, but also the person's conviction that he or she was not ill. In addition, a psychosis brought a 'thrill' to some patients:

> At that point I was admitted to the hospital and I did not want that, because I really felt on top of the world and I did not want to be admitted. So they took me, they took me into custody and admitted me and afterwards I realized that it was the right thing because I was very confused.

When patients were isolated it emphasized the aspect of danger and people fought to retain a feeling of freedom:

> Yes, I was in the isolation room. Yes, it was bare. There are just a few things that catch your attention. Just those lamps along the side. When you look out through the little window you see a set of those lamps. That made you look for a meaning. And I had the idea that I could make myself very small. As if I could crawl under the door.

During the first phase of psychiatric treatment serious behavioral problems occurred which according to the psychiatric literature were mostly due to the psychosis, but masked by medication. The antipsychotic medicines often caused a feeling of alienation and numbing.

> Because at one point they prescribed Cisordinol for me. That made me very sleepy and very dull. You know, I just wasn't myself. So I protested and I was allowed to stop for a while . . . One night I asked H what kinds of pills these were and what they were supposed to do, that sort of thing. And when I heard that it was Cisordinol, and that this was administered in cases of psychosis . . . yes, then I knew what was wrong with me.

Involuntary admission and isolation meant that the contractual relationship between hospital staff and patients often turned to conflict. When people did not feel ill or if their experience was one of great freedom, therapists found it difficult to present convincing arguments about how good and necessary it was to restrict their freedom. The distance between patients and the agencies that arranged the involuntary admission was so great that people were often unable to protest or formulate their own sound judgment about their condition. Objections and resistance were then transferred to and expressed by agency of hospital staff members, who had to deal with the moral aspects of the admission. It seemed that coercive measures were contrary to the ethical medical code, which stated that intervention and treatment should take place at the request and with the approval of patients. However, staff members felt that if they did not intervene, they were being morally negligent. One therapist stated: 'Suffering justifies intervention, often psychosis is hell.' Patients looked on individual mental health workers as substitutes for the authority that ordered their admission and therefore therapists were likely to encounter criticism and resistance. Another reason why relationships between therapists and psychotic patients tended to be fraught with conflict was that initially they disagreed over psychiatric, internalizing ideas around the causes of illness. Patients referred less to illness within themselves and more to the consequences of ill-making aspects of their culture and society. Almost every patient points therapists to a deviation somewhere other than within themselves: 'This is a power outside of me.' The psychosis originated in collaboration with others, with the other. Eva said:

> The world is a kind of tower of Babel and the world is coming to an end . . . I think that, because I am Eve, I am the smartest of all the people and I am murdered. I am a kind of sacrifice . . . Those who nurtured me made a kind of Christ-figure out of me. Abraham also went to sacrifice his little son, but God put a stop to that . . . I must die.

As seen by patients, their dilemma stems from an outside world that is evil, indifferent and cold:

> I have passed through great dangers. B is an evil city. I notice that B is kind of closed to me. Everyone can hack away at everybody else, whenever he wants. I went through a lot of things in B. It is a mess out there . . . Just do your own thing, as long as you don't bother us, they say.

A mental health worker's comment on the above statement shows how widely views differ:

> He has delusions, or let's say the delusion that everybody in B is bad, that they are all after him . . . He has no insight into his own condition.

Although therapists do point out the negative processes in society that can contribute to psychological problems, they primarily address the individual, rather than the significance of external events. A therapist:

I, too, think that this is disgraceful. But if I tell you this, what happens? What happens is that I think I'm leaving you in the lurch with your problem. What happens is that I would join you in the shit and wail along with you – and while I do that I'm really taking you for a ride. You hope I can do something, but on this thing I'm powerless. That doesn't help you.

What counts, ultimately, is the psychotic individual. Whether the admission to hospital is voluntary or induced, psychotics are cut loose from everyday life and placed outside of reality in three ways. First, the person's behavior is abnormal and this leads to admission. Second, his views on what causes his problems are framed as unrealistic. Third, patients find themselves marooned on a therapeutic island. On this island the patient is at the beginning of a new career, a career that is by and large identical for each patient. Progress is marked by an incremental freedom to maneuver and more opportunities to interact, as the patient keeps pace with a growing sense of reality and constructs a new reality. Patients are allowed to move from the restricted ward to open units, then to resocialization units, day care and treatment, sheltered housing and finally, depending on the situation – back home.

Sometimes there is a complete break, as when people are placed in a restricted ward. The period shortly after admission, prior to medication, can be compared to a condition of liminality (cf Turner 1974, 1975), marked by chaos and lack of harmony. Staff members redress the situation by administering antipsychotic medication. When the uncontrollable chaos has been checked and the patient is no longer subject to the caprices of his psychosis, he can be moved to an open unit. Open units do not comprise a group of 'similars', but are rather composed of patients with diverse problems. Reintegration into society follows within the symbolic domain of psychiatry, and this is the perspective used to analyze complaints and their background. The psychotic crisis is defined as a reaction to the patient's inability to cope with transitions in life, and to deal with crises. Therapists and patients must come to embrace this explanation if patients are to gain faith in the therapeutic myth that the employment of a specific therapy can improve the condition, that is, 'heal' the patient. The path leading to this faith is via therapeutic rituals such as conversations with the therapist, 'living-room' conversations, and group therapy sessions consisting of narratives with significant elements that help to explain the illness and its cause or origin. By way of these rituals, a new reality is constructed which, if it is accepted by patients, offers enough of a perspective and foothold to return to a 'normal' life. However, I frequently heard it stated that 'I had to do something to get back into society and live normally', which may have indicated desperation for change rather than faith in the therapeutic myth. I found it difficult to determine whether patients really wanted help in the initial stages of hospitalization, but I noted that in time people who had resisted or denied feeling ill, said that after reconsidering matters, their admission had been necessary:

> At the time I did not consider myself ill. I went along with it completely. It was reality for me and I kept myself preoccupied to the point that I had time for attention for other things. I saw all kinds of images. I saw a lot of people at one point. I saw many delusions. And because of that I could cope no longer. I simply had to be taken into the hospital.

Once the patient has accepted the myth, action becomes possible and it is time to look for culturally acceptable techniques to control the psychosis in order 'to be able to return to society'. In effect, meanings are being transformed (the manner of these transformations is explained in Chapter 6). The drama of a person's psychosis is highly individual and from the outset it is filled with conflict. The potential space (cf Winnicott 1965) for subjective and intersubjective communal experiences is very restricted. The psychotic's relationships with health workers are asymmetrical and those with fellow patients do not lead to communal experience; at most they are recognized or rejected. In the social arena, the therapeutic myth is fragmented. It is not based on a comprehensive world view, but rather on a fragmented model as applied to the individual patient in adjusted forms (cf Van der Hart 1981: 535). In addition to this social fragmentation there are two other factors: the metonymic nature of psychiatry, and the fragmentation of the psychotic person's selfhood.

The battle for reality

Therapists' and patients' models of psychosis

Therapist: His is an attitude of rejection. He hardly adjusts to his environment. He has no test to see if something is possible or not, no criticism. He feels that we are doing something with him that he does not really want.

Patient [speaking of this therapist]: I don't want to disappoint him [the therapist], but I don't quite trust him.

These quotes illuminate widely divergent views on psychotic behavior. The therapist sees a relationship in terms of a patient's limited cognitive capacity and lack of cooperation, whereas the patient describes the therapist in terms of feeling (distrust). They tend to view their battle as a consequence of different ways in which the world is experienced and understood, and as the quote shows, reserve is seen as rejection. Differences such as this are a basic condition of therapeutic interactions, because the battle is fought out of necessity and with a specific purpose. The goals may vary from improving productivity (i.e. the number of discharges from the hospital, a frequent objective in the case of short-term stays), to improving the quality of life of long-term residence patients. In interacting with psychotic people, the importance that hospital staff attach to these differences is so great that they function as criteria of whether or not a person is psychotic. Thus, reality awareness and reality testing (and more particularly their absence in a patient) are important concepts in the stories that mental health workers use when working with psychotic people.

Models used by therapists

When mental health workers attempt to determine a patient's degree of reality awareness and reality testing they can make use of certain diagnostic criteria and psychiatric models. The professional or expert models (Keesing 1987: 371; Gaines 1979) should be distinguished from the models used on patients. The latter are based on direct experience whereas professional models are seen as 'experience distant'. This means that one can expect a distant, more or less neutral value and emotion-free therapist description of the patient's condition: in fact, therapist models are far from homogeneous. Research in this area suggests that the interpretations and descriptions given by therapists are embedded in cultural ideas that preceded their formal training but have continued to influence their judgment (Light 1980). Analysis of the formal diagnostic systems indicates that these are not free of cultural prejudice (Gaines 1992; Richters 1988; Young 1988). Therapists do not describe the condition of their patients in neutral terms. Their descriptions are couched in cultural terms of what is and what should be, since the picture of how a person *ought to be* is implicit in psychiatric diagnosis and terminology. Moreover, the descriptive terminology is not free of idio-syncratic elements and emotions. In particular, the emotional involvement of therapists with their patients becomes clear in descriptions of patient behavior. In simple terms: therapists are ordinary human beings who use ordinary (everyday) images and words and who seemingly have little interest in formal terminology and professional language. Their concern is their relation with psychotics. The problem is that in this pursuit they do not (or cannot) explain their own view of reality. Terms like *psychosis* and *psychotic* are used to describe a vast complex of phenomena associated with disturbances in reality testing and awareness. The ways in which mental health workers describe patients may be divided into the six categories shown in Table 3.1.

Therapists usually describe the experiences of psychotic people in terms of what they lack: 'has no confidence'; 'unable to cope with sorrow'; 'lack of awareness'; 'unrestricted experiences'. Implicit in this is the sort of experiences that people ought to have in order to be healthy: confidence, power, controlled experience, and so on. In the descriptions of therapists, behavior is the most import-ant since it gives a concrete indication of the degree to which patients are realistic and have insight into their situation. The type and frequency of patient behavior can reveal the lack of awareness of social norms, which is why in the

Table 3.1 Mental health workers' descriptions of patients

Type of description	Mental health worker statements
Personality	"He is a vulnerable person."
	"Her limits are vulnerable."
Character	"Untouchable."
	"Impulsive."
	"Individualistic."
	"Negative."
Cognitive functioning	"Unable to make things bearable."
	"Unable to interpret his own situation."
	"Unable to state objectives."
	"Hardly able to situate oneself in history."
Psychological capacity	"Chaotic and unstructured."
	"Delivered up to powers."
	"Self-alienating ideas."
	"Confused."
	"Flighty."
Psychical condition	"Catatonic."
	"Pacing around."
	"Having the jitters."
Emotions	"Without emotions."
	"Cold."
	"Mood changes."
	"Loss of emotional depth."

hospital more attention is paid to what people do than to what they say. The terms used to describe the behavior indicate how therapists view the interaction and how they experience the behavior of psychotics. The approachability of a patient is important and the descriptions indicate that therapists consider themselves to be the active and well-intentioned party in the interaction: 'He shows flight'; 'she is hard to approach'; 'you cannot follow him'; 'I can't get a hold on him'.

Therapists consider the patient to have closed the door on a productive therapeutic relationship. Proximity plays a major role: 'he is losing distance'; 'he draws me into his world'; 'there is a wide gap between him and me'; 'he keeps his distance'; 'she draws back from suggestions or advice'; 'there is irrationality and unfriendliness'. In the interaction the patient is like a container, a space that the therapist can decide whether or not to enter: 'he is quite open' or 'he locks himself up completely'. Once the therapist enters the space he is confronted with certain tactics: 'his attitude is one of rejection'; 'he leans on me'; 'his jokes are intended to avoid the issue'; 'he tries to provoke me'; 'he makes bizarre moves'; 'he is aggressive'; 'he is impulsive'; 'he is playing a game'. The descriptions clarify the expectations regarding the character of interaction with patients. In dealing with psychotic people a therapist is engaged in a never-ending effort to decrease the interpersonal distance between him/her and the patient. The therapist is like Elmer Fudd who keeps trying to catch Bugs Bunny, but never quite succeeds.

The descriptions show that therapists and nursing staff base their statements on experience and interaction in daily clinical practice. They reveal the model of reality applied by mental health workers, a model in which behavior and the social-interactive aspects take center stage. The process of making sense of this and the meanings that health workers extract from it remain in the background. We might say that patients are turned into a collection of components: characteristics, behaviors, and experiences. In the interaction, one component stands for the patient and his disorder. In essence, the part represents the whole. Thus, psychiatry is metonymic.

Patients are unaware of the view of reality shared by therapists and other staff members. The views invariably remain implicit. When for example a therapist says of a patient that the latter is 'very open', the statement implies that the therapist presupposes that people normally should not be that open. Conversely, 'locking up completely' implies that a certain degree of openness is considered normal. On account of the obscurity of the reality views, the boundaries between normal and abnormal are blurred. Individual patients have different notions concerning things 'healthy' or 'unhealthy', depending on what transpires during the interaction. It may happen that one therapist describes a patient as 'unapproachable' while another mentions his 'unhealthy openness'. This depends in part on the behavior of the patient during the interaction with the therapist, but also on the predetermined views of the therapist.

In a sense the models are operational (Caw 1974): in interactions with psychotic people, they have a steering effect on the behavior of therapists and nursing staff. Such behavior is to an important degree preoccupied with management of the interactions. The models reflect the relationship between therapists and patients, in that they specify notions about power relations, positions and roles. They restructure and strengthen beliefs about psychotic people and the therapist's own position because they do not refer to a fixed, realistic frame of reference. 'Reality,' says one staff member, 'is the world as I see it.' That is to say, mental health workers have subjective frames of reference and these can sometimes lead to misunderstandings which in turn affect their interaction with patients. A misunderstanding of this kind is that certain expressions or behaviors of patients are called psychotic although, upon closer inspection, they prove not to be so. The following excerpt in which a female patient recounts that she is unable to sleep at night and keeps listening to her roommate's breathing, illustrates this (the roommate had been given sleeping pills):

It caused her to breathe very laboriously. I recognized that breathing from the time that I worked in a hospital. After a while it began to panic me, really, because the breathing kept taking longer, the periods in between breathing kept getting longer. So it seemed as if she was dying. Then I heard nothing, and I went to the nurse. I said: she is dead. And he said: Well, that is typically something psychotic. You have a psychosis.

The nurse called the panic reaction a sign of psychosis. The therapist to whom she told the story termed it an over-reaction:

> I would say that this was an overanxious reaction. No psychosis. That would be quite different.

The patient speaks of it as a kind of twilight condition:

> It just has to do with that at night everything is different. It is all quiet and you don't hear anything . . . If you cannot sleep you just lie there thinking and then you hear sounds and all that.

Three interpretations from three people: such fundamental differences in subjective interpretation can easily exacerbate uncertainty and doubt in patients:

> H [the girl with the difficult breathing] sometimes asked me: Do you hear that too? I said: Yes, I hear it too. Oh, she says, if we both hear it nothing is the matter. You can be talked into things, too.

When the term psychotic is used for all patient behavior, it does not necessarily conform to the criteria applied in a ward. Loud behavior, screaming with anger because of failure or disappointment, wanting to be left alone, dreaming of the future, are healthy expressions in certain situations, but they can be dubbed psychotic if the models are used in a manipulative or strategic way, when in fact the intention is to maintain a certain status quo. In many situations a psychotic person is expected to have the insight of a therapist and apparently they often rise to the occasion.

Models used by patients

Just as the therapists and hospital staff use models to make sense of patients, so too do the patients for their caregivers. Patient narratives are characterized by the awareness that madness is incomprehensible, fascinating and ultimately worth administering to. This awareness influences their behavior and has an effect on mental health workers. A short-term resident patient says:

> He does not understand me, but then, I can't be understood.

A long-term resident patient:

> I like to talk to people because I think I have much in me that is interesting.

In the hospital there is power in incomprehensibility, though it is the power of the powerless. A patient believes, psychotically, that he is God. He talks about

Table 3.2 Patients' descriptions of their disorder

Type of description	Patients' statements
Personality	"I am vulnerable." "I have no mastery over my thoughts." "I'm two people."
Character	"Of my own I am restless." "That's my character." "I'm kind of wild."
Cognitive functioning	"I say confusing things." "I cannot be understood."
Cognitive properties	"My brains are wrong." "There is something wrong with my mind."
Emotions	"I am overwrought." "I am always afraid." "I am never happy or joyful."
Accusations	"There is a power outside me." "The devils control my thinking." "Voices are telling me all day what I should do." "The world is against me."

this with his therapist and afterwards says that the therapist does not understand him. The therapist:

> My hypothesis regarding X [the patient] is that he cannot bear the sorrow surrounding his divorce. If you are God you are untouchable. So, when X says that I don't understand him, the very fact of 'not being understood' gives him more strength.

Patients describe their disorder in emotional and evaluative terms. Like the staff their models may be categorized into descriptions of characteristics, experiences and behavior. The characteristics are shown in Table 3.2.

Psychotic individuals associate their *experiences* with specific complaints: tiredness ("I am tired all over"); weakness ("I feel weak"); lack of feeling ("reality is a gray mass"); hurt ("I feel myself mentally attacked"); emptiness ("nothing interests me"). These complaints correspond with symptoms of depression and reflect the theme of loss (cf Foster 1983: 182–187). They are related to meaning: "Life has no meaning for me", and "I must regain joy in my life". Basic to these complaints is a feeling of helplessness, but there are experiences that point in the other direction. These are associated with energy ("in those days I did all kinds of things"); power ("in that case I can cope with life"); richness of feeling ("then I feel rich and happy"); fullness ("I feel the lives of other people inside of me").

In descriptions of their *behavior* oppositions also played an important role. Patients described themselves as closed monads: "I never say what I think"; "I don't want to say anything about that"; "I cannot put it into words". Or they saw themselves as open: "I had no inhibitions"; and "I want to tell everything". Their views on the position and behavior of mental health workers were as contradictory as their self-descriptions, and the contacts were most clearly characterized in terms of a struggle. Therapists were described as enemies ("they are all against me" and "they're out to get me"), as people without sympathy ("he understood nothing"), pedants ("she always knows better"), nags ("he keeps pecking at me"), scoundrels ("all nurses are bastards") or curt-mannered entrepreneurs ("but he is so businesslike"). Then again, therapists and nurses could also be "people who can take it", "people who understand me" and "helpers".

Patients described themselves and others by way of counter-images.[10] When they said that they felt weak, they not only differed from ordinary people whom they supposed to have adequate strength, but also attested to their own feelings of inadequacy. The accent here was not on the interactive level, as in the descriptions given by therapists. Rather, the point was an appreciation of disorder and an evaluation of the self. Counter-images, in turn, also raised questions about norms and values, and the staying power of individuals. This aspect of appreciation also applied to the dimension of interaction.

The counter-images fix 'the difference that makes a difference' (Bateson 1972: 481) from the perspective of the patients and they help to clarify why mental health workers and patients hold such incongruous views. The idiom of distress used by psychotic individuals often gives expression to tensions between the individual and his culture. Others, however, do not understand it as being a commentary, but as an indication that something is wrong or a reason to temporarily isolate someone. As stated above, an assessment of what psychotic people say and think is of less importance than what they do. Accordingly, it is conceivable that the subjective experiences of psychotic people do not play a large role in interaction; that role goes to the subjective experiences of others, as gained in dealing with psychotic people.

During residence in the hospital, patients are supposed to internalize the explanations and psychiatric ideas about therapy and healing, although they are left guessing as to the basis – perhaps it can be termed a world view – in which these assumptions and ideas are embedded. The fragmentation that is typical of psychiatry renders perspicuity impossible. For this reason it is plausible that subjectivity, in the sense of shared tensions or joy experienced between the individual and culture, is not a part of the interaction. Mental health workers and patients offer incongruent models of the disorder and selfhood of patients. This would explain why the values, norms, rules and beliefs of therapists clash with those of the psychotic individual, who considers his own concepts to conform to the values and norms of society and to his image of his own fate. This enduring dichotomy hinders interaction and causes confusion for both the therapists and the persons. Not only does it create confusion, but it also places the psychotic world 'outside' culture. The differences between patients and others in the meanings attributed to the disorder, the behavior and the interactive language are considerable and they constitute the backdrop of problems in interaction.

Chapter 4

Hope and hopelessness, healthy and sick parts

When Juries, a psychotic man, says: 'I'll take the long-term residence', his choice reflects surrender and despair. A significant proportion of psychotic patients at Saint Anthony's hospital are considered to be chronic, which usually means either long-term or permanent residence in a psychiatric institution. A fragment from my conversation with Juries suggests the impact this can have:

> My illness has turned my expectations for the future upside down. I wanted to get married: children, a house, a garden and a dog. But things went differently. All I want now is to go to a small long-term residence apartment. Then I would volunteer to work with the elderly and do fitness training.

In psychiatry, lacking hope epitomizes low self-esteem and ultimately suicide. To have hope is 'healthy', to be without hope is 'sick'. At Saint Anthony's an absence of hope is seen as a symptom of illness, because hope is considered to be a moral imperative, albeit a complex and ambivalent one. Hope normally stresses the individual's will to overcome illness, but this concept would be inconsistent with staff views of psychosis and schizophrenia as illnesses that affect people whose cognitive, emotional and reality-testing capacities have been severely disrupted. At Saint Anthony's hope has another dimension in which therapists and nurses serve as 'anchors' to life and survival. For the patients to be without the hope that this brings would be a sin, because it would mean that they have lost faith and do not believe in the staff's capacity, or the healing power of psychiatry (Van Dongen 1998). Many staff members find this so ambiguous that they eventually lose faith in both the capacity of patients to overcome their illnesses or crises, and the effectiveness of psychiatric treatment. The changes brought by serious psychological disorder are so radical that attainable notions such as having children, a house, a garden and a dog, are transformed into a rather truncated version of what may still be possible. In a psychiatric hospital, optimism about medical progress is confronted by the limitations of existing therapeutic interventions for mental illnesses, in particular chronic disorders such as schizophrenia. Yet, hope is kept alive.

The hospital is divided into two characteristic sections, for short-term residence (STR) and long-term residence (LTR) patients. The two differ distinctly in their objectives and philosophy, and this affects interaction with patients. In both sections expressing madness or speaking about psychotic experiences are mostly seen as counter-productive. Mental health workers in the STR section assumed that they could block access to patients and this presented obstacles to inter-action and treatment. Workers in the LTR section assumed that talking about psychotic experiences would lead to 'unrest' and decrease the level of patient wellness. In truth, it is difficult to examine the psychotic world, and the task becomes doubly intractable given the assumption that the psychotic world cannot be integrated with the 'normal' world. This barrier to clinical interaction impacts on the lives of psychotic people, as illustrated by what a patient and a therapist had to say about psychosis.

> I think my experiences are unreal. I keep saying that, because I think that others think them all unreal. They don't understand anyway. For me it is real, but so are other things, and sometimes I can't keep the two apart. I want you to understand how difficult it is to give everything a meaning, since many things that I saw as images are just things which I experienced before. Those things come back.
>
> (Fatima, STR patient)

> For Fatima, reality and the world of psychotic experience can exist along-side one another. She is very open and talks about it quite freely. At some point, though, I stopped her, because I wanted to stick with reality. The voices, for instance, are threatening. If you don't talk about them any more they recede and become less of a threat.
>
> (Fatima's therapist)

If talking about the psychotic world and expressions of madness are deemed to be counter-productive, it is a small step away from 'censuring' madness. Expressions of psychotic experiences were assigned a minor place in the inter-action process at Saint Anthony's, and prohibiting these expressions required a number of institutional rules backed by specific implementation by health workers and managers in the two sections.

In this chapter, I expand on observations and excerpts taken from my conver-sations with patients and therapists. The conversations reflect on interactions between therapists and patients, and the stories that they tell each other about the future.

Short-term residence and the story of hope

The short-term residence (STR) section takes in people with diverse psycho-logical disorders. More than 30 per cent of its patients are diagnosed as schizophrenic, paranoid or suffering from an unspecified psychotic illness. This proportion is likely to be much higher because people with psychotic disorders are also subsumed under the heading 'mood' disorders.[1] The stated objective of STR is to use care and treatment to heal as many patients as possible, to the greatest extent. An important intervention implemented by the nursing staff, is 'care to measure'.[2] Help is tailored and nothing is offered beyond what is strictly necessary. In relation to care, mental health workers adopt the image of the mother formulated by Winnicott (1965: 58, 145): 'a good enough mother', who successfully adapts to the expressions and needs of patients. This process of adjustment to the individual patient is one reason why we take cognizance of fragmentation in psychiatry. The goal of therapy and treatment is 'depth', the intention is that care should recede over time, and the objective is eventual release. This means that people gradually gain greater insight into their problems, so that treatment can attain a more profound depth.

The short-term resident's interest is expressed in terms of productivity. The STR story is always one of hope, which plays an important role both in caring for and treating patients. In treatment, hope is directed at the 'restoration of the internal dialogue', as one psychiatrist has put it. The important concept here is insight, an insight that is linked to the past. The history of patients and the reasons they give for being ill are prominent in therapeutic conversations. A perspective on the future takes form in the treatment programs, and depends on the career of the patient in the hospital; the clearer the insight, the more favorable the future perspective. Time is a diachronic process, with past and present opposed. Treatment begins in the patient's past and proceeds into the future. The story of hope is also a mirror of faith or belief in progress: it is by *doing* that people improve their situation. In the STR section patients participate in many different therapies. These therapies are subdivided into group and treatment programs intent on the construction of new meanings, as well as an exchange of meaning among patients and between patients and therapists.[3] One such communal program is the 'living-room conversation'. Led by a staff member, the patients discuss their experiences: the topics are personal problems, individual experiences and interaction with others, while treatment programs are divided into group treatments and group therapies.[4] There are consultations between patients and therapists at various stages regarding intakes, evaluations and progress.

Hope and belief in progress are very evident in the care routines. The lives of patients are arranged in minute detail. The day's order is fixed and patients sometimes carry their schedule for the day in their pocket. Routine chores such as shopping, washing the dishes and cleaning the bedrooms are done by patients. Responsibility is restored in increments as a person begins to cope better, and patients gradually take on more self-care tasks during their stay in the hospital. The process runs parallel to a growing insight into personal problems and opportunities. Frequently, psychotic people can confirm the stories that mental health workers tell about those who are psychotic. Hence they can be said to 'assist' therapists in fabricating the story of hope. Although care and treatment are partly the same as that extended to patients who suffer from other disorders, the story of hope and progress is adjusted in the case of psychotic people. 'Hope' in this sense is not intent on healing but on acceptance. As a therapist described it, people 'must learn to accept their illness and learn to recognize their positive points'. We hear an echo in the words of a patient:

> I think that I am getting worse all the time and nobody can do anything about it. I want to get rid of it, but I guess I have to learn to live with it.

Progress at Saint Anthony's was not measured in terms of growth of insight on the part of patients, for insight was lacking in the treatment. Instead, it addressed itself to simple repairs (cf Habermas 1988), and patient care focused on expanding social skills. Patients did not always echo the story of hope, nor did the manner in which it was given form meet their needs. One man commented to me:

> I just sit here and drink coffee. All those people around. They bother me. Not much is being said here. I have nobody who talks to me.

The patients could also disagree with the emphasis on 'belief in progress'. This became clear when I talked to them:

> I expect very little to come of this. I want to get out. Live with my mother and then an apartment of my own.

Psychiatry has managed to find an appropriate method of keeping psychotic disorders in check. Patients note this improvement, but they also express resistance to covering up the madness:[5]

> They do nothing here all day. You are not stimulated here. Games and tinkering, you can't fill your life with that. All you do is drink coffee and wash dishes once in a while. There is just nothing going on. In the past sometimes things did happen. Somebody cut himself or tried to kill himself. Now there is nothing. The whole staff keep saying things we knew long ago. The staff have the power. All they think about is things like society, family, rules – there is no room for anything else.

This reaffirms the notion of 'house, garden and dog' that is important to many, and it strengthens the feelings of abnormality felt by psychotic people. In due course patients must be discharged from hospital and this raises the question of their future, which basically means facing life alone. Mental health workers take cognizance of factors that might disturb the normal story of hope and progress: individual factors such as pathology or dependency, or therapeutic factors such as therapy stop and chronicity: because they could impede independence. The prognosis for psychotic disorders is mostly poor and dependence on others is common. There is only a slight possibility that treatment will bring sustainable personal growth, and a slim chance that it can be terminated. Psychotics confirm this story and because it is retold constantly, it takes on a life of its own (Taussig 1980). Patients fear the future and do not know what to do because when they were admitted their networks were decimated and they experienced social death. Juries:

> I now have a relationship with X. We slept together. That was wonderful. But we don't talk about the future. It scares both of us, I guess. I want to go to the LTR and she wants to go to the Hostel. So, I don't know.

Astride the glimmer of hope stands the patient's narrative of despair, which often leads to a stalemate that therapists must break through. In turn, extensive bargaining regarding the future, discharges from the psychiatric hospital, and repeated readmissions follow.[6] A costly discourse arises in terms of expense, time, effort and suffering (cf Habermas 1988) between therapists and patients. The compromises that are reached are seldom realistic. As it is, psychotic people find it difficult to accept the hope-and-progress story, especially when that story ignites their expectations. Discharged patients can have a feeling similar to that experienced on admission, the feeling of being under duress:

> Yes. And now I have the feeling of, again, they are pushing again. I feel as if I am put out to the street with everything I own. A feeling of, go ahead, rot in the gutter.

Besides resistance to admission or being discharged there is another kind of resistance: to future life as a *psychotic* person. The narrative of mental health workers about psychotics holds out little hope of complete healing. Patients have an insufficiency, so the likelihood of healing is slight. The story is based on the models used by therapists, as described above and continually fleshed out and confirmed in daily practice. This is expressed in the expectations that therapists have of their patients, as evidenced in mutual interactions and therapy in its various forms. The goal of therapy is to let patients understand their insufficiency and accept their limitations. To the extent that it is possible, acceptance and insight are more or less forced. This is not only a matter of the authority, expertise and techniques available to mental health workers; it also reflects the wishes and expectations of society. These often encourage therapists to take refuge in standard stories and techniques, since the story of the therapist becomes a truth that outranks that of patients.

There is a paradox in these truths, in that patients are taught simple skills in order to live and function normally in society, but they discover from stories in the hospital that their future will not be like that of others. Seeing and accepting this fact are inculcated quite forcefully, and this process generates inherent defects and resistance in its wake. Feelings of shame, anger, sorrow and helplessness rapidly transform into resistance:

> They do not take me seriously. Every suggestion you make is shot down.
> They send me from here to there and back again: the RIAGG, the therapist,
> the doctor. If I want to develop myself or if I comment on things I am
> psychotic. Therapists have too many roles. They give treatments, they
> arrange things, they are the doctor, the gatekeeper, the father, the know-it-
> all and so on. That's impossible, isn't it? They rob me of my chance to
> do something with my life. My doctor wants me to go to LTR. What am I
> supposed to do there? Get bored to death?

Transfers from the hospital to sheltered housing or the introduction of other
forms of treatment are marked by crises. These crises are not only the product
of individual psychotic disorders, but also the abrupt breaks that mark the world
of psychotic people. Ultimately, patients have to accept the truth that there is
no other way or place for them to go:

> Three or four years ago they already asked me if I wanted to go to the RIBW.[7]
> I didn't take to the idea at all. Gradually I came to accept it and now I am
> going there.

A number of patients surrender and openly say that they will not be 'cured'.
From a conversation between a nurse and a patient:

P: Yes, the other day I told X [the therapist]: go ahead, put me in the LTR.
       And he said: We are not doing anything with you, he said.
[*Nurse laughs*]
P: And he was right, too.
N: [*laughs*] Well yes, you can eh; I think you can take in that sense, too.
P: Yeah. [*both laugh*]
N: I guess he did not mean it that way, no. And if you are going to go home,
       eh, they try that first, don't they?
P: Yes, I have the idea that . . .
N: Hey? In your case too, eh?
P: I have the idea that it won't work.
N: Won't work?
P: No.
N: No?
P: Yes, it really won't.

The contractually stipulated principle of 'care to measure' gives patients the
freedom to choose forms of therapy with which they have the most affinity,
but it is also manipulative. The statement: 'Put me in the LTR' illustrates the
powerlessness of both psychotic people and hospital staff. To impose order is
a crucial aspect of institutional 'reality construction', whereas a psychosis is always
related to chaos. 'Chaos' is understood in this context as disorderly behavior and

continuous breaches of social rules. When psychotic people cross boundaries, their transgressions are often interpreted as signs of madness. In terms of its specialist knowledge, psychiatry adds yet another important element. Mental health workers view psychosis as loss of structure on the cognitive level and chaos thus refers to 'wild' associations made by the psychotic, the ebb and flow of ideas, and disturbed thinking. This leads to a complete absence of order in behavior: unpredictability, aggression, degrading actions and wandering.

Mental health workers have explicit ideas about the contrast between *chaos* and *structure*. The observable social dimension of chaos is restricted in Saint Anthony's. This restriction begins as soon as a person is taken in, via medical treatment and possibly a spell in a closed ward. The psychotic reality is taboo, but different members of staff have different ideas as to what comprises psychotic reality. One worker may understand something as an expression of the psychotic world of experience while another may consider it a somewhat exaggerated reaction. The phrase 'Reality as I see it' is a telling one. The psychotic world as it appears in hallucinations and delusions is not in itself viewed as 'unclean' or unhealthy. In the hospital people's thoughts and beliefs are not considered objectionable, just as they are not considered objectionable in society at large. Mental health workers do not contradict the psychotic world and even recognize it to have a degree of value:

> Sometimes people design complete systems containing very worthwhile thoughts. That is interesting, because it can cause us to reflect. In those situations I say nothing, for who am I to say what I think about it?

This statement not only shows that in the hospital psychotic reality is credited with a degree of surface value, but also that the cultural norm of freedom of thought is observed. Therefore, from the theoretical point of view, psychotic reality is not a threat to objectivity and after all there is no censure on thought. At times it is clear that mental health workers would like to discuss this reality, but feel they cannot do so in view of patient privacy and the need to maintain a certain distance from one's patient:

> You could have a talk with her that you would just love as therapist. So I have to watch myself, it would be like a kind of incest.

If this section tends to deny inter-subjectivity, it is not the intention. The position of the workers is twofold, with a modicum of contradiction. In the course of treatment a kind of intimacy and partnership arises that may be somewhat forced but is not without demonstrated empathy for the patient. There has to be a degree of intimacy, but the sense is that it should not be overdone for fear of trespassing on the basic tenets of autonomy and privacy. Therapists have by definition to approve of society and its strictures. If they did not, patients would never be willing to work towards a return to society. Mental health workers have to hide their subjectivity, and this attitude is the foundation of any relationship with patients:

Therapist: He [the therapist, EvD] cannot enjoy his own work. He is divorced from it.
Els: Would you explain that?
Therapist: I'll use a metaphor. As father you cannot enjoy your children directly. Ultimately the children no longer go to the father. They go elsewhere. If he tries in any way he moves towards incest. It is not for you. If you want to share the enjoyment you have to distance yourself from your job.

The therapist attaches so great a value to privacy and autonomy that family intimacy is compared with a most intimate violation, hence the image of incest. In terms of pedagogical reality, psychotic reality has a negative ontological status. It does not serve the wellness of patients and it is without therapeutic value. This becomes clear in what mental health workers say:

I do not respond, because if you do things only get worse. You can't go into it too deeply; otherwise you upset him.

'Unseemliness' is the 'waste' associated with psychotic reality, and its process of 'deterioration'. In the clinical interaction, expressions that concern this reality are dysfunctional. They get in the way of progress (STR) or stabilization (LTR). This is not the only reason why the psychotic world is taboo. It violates the world of others, in this case the mental health workers' world – and it upsets them in certain ways.[8] In this connection I have mentioned the phenomenon of countertransference.

While formally and institutionally mental health workers are considered to be authorities and representatives of normal reality, a loss of authority and control affects their subsequent inter-subjectivity, and in turn, their interaction with psychotic people. On the level of interaction this implies confusion and one of the effects is to consolidate countertransference.

I do not intend to pursue the debate on countertransference and how it is to be understood. Good *et al.* (1985) review a number of thoughts on this concept in an article on reflexivity, countertransference and ethnography. Suffice it to explain that the authors understand countertransference as the totality of emotional reactions of mental health workers on patients, which in turn influences the interpretation process of the mental health workers.[9] They suggest that counter-transference is a special, important subtype of more general cultural phenomena: individual interpretations of reality and idiosyncratic networks of significance, which meet in an interaction and sometimes collide, as in the interaction between mental health workers and psychotics. The therapeutic process has a markedly affective dimension. Phenomena of countertransference occur unmistakably in every psychiatric interaction. Whether consciously or not, a mental health worker in interaction with patients is involved in the dynamics of incessant power transitions and colliding realities. These disturbing processes in the interaction with psychotic people keep recurring and may evoke countertransference. This prompts varying reactions from mental health workers. They might say that the patient is presenting nonsense and that the patient is incomprehensible, or there may be a long silence in the conversation if the mental health worker does not react to the disturbance. Therapists may become irritated and show it, but these responses are not by definition proof of incapacity. Assumptions, qualifications, knowledge and emotions all play a role in the interaction. The effects of the countertransference are not always identified, but considered to be a normal part of the interaction with psychotic people, in which case the countertransference will consolidate itself. Mental health workers want to learn about the peculiarities of their patients in order to limit the effect of countertransference. Equally, the patients will get to know the peculiarities of the workers and become familiar with their reactions. A pattern of interaction becomes established, based on routine and familiarity. As seen by a therapist:

> In the LTR he feels secure. I am a kind of father figure and there is a kind of bond of trust between us.

Routine and familiarity are conducive to consolidation of countertransference. The consolidation, in turn, leads to a specific discourse between therapists and psychotic people. In the discourse the countertransference is experienced as a fixed pattern of institutional behavior rather than as disturbance. The pattern arose in the immediate intercourse with psychotic people and is confirmed in the exchange of experiences during team consultations, joint case reviews, supervision, etc. (Light 1980). Mental health workers sanction patient reactions to these disturbances. Countertransference is hidden and absorbed in a perspective on reality in which the behavior of patients is pathological and beyond therapist control. Conversely, the interactive behavior of therapists is realistic, sensitive and corrective. Therapists have command over their interaction and know what it means. 'Containment and manageability are the priorities', according to therapists.

In *Totem and Taboo* Freud (1913) showed an awareness that a taboo serves to protect the psychotic person, but equally to protect mental health workers and the therapeutic process. A therapist said:

> I saw the sorrow and the tension. I was afraid that it would be too much . . . It was somewhat like 'get out of here, this is getting too heavy'.

The fragment illustrates that emotions can play havoc with therapists too. After one consultation the therapist's first reaction was: 'I was profoundly moved by that conversation'. Certain utterances that arise from psychotic experiences are forbidden because they may lead to behavior that oversteps moral limits.[10]

In effect the taboo is a *moral* prohibition, founded on the assumption that chaos leads to immorality. However, I began to wonder if this was the case, since chaos should be equated with anarchy rather than immorality. When psychotic people violate the taboo, in a sense they become taboo. In Saint Anthony's, people were sometimes isolated. This was not done merely to protect the patient but also to protect others against 'infection', since staff were always conscious that patients who displayed overtly psychotic behavior could encourage others in the section to become restless.

A taboo implies that certain aspects of the individual are negative and should be denied by others (Gell 1979). It is the psychotic world that is being denied, although in fact it determines an essential part of patients' experiences. One of the basic characteristics of a psychotic disorder is the phenomenon that people continually move back and forth between the psychotic and the normal world (Jacobsen 1967; Frosch 1983). I did not go into the question of whether this aspect belongs to the symptoms of psychosis or whether it is a consequence of the taboo on psychotic reality. In psychiatry, it is considered to be a symptom of the disorder. As long as psychotic experiences cause no problems they are 'left alone'. Mental health workers continually place behavior, including verbal expressions, on a scale ranging from extreme and seriously disturbed behavior to normal social behavior. Patients are psychotic to a greater or lesser degree depending on their placement on the scale. Normal behavior implies a shift on the scale:

> They still have rather normal behavior, of course. Fortunately, there is still a fair amount of that.
>
> (Therapist)

When patients transgress the taboo on psychotic experiences it is significant, because it shows how important the partitioning of the self is in the therapeutic process. Transgressions indicate how effective treatment is; the less the psychotic world emerges, the more effective. The meaning of the taboo becomes clear through its being violated. In this, there is an important difference between the STR and the LTR. In the STR, boundary crossings between the two worlds are indicators of progress or the lack of progress by patients. The part of the patient that is ill gets in the way of socialization and the number of recurrent taboo violations are a measure of how far people have moved in the direction of renewed socialization. Transgressions are marked as failures and determine the amount of time that the patient must remain in hospital. In the LTR, boundary violations imply fear and unrest, though they do not obstruct the process of resocialization. Both staff and patient have accepted that the psychotic disorder is chronic and will remain obvious. Crossing the boundaries is not interpreted as failure, but possibly as expressing conflict in the ward. The violations strengthen the story of helplessness and reaffirm the need for constant, intensive supervision. Nevertheless the two parts – the healthy and the sick – are interrelated again. The healthy part is activated to gain insight into the ill part. A therapist stated:

For me the point is: Does he have insight or does he not? Is he capable of grieving over his loss?

To this end the biographical experience of the psychotic patient is constantly objectified. The patient becomes a subject only if he first becomes an object for himself, and this is achieved by adopting the mental health worker's perspective. A therapist said of a woman with a paranoid psychosis:

I try to find out, and to let her discover, the basis for her suspicions.

The woman believes in a conspiracy. The therapist does not elaborate on her conspiracy theory; it is transformed immediately into a theory about her history.

As a rule, maintenance of objective reality is a routine matter. In a psychiatric hospital this requires special management, on account of the propensity for repeated disturbances of continuity and consistency. In such management it becomes clear how interaction with patients is based on the dualistic position of the staff. It is a process of constantly weighing and reweighing the balance of power, which is especially precarious in intimate interactions with patients. Mental health workers did not appear to be blind to the suffering and existential quest of their charges, but to borrow a phrase from Lacan (1966) 'their mastery was needed to control chaos':

I do not go along with it. I want to prevent him from becoming overactive.
(Therapist)

The division of a patient into a healthy and a sick part takes place in order to control the chaos of the psychosis. The 'healthy part' of a psychotic person makes explicit and intensive reality confirmations and confrontations possible. A therapist said: 'We decided to turn to continual reality confrontation'. In a confrontation, a patient is shown the consequences of his views and behavior for society; for instance, when a psychotic man in a group watching television repeatedly bursts out laughing for no apparent social reason, the therapist will have a talk with him and take a step-by-step look at the possible effects. It is pointed out that laughing has a social function and originates in a specific frame of mind; otherwise laughing is 'strange' and 'incomprehensible'.

The frequency of the reality confirmations and confrontations is important. In the hospital one can rely on a division of tasks between therapists and nursing staff. The division of tasks is best summarized in the words of a therapist: 'With the therapist you have *talk* about it; in the ward you have to *do* it.' Therapists are the managers, and in consultation with the entire staff of a ward and the patient, they determine how the treatment should be arranged. The therapy they offer is mostly verbal and they work primarily on the cognitive level, that is, their conversations with the patients mostly turn on reality confrontations. In these talks the 'healthy parts' of the patients are displayed as the insight that they have into their own problem, the degree to which they adhere to social rules of conversation and how approachable they are, and the degree to which they accept the interpretations offered by the therapists. In addition, therapists maintain contact with the patient's parents and/or relatives.

The nursing staff must implement the plans devised for specific patients. In addition to having conversations with the patients, they must closely monitor patient behavior in the ward, correct it and stimulate it. The 'healthy part' is displayed in the willingness and capacity displayed by patients to carry out certain tasks, conforming to ward rules, interaction with others in the ward, keeping appointments, and so on. Contact between patients and nursing staff is more personal, frequent and intensive than with therapists. Patients, especially those in the STR, do not always find them more intimate:

> I like the therapist better. The nurse is different. I have more confidence in the therapist. I can tell him a lot more, maybe because he is a psychiatrist.

Another patient:

> I tell the therapist more. I am more open to him. I talk with him more, because he is a psychiatrist and because I hope he can solve things. With the nurse I talk more about the group and about practical things. The therapist is more intimate, more involved. He knows my mother and my relatives.

Introducing order according to a standard scheme in the behavior of psychotic people, referred to as *structuring*, is a very important hospital procedure to maintain the taboo on the 'ill part' (the psychotic reality), and to master chaos. When the psychotic reality becomes apparent in a patient's expressions and behavior and this impacts on social processes, it indicates the need to structure immediately, both in conversations with therapists and daily routine.

Generally, structure embraces a series of rules regarding eating and sleeping, going out, the patient's place in the ward, the administration of medicine, the amount of supervision, the number of social contacts a patient is allowed and the duration of the structuring period. The degree to which structure is imposed corresponds to the severity of the chaos. If there is an obvious threat in a chaos situation the structure will consist of 'hand-in-hand' supervision, which means that a nurse is constantly near the patient, eating, talking, walking together and so on. Imposing structure sends a message to patients that certain boundaries of reality are being violated. It was used at Saint Anthony's both to protect and safeguard psychotic people and others, but also as 'punishment' for the status of being psychotic.

Structuring is not an arbitrary decision taken by an individual staff member when a patient is bothersome. It is a ceremony that binds mental health workers to institutional and social rules, and it involves consultation with the staff in order to pursue problems arising from the psychotic world collectively and according to institutional perspectives. In a multidisciplinary consultation the decision is not reasoned on neutral, objective grounds. The participants speak subjectively, using pregnant formulations, metaphors and analogies.[11] This sort of consultation makes it possible for mental health workers to discuss non-professional feelings regarding psychotic reality. In the discussions it becomes clear how counter-transference tends to consolidate. The 'special story' about psychotic people is confirmed, and at each juncture the chaos is emphasized. In the hospital each individual patient is regarded as 'an episode' that existed as a story prior to being admitted. There was little one could do to change it, because even if the ill part was no longer visible it still did not detract from the story. In that case the psychotic person confirmed the 'truth' of the story and the effectiveness of the structuring that was imposed, was reinforced.

In psychiatric practice, structuring is often similar to proceedings in the pedagogical process. As a nurse remarked:

> He cannot look after himself. You have to structure him a lot, continually. You have to keep telling him: clean up your room, keep yourself neat, come on time, look after your pocket money.

Such practices are part of resocialization as described by Berger and Luckmann (1966). The everyday world has to be internalized anew, and people must begin to feel a certain affinity with that world. But in the biography of psychotic people everyday reality is a source of suffering, from which they have distanced themselves. It became clear that while patients had great difficulty accepting or internalizing daily reality, the psychotic reality continued to retain a degree of attraction. A principle of psychiatric conversations is that the past is placed in constant relation to the present. The contents from the psychotic world are not attractive to mental health workers and are avoided. This has the potential to create problems, and mental health workers have to make sure that there will be no 'backsliding' or 'being propelled into psychosis'. The danger of this happening can be reduced and even avoided by using structured conversations. Structuring implies that therapists have a specific plan or intention before they launch into conversations with psychotic people. A therapist:

> Of course, I have a plan. I try to bring out everything I thought of prior to the conversation.

The mental health workers could keep the conversation in check by means of their plan. During those conversations they would make an effort to maintain contact, partially because they were afraid that the psychotic world would re-emerge ('The contact should not weaken, otherwise they become psychotic again'). For another part contact with the patient had to be retained in order to carry out the plan. 'Insight' was a prerequisite in carrying out the plan, which meant that the patients were continually encouraged to find words for their feelings, to attain self-insight and to forge links between the symptoms of their illness, their life history and emotions.[12] In the case of psychotic people it was assumed that because thought processes were disrupted this basis was partially or entirely lacking. In the words of two therapists:

> It is difficult to structure. It is difficult to point things out. He does not understand.

> They don't have any insight.

On the surface of a psychiatric conversation mental health workers would deny their role as expert and authority, although admittedly not everything the patient said was considered equally valuable (Ten Have 1987: 164). Mental health workers had to assert their authority much more emphatically with psychotics and it had to be made abundantly clear when something was not valuable. The 'sick part' was of little value in psychiatric interaction, and it was kept suppressed as much as possible. Structuring meant, among other things, that patients were repeatedly 'brought back to reality'. When a psychotic man used images of force and firearms to express his fear of others, the therapist switched to an everyday topic to prevent contact from being broken:

> Those guns are a symbol of fear. If I allow him to pursue this symbol he would perhaps have cut off the talk. Moreover, it is too much of an exaggeration and I wanted to move to something more realistic.

The reality to which therapists try to lead is that of the actual and of 'doing':

> The here and now, what we are to do, that comes first. Only after that, I step back some. In his treatment and in my conversations I am always dealing with the here and now.

> In her case psychosis is especially clear at the beginning of our talk. I let her talk about that first, and then I move to things she actually does.

> I want her to do things.

Conversations cannot be structured too rigidly, since professional knowledge about interaction with psychotic people and everyday views about conversing dictate a more open-ended approach. Principles such as cooperation, interest, respect for privacy, sympathy and the like also have a bearing on this. Grice (1975) calls these characteristics of normal conversations 'principles of cooperation and politeness'.[13] In interactions with psychotic people, mental health workers find that they repeatedly need to violate these principles to some degree to obtain the information necessary for treatment. A therapist:

You have to think of privacy. I always ask myself: What can I ask her and what should she keep to herself?

Structuring is not an isolated matter. Mental health workers seem to hesitate between transformations and the status quo of the patient's selfhood:

You should not confront them too much. You should let them be themselves.

This leads to an ambivalent attitude:

I am in two minds about that: on the one hand I want to give him room to talk, on the other hand I want to show him what he is actually saying.

Being cautious helps to retain the contact required to supervise people and for therapy to work, two aspects that present great difficulties to mental health workers. Patient resistance to therapy and contact, combined with expressions of psychosis and the like, lead to contact disorders. Van Haaster (1991) remarks that this is why mental health workers emphasize the vulnerability of psychotic people in social interaction, and stress the innate contradictions in psychosis. They speak of the need for contact and, simultaneously, the patient's fear of it. They experience both the 'cry for help' and 'rejection', which is why there is an extra dimension to the principles of interaction with psychotic people.[14] The professional dimension contains rules for conversations with psychotic people, and the first rule is the taboo on psychotic reality, mentioned earlier (Deane 1963). Conversations should also not be subjected to overt strain (Van den Bosch 1990). This means, for example, that mental health workers may have to accept rejection:

If he refuses to respond to something or refuses to talk about a certain topic I will immediately respect that. I certainly do not push him.

However, conversations must be 'a confrontation with reality'; for example, when a patient talks about solitary confinement and notes that he never felt as good as then the therapist must pose the question 'How can you feel at home in solitary confinement?' Such a confrontation is curbed by the implicit rule of being attentive and sympathetic to patient feelings that arise from experiences of psychotic reality. Patients have to have the feeling that they are understood, but when psychotic reality comes into the picture, the contrast becomes acute.

Long-term residence and the story of hopelessness

Please, just leave us alone, because, doctor, surely you understand that we who are here for so long already don't dare move to society. That would be the end of us all. The old doctor always said: 'You are a chronic patient' and that's true, because nobody knows how people think about things inside. This is an illness that nobody will ever understand, even if they have all kinds of diplomas.

(Quote from an institutional report)

The dilemma in psychiatry is that patients and therapists have 'to give up' when the disorder is chronic, because the 'sick part' all too often triumphs over the 'healthy part'. If the therapy team decides on a different approach the patients are sometimes transferred to apartments, where they live on their own with minimal assistance from the psychiatric staff, or to the wards where they will have full-time supervision and assistance. The LTR was built in the 1980s and looks a bit like a spacious section of suburbia. The design of the houses was guided by the idea of 'ordinary people living in an ordinary street'. The 13 LTR patients in my research were from the cluster under intensive guidance, consisting of two closed wards, an open ward and four apartments. Psychotic people were *housed* in Saint Anthony's; they lived there, each with a house number and a room of their own. The psychiatric story in the LTR was not one of progress, as it was in the STR; it was one of being without hope. Patients did not receive treatment, and the staff's objectives were to adapt and regulate behavior. They also wanted to gain control over chronic psychoses, and to achieve this they made copious use of psycho-pharmacological support. The patients lived under continuous guidance and supervision, and human interest was expressed in terms of quality of life. They had put a decisive distance between themselves and factors that might impact negatively on their lives. The LTR patients accepted their fate with its attendant illnesses and thought a different way of life impossible: their future would be more of the same, or worse. The pressure of adjustment and change aimed at returning to society fell away once they were taken into the LTR. While it might disturb society that they had become 'invisible', the patients felt alienated and expelled, and at odds with society.

The effect was that people had shorn life of its trimmings. Cultural values, norms and concepts such as cooperation, self-responsibility and responsibility for others were perceived as obstacles in the life of a chronic psychotic. As the patients saw it, cooperation and responsibility were not necessary, while mental health workers thought it highly unlikely that patients would cooperate or show responsibility, so once again, the 'story' about psychotic people had been strengthened. LTR patients displayed little mutual involvement and a markedly individual orientation. Even those who knew each other from many years before did not know where the others were housed. In the common rooms, such as the coffee shop, people would sit together for hours without exchanging a single word. It frequently happened that people selected a table for themselves, sat staring blankly, drank coffee and left silently. Conversations were brief and restricted, as illustrated by an exchange between patients:

P1:   I know you from the Binnenhof.[15]
P2:   I know you too.
P1:   That was sort of fun, wasn't it?
P2:   Yes. Where are you staying?
P1:   In [house] number 5.
P2:   Where is that?
P1:   Behind the restaurant.
P2:   Oh. You doing all right?
P1:   So so, eh?
[*Silence*]

The will to participate in anything active was slight, but drinking coffee and eating were two important common activities. On these occasions, people sat together for some time without speaking and while they seemed to be completely introverted, an unexpected utterance might indicate that they were quite alert about their environment. The group of patients sitting in the coffee shop was silent. Suddenly:

P1:   I am the king of Rock 'n Roll! My name is Jansen!
P2:   My name is Bugs Bunny!
[*Complete silence is resumed*]

Often, the conversations that took place were brief and terminated abruptly:

P1:   That's good music, the Beatles.
P2:   Yeh, it's my tape. I took it on tape.
P1:   Is that yours? Nice.
P2:   Yes, and a new record.
P1:   A new one?
P2:   The Beatles 1981–1991.
P1:   Huh? What? Oh, I see what you mean. Fine.
P2:   [*Gets up and walks away*]

Therapists, who were sometimes referred to as 'father', represented authority, the rules of the LTR, and they were the custodians of pocket money and medicines. In times of crisis they assumed most or all responsibility for others, and they had the keys to the ward entrance and exits. The staff thought of patients in somber terms (Van Dongen 1989). Psychotics were described as follows:

> Easily confused, reacting chaotically, clamoring for attention, getting enmeshed in ambivalent feelings and conflicts, and beset with fears, feelings of alienation and misery. Expressions of self-mutilation, suicide attempts, 'acting out' and aggressiveness could be consequences of this.
>
> (Hospital Annual Report 1991)

'People get a kick out of it when things go badly,' said a nurse on a closed ward. Heavy demands were placed on the staff, whose staying power was severely taxed by the extreme individualism of patients, by their attempts to manipulate staff and by a wide array of crisis situations. Patients, surrounded by others equally bereft of any hope of being healed, knew what the mental health staff thought of them. Drug and medicine abuse (Van Dongen 1990), manipulation of others, dramatic outbursts and sudden eruptions of emotion were constant reminders of the story of hopelessness, like an incantation repeated to reinforce the notion that people were seriously ill. Time in the LTR was synchronous: problems were not explained in terms of the patient's past, but in terms of that particular moment. When a patient fell into a psychosis, the immediate question was whether something had happened on the ward. There was a kind of immediacy in explanation and activity, expressed by patients in a variety of ways. It seemed as if they could be driven together by their own interest and its direct satisfaction. On one occasion, I observed a female patient move toward another patient, sit next to him and caress his hair. She spoke to him in loving terms, complimenting him. Eventually came her question: would he go to town for her groceries, because she was temporarily not allowed to leave the building? The man went. He returned half an hour later with a shopping bag and walked to the girl's room. The bag was accepted and the door was closed in his face. Liaisons between patients were temporary in nature and sometimes they were terminated abruptly:

P1:   You said you'd come to me, but you don't come to see me at all.
P2:   You shouldn't bellyache like that when I'm talking to someone else.
P1:   Just get lost.
P2:   Ciao, bitch!
P1:   You don't need to come any more.
P2:   You always say that, pisshole.

Acting on impulse was commonplace. An unsuspecting visitor in the coffee shop could suddenly be hugged and kissed by an acquainted patient (male or female), and some time later the same patient might pass by without saying a word. At unexpected moments and in arbitrary places patients would begin to tell stories or let their thoughts be known. 'I want to die, Els,' a woman said to me at around nine o'clock in the morning when I entered the ward, before I had a chance to greet her or take off my coat. Immediacy was also displayed in quite unusual circumstances. Anna, an older patient in a ward for intensive supervision, was walking in the street when she saw me driving an automobile and signaled for me to stop. I parked and got out. 'I have to be shocked this afternoon,' she said without further preamble. 'Well, I guess you will have a bad headache this evening then,' I answered. 'Maybe they do it at least three times.' (Shock therapy was not administered at this hospital.) Anna began to laugh and took me by the hand. She started singing an evergreen song and wanted to dance in the rain. We danced, but as abruptly as we began Anna stopped and walked on.

Another form of immediacy was being able to converse day or night with the staff on the wards. Unusual accounts, psychotic experiences and experienced problems could be related any time of day at the LTR, just as long as they did not precipitate a crisis, and provided there was the capacity for an immediate response to any crisis. Sometimes a person was ushered into another room when the crisis event should have been treated from another perspective. Memories of a personal history or events in society could cause a crisis, but the intervention of fellow patients could help to hide this from the staff.

> *Diary entry*: When I enter the ward Anna rushes up to me, crying. She says something and points to her belly. I have difficulty understanding her. I am given to understand that she has a child in her belly and that the child is dying of hunger. She cries louder and speaks again. She cries for all the children who are dying of hunger. She saw them on television. She found it a terrible thing. She complains and is out of sorts. Eric comes in: 'Come on, dear, be calm.' Anna threatens him and he bends backwards: 'Help, I'm getting hysterical! I'm going to make a parabola.' Attention is shifted from Anna's sorrow to Eric's clownish behavior. There is no further talk of children going hungry.

Events in society continually confirmed what patients already knew, lending more credence to the story of hopelessness. When there is a crisis or a threat, immediacy was required; all or part of patient responsibility was immediately subsumed. People were removed from the group (or apartment) and supervised in an isolation room until the crisis had passed.

> *Diary entry*: Marijke sits in the common living room. She is crying. Her fellow patients in the ward are there too, silent. 'What's the matter?' I ask. 'I am very scared.' 'Scared? Why are you afraid?' 'There is a war. In Yugoslavia. Next thing you know it will be here. We'll all die.'

Yet another form of immediacy emerged when attempts were made to meet the wishes of the patients. During my fieldwork one of the long-term residents who had formerly lived in a caravan indicated that he would like to do so again. Plans were made to purchase and install one as quickly as possible in the hospital grounds. Patient initiatives were acted on promptly – if a man wanted to raise pigeons, a pigeon coop was built for him. The objective was to help the patient live more or less adequately and with the most satisfaction and pleasure that circumstances would allow. Finally, immediacy played a role in the direct communication between staff and patients, in what is termed *reduction* and *redundancy*. Reduction occurs when there are no regular therapeutic consultations. Therapists and staff speak to one another when they chance to meet or deem it necessary. When a senior therapist arrived, a number of patients might want to talk to him at once. These conversations were fragmented and 'phatic' (Alverson and Rosenberg 1990: 174). In other words, the words were aimed more at establishing and strengthening the relationships between therapists and patients than at an actual exchange of information. For this reason, personal experiences were often represented in reduced ways. Mutual familiarity, sometimes spanning a number of years, conferred a kind of restricted code (Bernstein 1964) on the conversation. In addition to reduction, the conversations contained redundancy. When the topics turned to wishes, complaints, and daily cares, the patients offered a great deal of redundant information. On a superficial level, the history of patients played a small role in the daily life in the LTR wards. One patient told me:

> For me the past was a sad time. I'd rather not think about that any more. I go swimming now, or sit in the sun, or play badminton. I do things that are fun. Those few years of life I still have ahead of me, I want to live happily.

Sometimes history is treated like a book which has been closed and set aside. Chronically psychotic patients are able to tack quite stubbornly between good and bad moments, ever onward, vacillating between periods of intense psychotic experiences, fear, anger and despair, and periods of brittle peace and quiet. These fill their days. A schizophrenic patient explained how he experienced this kind of life:

> It's not nice to keep hearing all day that things are a mess in the house and that sort of thing. What a mess, what a pigsty, or even worse. That is not nice and I can't stand it, because I still feel some positive aspects in this apartment. A. keeps trying to walk. My foot always hurts me, but I still go out at the agreed upon time. H., who has gone through much suffering. And in spite of all this we take up our burden every morning, go on with it and so on. I think that you need a lot of pluck to be able to do that. Sometimes I think: I'm going to lie down on my bed and I will just sort of come to my end and so, but at those times somebody always shows up and says, No, damn it, you've got to go on. But there are times when everything runs together.

'To keep things manageable' is a top priority for therapists in the LTR, but even this edict can become part of hopelessness. To understand why the world of madness presents so many obstacles to mental health workers, one must appreciate therapeutic views of reality. These views can remain hidden during interaction with patients and only become clear indirectly, e.g. when patients break the rules. Two levels of managing may be distinguished in the reality views of hospital workers: a manipulative level and an inter-subjective level (Berger and Luckmann 1966). On the manipulative level an important role is played by pragmatic motives such as forestalling unrest and maintaining contact with patients. The criteria regarded as significant in orderly behavior are seen in terms of personal traits: self-reliance, responsibility, autonomy, social skills, ability to resolve conflict and the like.[16] Mental health workers feel that psychotic people do not meet these criteria and 'must relearn them'. Psychotic experiences are deemed to have a seriously incapacitating effect and to talk about them with patients generates tension. A therapist said:

> He is always full of great plans. He wants to leave the institution and be healthy again: to study, and so on. These things are normal for him. They are mentioned often. But there is a gap between his plans and his behavior. He cannot even do some simple carpentry and he does not work much. Most of the time I don't question his great plans. This time I did and it made him very nervous.

To allow experiences and manifestations of psychotic behavior to be displayed in public is dangerous for the patient:

> We have to keep an eye on her, because some bizarre urge would lead her to commit suicide. She tried that before. In those situations she acts impulsively, following a psychotic experience. It is not from a depressive condition. In the ward we can protect her. Not that we keep her in our sights the whole day, but she is not alone and [she is] more shielded.
>
> (Therapist)

The inherent danger of expressing or discussing psychotic experiences hampers the reality of autonomy and threatens not only the patient, but also inter-subjectivity between workers and patients. A therapist explained that patients became dependent on others, in this case on mental health workers:

> To turn psychotic images into communicable experiences is impossible. It is [like presenting it as] a law-abiding, submissive man. That goes very far and is therefore dangerous.

'To make communicable' – by this the therapist meant discussing the experiences and gaining insight into their meaning. The patient in question responded so well to instructions that the therapist feared he would become too dependent on others. Primarily, mental health workers have a pragmatic interest in the reality of danger, which means threat of suicide, aggression, unrest, and so on. Workers indicated that this danger was always present and that it loomed large when psychotic experiences were discussed or psychotic expressions were allowed. A therapist said:

> His psychotic experiences, such as when 'his vocal cords dry up', probably have a profound significance for him. These experiences hit him hard and at such times he raves and rants in the ward.

There was a lot at stake and a strong sense of danger, for the patients themselves, and danger for others. A therapist said:

> X spent a long time in the closed ward. He was very psychotic. He would strangle women to protect them. He was also trying to strangle himself with a scarf. . . These phenomena were serious to the point that the ward therapist finally administered a very potent medicine.

Recent discourses on suicide and aggression in mental health care[17] make it clear that moral, ethical, legal and social aspects constitute a major obstacle to a clear-cut action model in these matters. Similar discussions are continually encountered in the clinic when coercion is an issue. Aggression and suicide are not always predictable; optimistic, life-praising remarks will often have a negative effect (Jenner 1992). Mental health workers proceed with great caution when they suspect that certain experiences, including psychosis, will evoke this world of danger. In Saint Anthony's, the world of danger could be manipulated not only through increasing drug dosages, patient isolation and intensification of supervision, but also by inducing silence about the psychotic world.

Inter-subjectivity can include reality that can be shared with others but is clearly distinguishable from other, more individual realities, such as dreams and psychotic experiences. In daily life people simply assume that they function in the same reality, but in the relationships between mental health workers and patients this is expressly *not* the case. Therapist assumptions that the psychotic reality cannot be shared and that sometimes 'ordinary' reality is difficult to share with psychotic people, lead ultimately to patients having to employ the reality of the mental health worker. In the clinic the idea of inter-subjectivity is given a meaning different from its everyday one. It is restricted to a world in which the rules of social intercourse are respected, where communication is meant to improve the patient's situation and where the meanings intended by patients correspond with those of the workers.

In the hospital inter-subjective reality is based on exchange or trade: complaints are traded for a diagnosis and a diagnosis for a therapy (Oderwald 1985: 162–176). This latter exchange is special, compared with trade processes in other forms of medicine. Rather than being intended to remove the illness,[18] the original identity of psychotic patients (people who *have* a psychotic disorder) is turned into an identity of a person who *is* psychotic:

> I want to show her that I understand her and that what she is doing is right. She keeps picturing herself negatively. And I want to lead her to: that is how X [the patient] just happens to be. I want to stop looking for solutions. You have to make do with it. My frame of reference is: self-acceptance.
>
> (Therapist)

This trade is based on the premise that mental health workers are neutral and operate 'technically', based on assumptions regarding 'healthy' and 'unhealthy' identities. However, there are two factors that destabilize this inter-subjectivity:

disturbance in the social intercourse and disruption in the process of exchange. Mental health workers indicate that the capacity of psychotic people to communicate in rational and purposeful ways is badly disrupted and the chances of meaningful conversation based on mutual empathy are limited. The dynamic of the inter-subjective process is that mental health workers are confronted with unpredictable breaks in the therapeutic process. At one point there may be unexpected and unreasonable eruptions; at another the worker gets the feeling of being ignored. At times, getting the patient to talk is like extracting teeth while at other times stories are churned out endlessly. This dynamic strengthens the patient's power. Mental health workers indicate that usually the dynamic occurs outside the conscious mastery and manipulation of their patients. This, in turn, parallels the idea that thought processes are disrupted and that hence processes of communication are disrupted as well: 'they can't help it'. Nevertheless, the position of power that patients have in the interaction is strengthened. In another respect, patients have the upper hand because they do not want to establish contact while mental health workers do. A therapist explained that this hampered the authority of the mental health workers:

> I am inclined to introduce some structure; otherwise he cannot cope with it. But during the conversation you feel that things are getting out of hand. Actually, you should rise above it, but during the talk this no longer works. So I let him go ahead and then things become even more confused.

The obstacles formed by psychotic realities such as delusions and hallucinations are worth examining. In institutional discourse these are part of what Berger and Luckmann call 'finite provinces of meaning' (1966: 24). These 'provinces' are delimited areas that deflect attention from the daily clinical reality. It is a problem to make this reality agree with the reality of the hospital. The transposition from psychotic to inter-subjective reality usually diminishes the intensity of the experiences. The language of the average psychotic person has no words for these experiences. A patient:

> I find it hard to say the 'truth', although I want to. Deep in my heart I want to very badly, but I can't put it into words.

Some events in the psychotic reality are rather shaming and in retrospect patients are very keenly aware of the 'other' nature of their world. For the staff, agreement between the psychotic and the inter-subjective reality is just as much of a problem. They have frameworks to identify and explain this psychotic world, one of the best known being the psychoanalytic framework. In this school of thought, the significance of delusions and hallucinations is usually reduced to suppressed, infantile, historical or sexual conflicts, or a persistent narcissism.[19] A framework that plays an important role in the hospital is one in which psychotic reality is understood as a reaction to individual social circumstances and history. This perspective places less emphasis on sexual conflicts and accentuates the system of which the patient was formerly a part.

Sometimes mental health workers at Saint Anthony's did allow patients to talk about psychotic experiences. In these instances the aim was not to 'turn them into communicable experiences' but rather to provide an opportunity to 'let off steam'.

> She has a serious depression and a big delusion. The psychotic element occurs especially at the beginning of a conversation. I let her talk about that first and then I move on to the things she does. When during the conversation the contact between us fades the psychotic element returns.
>
> (A nurse)

Mental health workers did not steer away from the psychotic reality altogether. What they generally did was refer to it in rational terms of causality and individual history:

> What I try to do is that I bring out my own interpretations of the cause of the psychosis. I want to know if he makes that connection too. His answer was grist to my mill. If he had felt sorrow back then he would never have become psychotic.
>
> (Therapist)

Patients did not recognize or 'feel' the interpretations offered by mental health workers, so there was no basis for inter-subjectivity:

> With the right effect you could talk about the psychosis. But you don't get the chance to find a way via the psychosis. Psychotic experiences cannot be actualized.
>
> (Therapist)

To 'actualize' a psychotic experience was to (attempt) to turn it into a communicable experience, so that it could be 'experienced' by others and perhaps play a role in the therapeutic process. Mental health workers recognized that psychotic experiences had a function; they were understood as defense mechanisms:

> I certainly assume an experience when he walks around laughing without any apparent reason. I do not think it is adequate. His laughing is functional. It is a way of coping with sorrow. He just had a very painful experience. And so he walks on the lawn here for a couple of days, laughing.
>
> (Therapist)

The therapist holds that such laughter is not a viable way of solving problems or coping with sorrow. As health workers see it, delusions and hallucinations have certain intent, related to the dynamism and development of the personality, and in this sense they are important sources of information. To the mental health worker they reveal someone's personality, where its development was disrupted and what caused the disruptions. At the same time delusions and hallucinations are obstacles to the therapeutic process, because due to 'lack of insight' on the part of patients they cannot be transformed into a shared reality:

> This boy suffers serious defects, so that little can be done with the voices he hears.
>
> (Therapist)

Mental health workers do not deny existential experiences and themes, but there is little room for them in the discourse with patients because mental health workers question their value for the therapeutic process:

> I doubt if bizarre stories have anything to offer. My feeling is that sometimes they are very far removed from the life-world of the client. The feeling that this is indeed communication without meaning. Can you do anything with that? I doubt it.
>
> (Therapist)

As a result, the psychotic world of experience is isolated more and more, and becomes a matter of the individual patient (cf Perry 1976: 9).

The stories of hope and hopelessness are stories from the STR and LTR respectively. Even if the health workers know better, the story of hope (albeit in attenuated form) is at times kept alive in interacting with patients. We have noted that the experience of time is diachronic in the STR and it is characterized by a belief in progress and productivity. The hopelessness of psychotic people and the attempts of therapists to break through this leads to discourses in which the consensus reached is often no more than an appearance. The story of hopelessness in the LTR implies that patients are beyond treatment. The staff strive for stability, and the hopelessness is made palatable by the immediacy of responses to the wishes and various forms of behavior of patients. LTR experience of time is synchronous, and immediacy is asserted in many areas: in the interaction between staff and patients, in satisfying needs, interventions of therapists, and so on. The patients consistently confirm the stories of hope and despair as they move back and forth between contradictory feelings about themselves, their disorders, their futures and their lives. The result is a vortex that confirms and reinforces.

The relationship between mental health workers and psychotic patients is fraught with ambivalence and contradiction. These stem from the psychic disorder of the patients as well as the institutional prohibition on psychotic reality, the split into the 'ill and the healthy parts' and mental health workers alternating between reticence and intimacy in their interaction with psychotics. Pragmatic considerations prompt the mental health team to be concerned mainly with repairing the consequences of the cognitive chaos, without making use of the potential value of the psychotic world. This pragmatic attitude can be explained in terms of the strong social pressure exerted on psychiatry and illumined by developments within psychiatry. Social and professional signifiers of madness come together in the daily management of the clinics. This leads to an interaction process between therapists/nurses and patients in which madness is simultaneously hidden and uncovered.

In the following chapters I attempt to show how the processes of revealing and concealing are shaped in the microcosm of interactions between the mental health team and psychotic patients.

Chapter 5

Hiding in talk

Perhaps you can convince him to talk.
Maybe one of you can lead him
To dig out the old diaries of his travels –
Who can say?

Rainer Maria Rilke, 'The Diary of Malte Laurids Brigge'

Diary entry: It is three o'clock in the afternoon. I ring the doorbell at the lodgings of Vincent and his brother, who are both schizophrenic patients in the long-term residence (LTR) section of Saint Anthony's psychiatric hospital. Vincent and his nurse come to the door. 'Do we have to do our interview over again?' the nurse asks. 'No,' Vincent says, 'she comes to ask me things she doesn't understand.' Vincent and I leave. We see and hear his brother coming home, cursing and swearing. 'I don't understand it,' Vincent says, 'he gets the same medicines I do, but he blames everybody. I did that for just three weeks. It's getting to him now. In my opinion it is because of Haldol. Hal*dol*!' Vincent makes a pun of the word. 'It drives you *dol* [crazy]. I don't need that.' I ask Vincent if he wants to take a stroll as we talk. 'No, let's sit in the coffee shop, I like the background music.'

Vincent begins: 'I think the conversations on the tape are very short.'

'Why do you think that?' I want to sound rational. 'Look, others don't think I am normal. I am somebody who is different. Am I really different?'

'Well . . . ,' I hesitate. Vincent begins with a conclusion that is at once a question, a challenge and an expression of uncertainty. 'The hospital is not very big, you know. You keep running into each other. We talk until there is nothing left to say. Until we are all empty. [. . .] Your world is different from mine. People are strangers to each other. [. . .] I am talking to you in your language now. Dutch. It is Dutch, isn't it? 'Certainly,' I say. 'I should really talk in my own language. In English maybe?' 'Go ahead.' 'No, I'll stick to Dutch. Humanity puts pressure on me so I have to talk in your people's language.'

In this fragment, Vincent's statement that people talk until they 'are all empty' indicates the importance of vocalization in psychiatric settings. Communication and intensive social interaction within the confines of the hospital help to generate ideas that transform reality and enable people to address their problems, even though patients are said to 'resist' staff from the outset. I have noted that reproduction of psychiatric postulates about psychotic people leads to specific 'cultures' developing in the long-term residence (LTR) and short-term residence (STR) sections, and that staff and patients have different ideas and explanations of illness. Psychotic reality is forced to retreat because it is regarded as chaotic. The hidden reality, the sick part, is regarded as taboo. Nevertheless the taboo, together with consolidation of countertransference and patient structuring, is intended to help restore order. Patient resistance, therapist postulates, the disappearance of the psychotic life-world, beliefs, ideas and incongruities all merge to shape a discourse within which concealing and revealing the psychotic world will alternate with therapeutically important issues. The power relations between staff and patients shape the conversations in such a way that they conform to a predetermined literary canon of what 'the narratives of patients' should entail. The narratives are produced in similar ways in many psychiatric clinics. For example, Young (1995: 227) suggests that in a center for the treatment of post-traumatic stress disorder (PTSD) amongst veterans, patients display a double narrative: life stories, and a story first told in the DSM-III. Thus, the veteran narrative becomes a 'narrative of splitting'. To describe and analyze this specific kind of discourse, I focus on conversations as the arena in which the protagonists – staff and patients – 'do battle'. In that context, both parties must laboriously construct a form of shared reality as a basis for continued mutual contact. The subject matter here is how psychotic people seek to conceal therapeutically relevant matters and how therapists seek to uncover that which they deem necessary, but patients do not talk about. My tentative interpretations emerge from but are not limited to the integrated source material gathered at Saint Anthony's psychiatric hospital.

Topics that are out of bounds

Concealing psychotic reality, or insisting that therapeutically relevant issues be discussed, is a matter of seduction and strategy rather than a power struggle. Seduction is inherent in *empathy*, a crucial basic attitude adopted and used by psychiatric staff and therapists, and considered to be a valuable skill. Based on the premise that empathy can both ensure continued contact and shed light on the emotional struggle and self-perception of patients (Good *et al.* 1985: 214), it is important that conversations and consultations leave room for the life experiences of patients. Empathy takes on a social and a clinical function, of necessity combined with the need to maintain a professional distance. Empathy reduces the distance, but never eliminates it. This apparent contradiction can be puzzling to psychotic people, since they experience life in two distinct ways:

psychotic and non-psychotic. Empathy implies an understanding of both ways, while the professional attitude of therapists would seem to inhibit a real understanding of the 'sick part'. For the patient, this presents a constant anomaly. How do they react? Vincent hints at his response when he says 'I am talking to you in your language now' and 'humanity puts pressure on me so I have to talk in your people's language'. We are led to conclude that psychotic people will adapt as much as they possibly can, and that conversational exchanges reveal much less than they conceal. Although patients at Saint Anthony's often did not hesitate to talk about their psychotic experiences, therapists reported that they tended to avoid reference to emotional experiences in personal histories. Precisely these experiences had to be forced into the open because they were needed to find footholds for change.

Ultimately, the therapists wanted to exclude the psychotic world from the picture as much as possible.[1] Things happened simultaneously: even while a new reality was being constructed, other elements were being veiled and an (apparent) reality was emerging. By extensive analysis of conversations, I illustrate the ways in which patients and therapists sought to cover up emotions, experiences, and psychotic reality. The relevant psychiatric literature prescribes various 'dos' and 'don'ts' for therapists during their talks with psychotics.[2] When therapists and patients conversed the usual conventions were observed: questions were raised, one or both parties remained silent, both talked at once or interrupted each other, etc. But there was a specific intention here, since the purpose of psychiatric conversations was to change the views and conduct of people. I refer to the goal of this process of change as a 'new reality'. Rather than looking for potential significance in a psychosis and its psychotic reality, therapists want to transform a patient's behavior and perceptions of reality. They seek to redirect the emphasis that psychotics place on their psychotic experiences and related complaints, towards a solution of problems. Accordingly, therapists will negotiate about the definitions offered by patients. In the course of such negotiation a new reality is constructed and the problem is transmuted into something 'presentable'; that is the experiences of patients are transformed by negotiation with their therapists into acceptable and understandable terms, thereby removing some of the barriers to finding solutions. In the STR a step-by-step solution was sought while in the LTR the aim was to find solutions for problems as they arose. In the process of transformation, the therapist's role was to lead and direct the conversation. Various strategies were used, comprising social and clinical elements, and not entirely distinct from each other. Social strategies included contact orientation and the emotional reactions of therapists (see Chapter 4 on countertransference). Clinical strategies included confrontation, transformation, evaluation, interruption, and a determination of goals. Patients used various strategies in response to therapist strategies or to express their own intentions and objectives; these included avoidance, silence and rejection.

While talking to me, a patient in the STR (René) suggests that he might die if he tells the therapist (Karel) that he has 'seen the Lord'. He wants it to be known that he has a secret, but does not want the secret to be discovered. This was the way with secrets in conversations at Saint Anthony's. People allowed them to filter through, although both therapists and patients hinted at things that were not to be mentioned. To reveal or interpret these hints, we can divide the conversations into phases that Ten Have (1987: 136) calls 'super-sequences', which when taken together comprise the structure of a conversation. In inter-action analysis, Ten Have gives various examples of a phased structure (1987: Chapter 3). An example of a global phased structure that corresponds roughly to psychiatric conversations is the structure of physician–patient consultations described by Ten Have (1987: 105) as *opening – complaint – diagnosis – treatment – closure*. Conversations in this book do not follow the usual sequence, since the subject matter is neither diagnosis nor treatment in the sense of medical intervention. There may be new complaints but as a rule they have been presented earlier.

An important difference between conversations with psychotics and those with other patients is an assumption in mental health care that talks with psychotic people are by definition chaotic. These conversations are not expected to comply with the usual socio-cultural rules regarding purpose. Therapists expect them to be structured alogically: 'muddled', 'chaotic' and 'unstructured'. The psychosis taboo also means that a therapist cannot structure a conversation at will. Patients will inevitably break it down, making the taboo even more evident than the institutional rules can do.

How patients and therapists set about their conversations

The beginning of a verbal exchange can be compared with listening to a weather forecast before one goes on a hike: it is at best a guideline. The possibility of unexpected disruptions or inaccessability became clear even before the process began.[3] Therapists could not dictate the structure or progress of the conversation with a psychotic patient, and they often considered the start of the conversations to be delicate and 'touchy'. Greetings were exchanged before the taperecorder was switched on. The video recordings show that this ceremony could vary from a simple 'hello' to an elaborate coffee-serving ceremony.[4] Before the conversations began, many patients (prompted by experience) took the seat closest to the door. In an ordinary visit to the doctor, one might sit near the door because people tend to wander in and out during consultation hours. In this instance, it was a conscious strategy on the part of the therapist, because as one put it: 'The client is always seated next to the door. This gives him a chance to run if things get too much for him.' This strategy is one of the 'Recommendations for careful therapists' (Van Haaster 1991: 98–100). An escape route is offered, because therapists do not want to disrupt relationships or breach patient privacy. The implication is that psychotic people cannot cope with reality or that confrontation may lead to fear and confusion. However, this dimension emerged only when there was an attempt to change the seating pattern. When a patient did not take the chair next to the doorway, he was transgressing the unwritten territorial law[5] that the space farther back in the room is the workplace of the therapist. It is considered 'natural' that the therapist should sit there, and changes in the spatial arrangement can be expected to affect communication. It also indicates the status of the relationship between the therapist and the patient at the time of the conversation. When the patient occupies the therapist's chair, he does not acknowledge convention. Sometimes, the effect can be quite comical. In the fragment below, Eric (LTR) entered, seated himself in Jochem's chair, and folded his arms. His body language made it clear that he would 'call the shots' today. Jochem took the 'patient's chair', checked the taperecorder and switched it on.

Jochem: Right, the tape runs.
Eric: Well, about the only thing that seems important to my Jewish interest. It works, doesn't it?
Jochem: Yes, it's running.
Eric: Oh, it's running.
Jochem: You find that important, that it's running?
Eric: No, but here we go again, just turn it on, because, uh. . . .
Jochem: It's on.
Eric: It's on. Thank you [etc.].

In addition to changing the spatial arrangement, the patient wanted to reverse the roles. He seized the initiative by introducing a topic, and with a play on words he expressly corrected the therapist, Jochem, who had said 'the tape runs'. Eric asked whether the taperecorder was recording or not, using the opportunity to question his therapist's competence. This is an aspect of the psychotic person as 'trickster', a clown who exaggerates in order to correct. An opening move of this nature restricts the rest of the conversation. If inverted symmetry is sustained and the patient continues to call the shots, the therapist is excluded and cannot take the therapy forward. In this way, Eric was delaying the specific issue that Jochem wanted to discuss, namely the arrival of Eric's brother from another continent and how he felt about it. Eric tried to shut this out and (at my prompting), attempted to direct the discussion towards his life in the hospital, and how the therapist fitted in. Therefore, he began by saying 'Well the only thing that seems important to me. . . .'. The conversation failed from the start, because they approached it with such different motives.

The beginning of a conversation can be a veritable minefield: when the process of tuning in to each other is laborious or it fails, the therapist must expend a great deal of effort to get it going. This happened with Karel and René. Karel (the therapist) was not sure about where one should sit relative to the video camera, and he left the room to find out. Meanwhile, the patient looked for his cigarettes and an ashtray. When the therapist returned:

René: May I smoke here? Yes?
Karel: Sure you can.
René: I'll get my cigarettes. I forgot to bring them.
Karel: Well, you'll just have to wait a moment, lad. [*turns the tape on*] Alright.
René: I did not comb my hair. Shit!
Karel: Right. Let's move this out of the way, it would distract us, wouldn't it?
René: Let me comb my hair.
Karel: Yes, in group therapy you are not supposed to smoke, are you?
René: Sure. But I forgot to bring them,
Karel: I see. You forgot them.
René: I'll get them. Be right back.
Karel: No, no, no. Please don't because . . .
René: Why not?
Karel: We only have half an hour. I have to keep an eye on the time. If you have to go all the way to the ward . . .
René: But I will be back in less than two minutes.
Karel: René, let's just have a quiet chat, shall we?
René: Yes, I am completely add . . . I am completely addicted to smoking, you know.
Karel: As soon as we are done here we will go for a smoke. I promise . . . How did things go at the dentist this morning?
René: Not bad.
Karel: Tell me about it.
René: Tuesday he is going to pull my teeth. Everything.
Karel: What? Everything?
René: Except for one molar in the back, all of them.
Karel: How many will he pull?
René: Nine. The whole lot.
Karel: The whole lot?
René: Yeah.
Karel: Uh, and, and
René: They're all rotten. [*muttering*]
Karel: How did that happen?
René: Sweets. Food. Well, not going to the dentist; scared to. All that.
Karel: But now you have to anyway?
René: Can't get around it . . . I'll get my cigarettes. [*muttering*]
Karel: Sit down, sit down, sit down. Please, do me a favor. We're grown-ups, having a chat, aren't we?
René: No, but I need a smoke.
Karel: We talk without a smoke, possible, isn't it?
René: Sure, but I am nervous. NERVES!
Karel: What, nervous?
René: My nerves, uh, uh, uh . . .

Karel: Why? Why, why, just stay put, sit down. Do me a favor.

René: . . . Well, I just am.

Karel: Why nervous now?

René: Because ah . . . I am nervous because of the camera.

Karel: It doesn't bite, man.

René: I know. But if I have a smoke I perform a lot better, man.

Karel: Are you sure?

René: Yeah.

Karel: No, wait. I have the answer, René?

René: Yes?

Karel: I'll get some for you.

René: Okay.

Karel: Just stay here a moment.

René: Pall Mall and shag in my room.

Karel: Right. I have tobacco lying around.

René: Do you? . . . didn't know that.

René seized the initiative by asking permission to smoke. His need to get his cigarettes from the ward made it difficult to start and Karel had to make various attempts to retain his authority. A first attempt is found when he said that René had to 'bide his time'. A second attempt occurred when Karel asked René to sit down (the video shows that Karel straightened his leg to block the passage). The remark about there not being enough time did not convince anyone, but the leg was more effective. René sat down again. The third attempt was when Karel used the common ploy of introducing a current topic (the dentist), to launch the discussion. This seemed to work until the patient unexpectedly rose again. Karel did not want the patient to leave since he was evidently not sure that he would return.[6] The ensuing battle rose to a kind of climax, when the patient shouted: 'Nerves!' The next adjustment resulting in Karel's compromise when his patient's argument was sufficiently pressing for Karel to fetch the tobacco. His final attempt to retain his position was to suggest a compromise, when René would have Karel go to the ward and he went to his office instead.

Conversations that begin like the one above are forms of 'tuning out' and hence deviate from the daily experience of 'tuning in'. In talking with psychotic people 'tuning out' is not uncommon and therapists blame this state of affairs on the disorder ('He is in the grip of rejection'). Not being 'tuned in' is a psychotic symptom and confirms our set ideas regarding psychotic people. Deviations, however, can have other meanings. The 'battle' in the opening was not restricted to this conversation, and contestations arose frequently in the broader context of resistance to hospitalization, comment on and resistance to dominant reality perspectives, power relations inside the institute and outside, social rules and norms, etc. Reflecting on the conversation, René expressed it as follows:

Everybody here is atheist. They laugh at me when I talk about God. Here they say that only heaven exists, but that is nonsense. If there is a heaven, hell has to exist too. It's as simple as that. All those atheists here will go to hell . . . they are all against me . . .

Repeatedly, René's views on the lack of belief of others were a source of unpleasantness, and at times hostility. It was difficult for therapists to 'gain access' to a patient, ironically because of their belief in patient privacy. The fragment below underscores this:

Therapist: [*coughs*] (7) Uh, well, yes, we've got to make a start.
Joris: Okay.
Therapist: (2) Uh, well . . . My first interest is, to start with, uh . . . your experiences in the past week.
Joris: You are?
Therapist: In uh, your town.[7]
Joris: Oh, that was fine.

A long silence at the beginning of the conversation marks an uneasy start. It is not clear what transpired during the silences but Joris's minimal reactions made matters difficult for the therapist, who seemed hesitant throughout. When the therapist introduced a topic relating to Joris's recent activities and his volunteer work at a school in his home town, Joris responded in socially appropriate ways but his replies lacked form or content. This set the tone of the conversation. Joris was reluctant and evasive while the therapist pressed ever harder for points of contact:

Therapist: At school?
Joris: Yes.
Therapist: That went well?
Joris: Yes.
Therapist: How did it go?
Joris: Just fine.

Not every conversation begins in this way. In the STR, the beginning usually consists of clarifying the positions of therapists and clients, after which the therapist introduces a familiar daily topic. Most often these are practical matters such as the recent activities of the patient or events in the hospital. Karel tried this approach with René, but it failed dismally at first. These opening moves contain a meta-message about the relationships. The therapist usually sees both parties in the context of the therapeutic relationship and tries to effect mutual adjustment to the situation.[8] An example:

Therapist: How are things going at the moment?
Cor: Reasonable.

Therapist: Yes? Do you think that there is some change since the last chat?
Cor: Well, I am not scared of anything
Therapist: I think we should move closer to that thing
Cor: Should we?
Therapist: It'll pick up our voices better. Maybe you can . . . just a bit . . . there. You're doing reasonably well, you say?
Cor: Well, in the morning I feel a bit strange.
Therapist: . . . In the morning?
Cor: Strange
Therapist: How does that work?
Cor: Uh . . . I feel rotten (2) Later on I don't feel so bad.
Therapist: You start the day feeling bad?
Cor: Yes (3)

In this fragment, therapist and patient 'tune in' to each other. They seek a balance between openness and intimacy, and respect for each other's privacy and position (Goffman 1961a). Introducing a current concern such as the patient's condition can be viewed both as an attempt to gain access to the patient and as 'alignment' (Goffman 1974), or mutual positioning. Long openings in which a current or safe topic is discussed before therapist and patient move to the core of the talk (the patient's life and experiences) are not unusual. In some conversations, the first minutes were spent on shared recollections, daily affairs or small talk, before the conversation gradually got underway. The purpose of these slow starts often seemed to be to raise more sensitive issues (on the part of the therapist) or to postpone these (on the part of the patient).

How various conversations began depended in part on the nature of the relationship between the mental health worker (e.g. nurse, therapist) and the patient, and the health worker's place in the hospital pecking order. Conversational beginnings between nurses and patients tended to be different from those between therapists and patients. In the hierarchy of the institution nurses ranked 'lower' than therapists, and their battle for recognition had to be more direct. In the fragment below, René was talking with a nurse.

1. *Nurse*:   Right, the tape can run now.
2. *René*:   It is running now, then?
3. *Nurse*:   Yes . . . Now, you can look my way.
4. *René*:   Why?
5. *Nurse*:   Because then you don't have to look at the machine.
6. *René*:   Huh? . . .
7. *Nurse*:   What shall we talk about?
8. *René*:   About nothing. I don't feel like it any more.
9. *Nurse*:   I thought of something. You haven't?
10. *René*:   No.

There was no long approach to a topic here. The nurse clearly intended to impose a structure at the beginning of the conversation and his authority was evident from the command in line 3. In line 8, René resisted. Like therapists, nurses began by introducing a current and usually (emotionally) safe topic, such as the patient's condition:

1. *Nurse*:   The tape is running.
2. *Cor*:   . . . It's running.
3. *Nurse*:   Cor, we're here to uh. . . .
4. *Cor*:   What is the date today?
5. *Nurse*:   What?
6. *Cor*:   Today's date.
7. *Nurse*:   The 16th, December 16th, to uh have a little talk . . . the two of us about you . . . Cor, I want to begin by asking how you are at this moment.
8. *Cor*:   Well, I feel kind of rotten.
9. *Nurse*:   Yes.
10. *Cor*:   Happens to me more often when I get up in the morning.
11. *Nurse*:   Yes?
12. *Cor*:   But it gets better after a while.
13. *Nurse*:   Yes . . . say, Cor, you have this only when you get up in the morning?
14. *Cor*:   Yes.

Having checked the taperecorder, the nurse wants to announce the objective of the conversation and ask a familiar question. Making use of the brief pause (line 3), Cor manages to interrupt him, but the sudden shift does not daunt the nurse. He gives the information requested and goes on to complete his sentence. This indicates a decisive speech act, and the nurse has indubitably planned the questions and conversation structure as illustrated by line 13. However, where the mental health worker has planned the conversation, there is a danger that relevant patient utterances will not be heeded or grasped because they do not fit into the planned structure. More than once when thinking back to the talk he had with a patient, a staff member lamented the fact that because of his planned structure 'important issues were not picked up'. The product required in the end is more like an information-gathering interview, with a 'hit and run' (Richters 1991: 24) element to it. This approach contradicts the psychiatric principles of involvement and intimacy, which is why most therapists use a different one. A mental health worker will seldom reveal immediately what he intends to discuss in the rest of the conversation. If the plan remains hidden it allows the patient greater freedom in his choice of topics, although it does hold the risk of countertransference when unexpected conversational disruptions occur and the planning goes awry.

Nurses are in contact with patients more frequently and for longer stretches of time, which partly explains why their conversations are different. Two fragments illustrate this: the start of a patient's conversation with a therapist, and one with a nurse.

Therapist: For me this is also the occasion to, uh, have a longer chat with you, right?
Marie: Yes. Things are not going well.
Therapist: What?
Marie: Not going well.
Therapist: Things are not going well.
Marie: Ringing ears, my head.
Therapist: Yes . . . yes.
Marie: Very serious, weeks already.
Therapist: Ringing, is that what you said?
Marie: Ringing.
Therapist: Yes.

Nurse: Okay. We act as if the thing isn't there . . . How's it going?
Marie: Bad.
Nurse: Bad?
Marie: [*cries*]
Nurse: Tell me. What's going bad?
Marie: Ringing in my ears. I'm wearing my hearing aid.
Nurse: You have a hearing aid in? . . . That's a small one . . . Let me see . . . Right, that's a small thing.
Marie: [*sobs*]

Marie presents her poor condition in different ways. 'Things are not going well' is qualitatively different from 'bad'. In response to the nurse's empathy and her invitation to talk about it, Marie lets go emotionally and cries. The therapist restricts himself to 'minimal response' (Schlegoff 1982) and repeats what the patient says. Both techniques are meant to move the conversation forward and to demonstrate a degree of involvement. Because the patient presents her problems in these different ways, the mental health workers can regard this as inconsistent and a symptom of the illness. However, Ewing (1990) shows that different self-representations are quite common in people's stories. They are related to a situation, and not a symptom. As noted in other areas, there is also a difference between the way conversations begin with residents of the STR and LTR sections. Patients in LTR commence more readily than those in STR. There is a different tone to the conversations and often there are ironic and playful openings. While this tends to soften the edges, the resistance of patients to the institution (and to life in general) is still evident:

Sjef: [*laughs*]
Therapist: Yes . . . well: you're gonna sit like this too?
Sjef: Yes . . . You know, your teeth are not all that good either.
Therapist: . . . No.
Sjef: [*laughs*]
Therapist: . . . Yours aren't either.
Sjef: No.
Therapist: You ever go to a dentist?
Sjef: No. Scared to.
Therapist: You're scared?
Sjef: [*laughs*] No.
Therapist: How is that? . . . Why don't you go to a dentist?
Sjef: It hurts.
Therapist: Pain?
Sjef: Yes.

Like Eric, Sjef took the therapist's chair. The latter served coffee, gave Sjef milk and sugar, and then sat down, leaning his arms on the table. Sjef copied the gesture exactly. For a number of seconds they locked eyes and the patient laughed. The therapist confirmed the mirror arrangement. Sjef agreed, and was silent for a moment. He looked at his therapist and then fired off the remark: 'Your teeth are not all that good *either.*' This is more than just introducing a topic; to be sure, the dentist was important to him at the moment since he had just been to one with a terrible toothache. By placing himself and his therapist in the same frame he indicated that the condition of his teeth (and the condition of his selfhood) was not as abnormal as he assumed others believed it to be. The therapist said nothing for a moment, which suggests that he postponed his response until he had decided (Ten Have 1991b: 68) on a retort. This opening shows that both a certain form of resistance and the current nature of events in the LTR may influence the way in which patients begin conversations.

Unlike conversations in the STR, the *present* is not used in the LTR as a preamble to a hidden plan: the present is the leading topic throughout the exchange. Therapists rely more on the incidental and are less inclined to structure the conversation, since there is no therapeutic objective in the LTR. Patients and staff members seldom plan their conversations. They talk to each other when they feel a need to or when they encounter each other. Words have become superfluous through the acquaintance of many years. Even so, patients continue in this setting to hide emotions and personal experiences. Both LTR and STR therapists conspire to hide psychotic reality because they worry about a possible crisis. The fragment below illustrates that planned conversations are unusual. Griet, the patient, makes fun of the nurse's plan:

Griet: What do you want to talk about?
Nurse: About you.

Griet: About me? [*laughs*]
Nurse: Yes [*laughs*], what we talked about before, how you are doing.
Griet: (3) How I am doing? (2) Just fine.

As noted before, opening moves are meant to tune in and gain access to the patient before construction of a new reality can begin. Therapists and staff members seek to establish rapport with their discussion partners, place the talks in context, and determine positions. From the outset patients can still intervene to set the tone of the talk, resist or resort to sabotage. If patients succeed in doing so, the 'face' (Goffman 1967) is at stake;[9] that is, which of the discussion partners can accept the other's leadership without loss of face? In normal conversations, this positional issue is usually handled with care and conversation openings evince 'an almost nonchalantly implemented complexity' (Ten Have 1987: 75). Such casualness is greatly reduced in talks with psychotic people. Given their institutional backing, the therapist or staff member will assume the leadership and introduce a safe, everyday topic. In the actual situation, however, nothing can be done but wait and see what the patient will do. Literature on interaction analysis refers to minimum means to get a conversation going (cf Schlegoff 1979; Sacks and Schlegoff 1979) – but the therapist's 'agenda' is often postponed. Staff and patients make great demands on each other: 'maximum effort' for 'minimum information' is the rule rather than the exception.[10] This has a strong bearing on the therapeutic objective of a new reality.

'Will you try again to get me out of here?'

Questions leading to concealment

Once a conversation is underway, it usually proceeds in question-and-answer sequences, with the therapist asking the questions and the patient replying. Hence, questioning is a core 'technique' of therapist–patient conversations. On the surface, the creation of the new reality is left to the patient. But questioning helps the therapists to conceal their purpose, while giving the patients scope to conceal matters as well. In literature on physician–patient interaction, it is suggested that the doctor's questions are meant to restrict the patient's story to therapeutically or medically relevant matters on which information is required (cf Mishler 1984; Berenst 1986). Physicians are said to use questions to interrupt the patient's story, keep it brief and direct it to certain topics (Ten Have 1991a). This fits in with the observed institutional efforts to restrict the role of psychotic reality to a minimum in the process of healing, but it also limits the role of questions to gathering information or restricting people. They can be used to confront, demonstrate involvement, make evaluation possible or offer space to change the subject, and each of these intentions leads to different elaborations. Questions are 'expressions creating a kind of space for a reply, a cognitive framework to be used by the next speaker to seek an appropriate answer' (1991a: 89).

Questions do not of necessity restrict,[11] and they can offer patients a certain amount of freedom when answering in order to explore issues or conceal them. In the process therapists may have to take care not to steer the process too strongly and thereby limit their access to therapeutically relevant aspects of the patient's experiential world. It is already difficult for therapists to achieve intimacy in conversations with patients because their contact is more limited. Karel remarked about his conversations with René that 'Maybe I talked with him for a total of two and a half hours' [over a period of seven months, EvD].

In the earlier fragment, when Karel came back with cigarettes it ends the contestation, and René quite willingly resumes talking about the dentist. Karel poses questions that are meant to keep the conversation going and achieve a kind of intimacy rather than to obtain information. Questions aimed at involvement and intimacy are easier when conversations gravitate to subjects that are of interest to the patient, or describe their own activities:

Karel: You have matches, I hope?
René: Yes, I have. (4) Uh (4) yes, those teeth I was not afraid, but it made me a little funky. Well, that's just fear of the . . . but it was not too bad.
Karel: You were what?
René: Funky.
Karel: Funky? What's that?
René: Well, that's just scared. (2) the only . . .
Karel: Oh.
René: It wasn't so bad, really. I was not really scared.
Karel: Oh, he was a good sort?
René: Yes. [*mutters*]
Karel: And, uh . . . one of the nurses was there, too, right?
René: Yes, uh, uh [name]. (2) Next time I'll go alone, I think.

Karel's first three questions are intended to indicate interest. The contact achieved after the initial problems are overcome, must now be retained. But Karel's closing question is perceived as a challenge by René, who feels inadequate because a nurse has to accompany him, an adult, to the dentist. He responds to the challenge by resolving to tackle the next visit on his own. Karel's last question and René's reply, taken together, are the prelude to a 'core sequence' (Ten Have 1991a: 89) in which René reopens the struggle. Karel recommends that he should rather take someone along to the dentist next time, and René agrees. There is also a long pause, during which Karel remains silent. Such silences in the conversations are common. They do not represent reserve, as might be the case among professionals (see Ten Have 1991b: 56), but rather a transition prior to a new topic being broached.

Both partners had space to introduce a topic, and René seized the initiative. All the while he had been trying unsuccessfully to roll a cigarette and finally he asked Karel if he would oblige:

René: My fingers are slippery, can you roll?
Karel: That's, uh . . . You are kind of mixed up, aren't you?
René: Nothing mixed . . .
Karel: Is it because of the camera? Or is it . . .
René: Nothing like that. No, nothing, nothing at all, no, no.
Karel: But you just told me that you're nervous?
René: Yes. But not mixed [*laughs*].
Karel: Okay, another word for mixed.
René: No, that's not true, that's not true, that's
Karel: You said yourself that you're nervous?
René: No, that's not true, no, I don't agree with that.
Karel: No? How are things at the ward?
René: [*mutters*]
Karel: How are you these days?
René: Fine
Karel: But yourself . . .
René: Very fine, in fact. (2) nothing to report. Just fine, things are going well,
           going very well indeed (1) that's for sure. (1) One hundred per cent
           certain, sure.
Karel: We talked a lot with each other this past half year about uh . . .
           transfer to another ward, didn't we?
René: Uhuh [*busy lighting a cigarette*]
Karel: An open ward?
René: I should be about ready for that I guess, or not?
Karel: You are ready for it?
René: Uhuh. I think so.
Karel: What makes . . . how can you tell?
René: (1) By you.
Karel: Tell me
René: Yes, you sit there making a list of what I have to do this week, and I
           just do it.

Karel's question ('You are kind of mixed up') was a new confrontation. René
responded with great resistance. The subsequent exchange was broken off by Karel,
who asked how René was doing. Usually, this question is asked at the start of
a conversation and is considered a 'safe' topic. Safe topics do not as a rule set
off a battle. But at that moment the subject was unwelcome (things were *not*
going well on the ward) and René fends off Karel's questions for two reasons:
first, the context of the conversation, i.e. the confrontation implicit in Karel's
questions; second, René has raised a barrier because of his feelings of inadequacy.
Karel could have pursued this, but he did not. By way of a question he changed
the subject and moved into calmer waters:

Karel: (2) How often do you go to Ward 2?
René: Uh, I don't have time right now, but normally speaking about three times a day.
Karel: And how, what do you do there?
René: Uh, sit, drink coffee, talk, listen to music, watch the telly, wash dishes. Yesterday I did the cooking, actually, cooking.
Karel: You don't say?
René: I cooked yesterday, for uh
Karel: You did the cooking yesterday?
René: Sure. And tasty, they all said it tasted good.
Karel: On Ward 2?
René: Yes
Karel: You cooked on Ward 2?
René: Yes, chili con carne.
Karel: Chili con carne (3) And that went alright?
René: Fine.
Karel: You cooked for a lot of people, didn't you?
René: About uh, twelve, I think (3)
Karel: All by yourself? Or did you have somebody helping you?
René: H. Well, I did the cooking myself. Well, H. helped. H.
Karel: H. helped you?
René: Yes.
Karel: I see

The question 'What do you do there?' introduced a relatively 'tuned-in' sequence. It often occurs in conversations that discussing and asking about 'do-things' and details (Tannen 1990: 112–113) generates closeness. René used the opportunity provided by the question to report on his activities on the ward. It offered him space for a success story and he hinted that he had something interesting to say. In conversation analysis, this is sometimes called a 'pre-announcement sequence' (Mazeland 1992: 109). Karel questioned him to confirm it. Alternating between fending off and tuning in is a fixed pattern in the conversations. When a therapist successfully broaches a sensitive topic, the patient becomes more evasive and inaccessible. This may take various forms: open resistance (as in René's case), explicit refusal, silence, or profuse vocalizing. If the therapist's question allows room to change the subject, the patient will do so. René successfully concealed a therapeutically relevant point. Karel described it as follows:

> He feels harassed about his ignorance; he feels that he invariably fails; he always thinks that people ridicule him.

Karel did not challenge the patient's effort to conceal; he complemented his story by using questions. The subject was less unimportant, since daily chores such as cooking were in any event a significant part of the therapeutic plan. During conversations between patients and nurses, a fair amount of time was spent on such matters and Karel's questions could be seen to indicate involvement. They also allowed him to save face because he appeared to redirect the conversation and retain control of it. However, when he asked 'All by yourself? Or did you have someone helping you?' the question tended towards confrontation and René abruptly changed the subject and disturbed the rhythm of the conversation by referring to the recording equipment. Karel managed to re-establish contact by rolling a cigarette and making a joke ('Let's say that this is a festive occasion') and in this way effectively brought René back to the original topic. The designated 'sick part' could resurface in the conversation.

Karel: Actually, I don't smoke much. Just once in a while. Let's say that this is a festive occasion [*gets a light*] (8) Okay.

René: [*laughs*]

Karel: How long have you been with us now?

René: I think uh . . . about six months, seven.

Karel: If you compare yourself with how you were when you were admitted . . . What do you think is different?

René: The difference is that meanwhile I'm better now. Not then, I was very sick.

Karel: Uhuh. In what sense are you better now? Can you do things now you couldn't then?

René: I am not afraid any more (2) of nobody, not the devil, not of dying.

Karel: You were in bad shape at that time, weren't you?

René: Yes, you can say that. But for me they just don't exist any more.

Karel: No?

René: No. (1) Exorcised. Try to keep them away. It just isn't good. The devil too.

Karel: What does it say

René: The Lord sets the devil at my feet

Karel: Sorry, I didn't get you.

René: The Lord sets the devil at my feet, a stumbling block.

Karel: Uh (4)

René: I had a conversion. I am converted.

Karel: You are?

René: Didn't you know?

Karel: But I always thought you had a religious upbringing?

René: Sure, but also a conversion.

Karel: Yes?

René: (3) God did that. I did it. Both.

Karel: Is that so? You did it yourself?

René: Uhuh. I even saw the Lord once.

Karel: You did? When?

René   I'm not telling. I'm not supposed to tell.
Karel: No?
René: No
Karel: The Lord?
René: No no (3) If I tell I might die.
Karel: That so?
René: Yes. Could be.
Karel: Well, then you'd better not.
René: No. That's why (2)
Karel: Gee, I didn't realize it already is . . .
René: Yes, I am allowed to tell but uh . . . really rather not. (2) I guess, I'm
            not really sure, actually (1)
Karel: [*mumbles*]
René: . . . . but I'd just rather not say
Karel: No, okay, fine.
René: Keep it to myself forever
Karel: But you are saying . . .
René: . . . goes into the grave with me
Karel: The most important differences between, say seven months . . .
René: . . . that goes into the grave with me
Karel: Yes, okay
René: . . . keep it secret
Karel: The big difference between then and now, between admission and now
            is that you are no longer afraid?
René: No (2) that's good
Karel: (2) I remember that you often had visions at that time?
René: Yes. Heard false prophecies. Voices, too.
Karel: ah
René: The devil
Karel: ah
René: That's all gone now.
Karel: All gone?
René: All gone. Thanks to the medicine I take.
Karel: ah (4)
René: And the . . . yes . . . uh and the . . . what do you call it
Karel: Is that it? Was it the medicine that did it?
René: I helped it some, I think, and with the help of the Lord.
Karel: What did you do yourself?
René: I guess. Not much, just uh, try to fight it. Leave the battle against the Lord.
Karel: Leave what?
René: The battle against God. I fought against God, but you shouldn't do that.
            You always lose. Jacob too. Jacob and Esau (2). You know that Bible
            story, don't you?
Karel: Yes.

Initially, Karel responded to René's remarks with questions. The question about the difference between 'then and now' offered René room to conceal his 'incapacity' as he did in earlier episodes. When he started to talk about the devil, later depicted as a dark being, Karel dropped the subject. He wanted to ask a question: 'What does it say . . .'. and René interrupted him. An overlap occurred: 'The Lord sets the devil . . .'. Overlaps like this are sometimes seen as an act that 'wipes out' the discussion partner's previous remarks:

> When overlaps are obliterative [. . .] one speaker clearly places his talk so as to blot out the talk of the another, the intruder's precise placement discloses him to have been attending the talk he overlaps very closely indeed. It is not faulty listening or imperfect participation. The mechanical image is of pinpoint bombing, not careless collision, of turns.
>
> (Moerman 1988: 21)

Karel noted that the overlap was not a matter of not listening or of misinterpretation, but something done on purpose to break down the talk. In pathological terms: 'it arises from René's fear of failure'. Overlaps are rare in the recorded conversations, while strict alternating is fairly frequent. If overlaps occur this is usually done on purpose, as in the above fragment from the conversation. Subsequently Karel seemed to be troubled by the new direction: 'Ah (4).' René pursued the subject and by resorting to ironic questions to counterpoint René's utterances, Karel attempted to silence the 'psychotic' world. He did not probe René's secret and when his diversion did not immediately succeed a series of overlaps followed, with concealment on both sides: these lines represent a delicate duet of contrasting voices, in which Karel seeks to keep the psychotic world out and to guide René towards a more therapeutically acceptable situation. The question about fear reintroduced turn taking and the conversation continued.

The next part of their exchange revealed different perceptions about reality and the effectiveness of the medication. It is characteristic of the institutional perspective that patients should demonstrably pursue self-improvement. As Karel saw it, improvement was due more to self-activity, but René maintained that if someone got better it was thanks to the Lord's help. During this episode Karel pursues René's religious frame of mind, asking about his religious background rather than his experiences or views. This kept the religious talk at the 'practical' level of denomination, the pastor, church attendance, the church's farming project, etc. René introduced the topic of 'sheltered housing' because the house was near the Pentecostal Congregation and he had lived there for a time. Karel responded and the conversation immediately focused on the quarrel that René claimed he had had at the shared house, because of his faith. René regarded himself as one persecuted for his religion. His own diagnosis was that he suffered from 'paranoid hallucination', but the religious dimension of his descriptions tell us more about his 'problem' than the DSM-III diagnosis does. It also indicates the nature of the therapeutic conversations. Karel may have overlooked an important aspect of religion: that it is not only about people persecuted because of their convictions, but has stories of comfort as well.

The conversations can have a fixed pattern. A patient introduces a subject and the therapist or other mental health worker asks questions about it. These convey an impression of empathy and involvement, and so give patients the idea that there is room to talk about certain experiences. Conversely, as in the following fragment, the subject matter can be specifically steered and structured:

René: That was not allowed there, M. didn't allow it. (2) Then he would get angry at me. (3) And there you go, another quarrel, I won't go there again, I'll never go there again.

Karel: If you had not left ... If you had not left there, you know, if the leadership had remained the same?

René: Uhuh

Karel: What would have happened to you? Would you be here then?

René: I don't think so. No, I don't think. (5)

Karel: Or would you?

René: Look, I think I am not going to speak out against the home.

Karel: No.

René: It is true that, well eh, let me see, it is eh:: let me think, I don't know, I've lost it eh, eh ...

Karel: Well, just try to think about it. What did you want to say? We were talking about the home, right? The home.

René: We were? Is the camera going, or something?

Karel: From the start (6)

René: Oh oh:: [*laughs and makes an obscene gesture*]

Karel: Don't do that! No sir, that's out.

René: Sorry, I am so sorry (4) [*laughs*] This could be fun.

Karel: We were talking about the home.

René: Right, the home.

Karel: If you had not gone away, then

René: Sure. I would not be here, that figures. If my father had not died, I would never have come here, never.

Karel's conjecture can lead to a confrontation. This route is used sparingly but consciously in therapy involving psychotic people. Once uncomfortable questions enter into the conversation, René's reply is evidently incorrect, or incomplete. The question 'Or would you?' suggests that Karel is thinking of another reason for René's admission to the hospital. 'Or would you' could be asked because René was silent. He grasped what Karel wanted and avoided it, saying 'I've lost it'. Karel asked a new question, and René did not want to pursue it. However, his dodging move – an obscene gesture towards the camera – did not have the desired effect. Instead, he was scolded. René now elaborated on the 'if' question: 'If my father had not died . . .'. Karel considers this subject important. He saw a chance to seek out individual, emotion-filled events in René's life, some with far-reaching consequences, but this did not happen:

René: First I thought he was putting me on, that was first, there he goes, dead, just like that. That can happen to you, too, and me, but now it doesn't matter, but do you know where you're going when you die? A heaven and a hell. Do you know?

Karel: Who, me?

René: Yes. Or don't you know?

Karel: I wouldn't know.

René: Uh, but you hope, don't you? What do you hope?

Karel: Nah.

René: Oh. Uh, you ought to know now already, see, before you die, otherwise.

Karel: Oh, you know what you hope, but you don't know what's going to happen. You don't either, do you?

René: No. (1) I know more or less. I uh:: people. Read a book, people who were in hell. Well, that's not for me.

Karel: What do you think it's like?

René: (2) Don't know. Never been there.

Karel: No. But you do have fantasies about it?

René: No (3) Don't need them (4) It can wait, till he returns

Karel: Till who returns?

René: The Lord. (4) Then we're all up the creek [*laughs*].

Karel: Up the creek?

René: Yeah, you people. Not me.

Karel: No? What's the difference?

René: Well, I'm converted, you aren't.

Karel: What happens to me, you suppose?

René: (2) Depends. (5)

Karel: Depends on what?

René: (3) Mmmm, if you are converted or not.

Karel: And if not, then what?

René: You'll go to hell.

Karel: Is that so?

René: Yes. (3)

Karel: And what happens there?

René: You'll be a prisoner there, forever. (2) Gnashing your teeth. Shrieking. You know.

Karel: Would you try to get me out of there?

René: [*laughs*] Of course not ah, cause I uh::

Karel: Of course not?

René: No (1) You do it yourself. You want uh:: dead, well go ahead, die.

Karel: Humm (2)

René: Makes no diff, hah: that does not interest me. If you throw yourself in front of a train you're dead, and you commit suicide and that carries the death penalty.

Karel: Ahah. (4)

René: Suicide.

Karel: Yes, you could say that. Why?

René: Well, time is up. I quit.

Karel: Really?

René: Yes. This was enough.

Karel: Listen, we've only talked for a quarter of an hour, man!

René: Yes:: no, not again.

Karel: Five more minutes?

René: No. It's finished, I said all I have to say.

Karel: There is plenty of . . . All?

René: Yes. There, turn that thing off.

Karel: Yes. But we haven't talked about your future yet

René: Yes. Not necessary. It's over now. I am leaving.

Karel: Give it one more try

René: No (4)

Karel: Why are you so scared?

René: I'm not scared. I just uh: (2) I think those prying questions of yours sometimes sometimes

Karel: Prying?

René: Yes. The questions, yes.

Karel: What am I prying into?

René: I don't know. I guess you know better than I (2) Or not?

According to Karel, one of René's secrets came to the surface: his preoccupation with suicide. Suicide was of great emotional significance for while at the same time his religion forbade it in the strongest terms. This complex and emotional fragment began with René and Karel battling for position, and René attempting to upset the roles (*he* would ask the questions now!). Karel indicated that he did not want to discuss his own ideas about the subject ('Nah') and took the initiative by asking a question: 'Do you?' Thus, the normal institutional asymmetry was restored. In the second place, the fragment was a 'pre-sequence' (Schlegoff 1968) for René's comment on how Karel was questioning him (see end of fragment). He felt hunted and rose to go to the door:

> Here I move in too closely. Although René has never talked about suicide or made an attempt I am sure that it has certainly crossed his mind. And it scares him, so he wants to leave. A mirror is being held up to him. Suicide could be an option because he feels himself an utter failure.
>
> (Karel)

I'm telling you: Karel was prying with his questions . . . They treat me rotten. I've seen the devil. He was black all over. Sometimes it seemed he talked to me in my head. But I overcame him. Not all by myself but with the help of [*points to the sky*]. Euthanasia is not allowed. You should never end a life. That is left to God.

(René)

Their idioms differed. For Karel, thoughts about what happens after death were fantasies and the idea of suicide and concomitant emotions needed to be expressed in a more idiosyncratic, a-religious idiom. René spoke in a religious context in which suicide was immoral. Speaking in different idioms need not create a problem, although in this case it evidently does. This was because the idiom not only expressed the problem or how one should feel about it, but also implied specific consequences for (therapeutic) activity. For Karel, this was an individual matter in which a patient was responsible for himself and had to deal with it himself. For René, it was a matter in which he was not only responsible to himself but also to God: a divinity, moreover, who can dispense the punishment of hell. He was confronted by two judges: Karel and God, and his fear was not so much of Karel, as a fear of hell. This fear was so great that it could not be expressed in the ordinary discourse of the hospital, only in a religious idiom.[12] One result of this was that the emotion could be interpreted as something else, e.g. as normalcy.

The ironic questions asked by Karel led to a break in the conversation, and brought it to a halt. Karel must have thought the recording was too short and he managed to lure René into continuing. It was very likely that the taperecorder was a factor here. He now tempted René by means of 'if' questions that referred to the future, not the past. René returned to the table and finally sat down again. 'Just imagine,' Karel said. The new subject was future plans, a relevant institutional reality.[13] René's stay in the closed ward would end soon. He would move to an open ward and Karel was worried about what had to be done next. One relevant issue was 'outplacement'. On admission to Saint Anthony's people's social relationships were often disrupted so traumatically that finding a way back was nearly impossible. The question of where patients would find a place to live was important and, hence, a major theme of the conversations. In almost every conversation there was an episode in which this subject was discussed and usually these particular episodes spelt trouble. There is an essential difference between the ideas about the future held by hospital staff and those held by patients. For patients, the quality of life outside the hospital is crucial and their concern with the future is existential. The practical sides of it seem less important.

Therapists and mental health workers approached the subject more pragmatically. Their thoughts dwelt on questions like 'Where will you find a place to live?' and 'Are you going to look for a job?' It was not that they were indifferent to their patient's happiness. Rather, the pragmatic side of their questions was a consequence of developments on the political–economic level[14] as well as the trend in psychiatry towards medication as a solution, and short-term therapies (Stein 1991). These developments and trends tended to obstruct discourse on existential issues. The divergent views of therapist and patient as to what the future holds can mean that problems arising during the conversation are incorrectly seen as generating from that particular patient. I have described (Van Dongen 1993c) how a patient's confusion arising from his therapist's questions on his future expectations led to a misunderstanding, with the therapist concluding that the patient was out of touch with reality. The basic problem was conflicting views on the future, similar to René and Karel, although the latter case was less extreme:

Karel: (2) I would just very much like to know how you, uh::: imagine that you will go to Ward 2, okay?
René: Yes?
Karel: How would things work out?
René: Fine.
Karel: Tell me about it.
René: Well, uh::
Karel: Move a little closer.
René: I can't say, I can't tell you, nobody knows what's going to happen normally. I'm not God.
Karel: Well, use your imagination, okay?
René: I'm not God!

Karel successfully dealt with René's resistance. He formulated the future strategy: first to Ward 2, which was an open ward, and then step by step towards being discharged. It surprised Karel when René told him that his mother would allow him to live with her in spite of earlier problems. The conversation moved on, but for René the subject was finished 'done!' He realized that Karel thought differently: 'Well, yes, but you like to be a caring person'. Karel would rather not hurry things: first there was the move to Ward 2. On René moving in with his mother, he was more cautious: 'We'll see how it turns out'. When René declared his 'trust in the Lord' he was referring to the quality of his life, not to practical matters. Karel's response was minimal and reserved, but his next question could be interpreted as a restriction. René managed to tempt Karel away from the future by talking about a girlfriend in the hospital. Again, Karel followed this up with provocative questions. The possibility that the conversation would end abruptly and that leave taking would be less than cordial was avoided by their having a smoke together. Karel's questions now turned to René's hobbies, his ornitho-logical and botanical interests. These episodes were examples of 'making talk' (Sudnow 1967). Karel deliberately directed the conversation to matters to which René would respond, and René even demonstrated how he had once caught a pheasant bare-handed. These extensions of the conversation were partly due to the presence of the taperecorder but they were not without therapeutic value. Up to that point, Karel's had cautiously been probing to bring out René's fear of failure, and frequently skirting confrontation. Now that the questions related to matters that the patient had mastered, it appeared to be quite a novel situation:

Karel: I know that every time they talk about you, that you are incredibly knowledgeable about birds.
René: That's . . . yes.
Karel: But you never ever told me about that, I think that's remarkable.
René: (2) No, you never asked, did you?

René vaguely corrected his therapist and the conversation moved to his much-loved work at a nursery. Karel said 'this was meant to bolster his ego, because in many ways he feels incapable'. Making talk in this way is meant to smooth the way for later progress. When René commented on his dismissal from the nursery and moralized about his boss and the industrial physician, Karel restricted himself to the slightest possible response. In this way he ensured that the conversation continued without an argument about René's boss or his failings being confronted. A transition to things that René was good at followed. He mentioned his guitar, and Karel pointed out the joy of making music: 'It's something nice to do, isn't it?' By the end of the conversation a new dynamic was developing around the guitar, but it was an ironic and playful argument, quite different from the other:

Karel: Why didn't you bring it along?
René: Yes, I keep forgetting to ask.
Karel: Pardon?
René: I keep forgetting to ask my mother.
Karel: You forget every time?
René: Yes.
Karel: You've been forgetting for months?
René: No, not that long.
Karel: Playing is something nice to do, isn't it?
René: Yes . . . I guess she should bring it.
Karel: No problem.
René: If she doesn't bring it I can't do anything about it.
Karel: No, but if you don't ask, she can't
René: That's true. I did ask once. Asked once. That's
Karel: One telephone call
René: True, you're right about that.
Karel: Hmm
René: But I'm not supposed to call my mother, you know, agreement with the nurses.
Karel: But she comes to visit you?
René: Yes, that's why. She'll be here tomorrow (2)
Karel: Well then, I would sure ask if I were you.

René: Yes, I'll do that

Karel: Those are the good things of life.

René: Do I have your permission to make a phone call? (0.5) My mother? (1) Your permission? And would you place the call to her house? (2) Right now? (1) Can you?

Karel: You are a pretty smart guy.

René: I'm just an ordinary normal human being, you know.

Karel: What is the agreement? You are not to make calls at all?

René: I can make one or two calls, but not my mother. (1) Do you follow?

Karel: I see, I get it.

René: Can I call? Am I allowed to call?

Karel: You said yourself that she'd be here this weekend?

René: Yes.

Karel: You can ask her then, can't you?

René: No. I want to ask in advance, then she can bring it for me.

Karel: Preferably in advance, of course

René: Saturday. Otherwise I have to wait another week.

Karel: (7) Let's wait and see if you really want to. This was just a spur of the moment thing, because I happened to mention it.

René was displaying his self-deprecating side as the victim of a dishonored agreement but his argument was not sufficiently convincing. Karel had to respect René's agreement with the staff, in spite of underlining the importance of the instrument. He hesitated, remained silent for seven seconds, and asked for a postponement. René laughed and changed the subject, quite aware of the predicament his therapist was in. He expressed dissatisfaction about another patient and on that note, the conversation closed.

The theme of this chapter is concealment. In the above passage there is concealment when confrontation threatens to break the exchange. A break allows patients to conceal therapeutically relevant issues and for this reason therapists do not use questions only in order to acquire information or achieve change. Questions that expand the subject help to achieve contact rather than unearthing further therapeutic issues, and the therapist can break through a patient's tendency to conceal by asking the right questions. The process can also serve to conceal psychotic reality (or another embodiment of what is or should be), and whatever action is required to address it. By asking the right questions, therapists can manipulate the conversation without creating the impression that psychotic expressions or moral comments are being excluded somewhat brusquely. Sometimes the manner in which therapists ask their questions makes it possible for patients to introduce or conceal subjects in unusual ways, because they seem to have no other option. But therapists are not faced with patients who have not mastered the art of conversation, due to their problems. On the contrary, patients become skilled at seizing the 'space' created by questions, and use it in an attempt to control the conversation.

Silence and vocalization

In this section two characteristics of therapist–patient talks are discussed: silence and vocalization, or verbosity. By verbosity I mean an abundant expression of seemingly irrelevant detail,[15] a detailing often rendered in quite graceful language. Silence always implies the absence of anything else. Both have many uses and meanings in a conversation (analysis of which would take us far afield) and are closely related to emotions. As with questions, they may be seen as attempts to conceal. I deal with both silence and verbosity as emotional 'language', since emotion plays an important role in both concealment and the therapeutic process. While it is assumed that silence and verbosity are used to keep strong and difficult emotions in check, the conditions under which they come into play can differ (Saunders 1985: 165). As the likelihood of a conflict in the interaction increases, people prefer to remain silent, using silence as a coping mechanism.

The term 'psychotic' refers to both disorders in individual emotional life and disorders in externally directed expressions of feelings. The two senses of 'disorder' are related in that the interpretation of the former takes place on the basis of the latter. Patients are described as 'lacking emotion', 'cold', or 'emotionally unstable' evidently because they do not express their emotions in expected ways. Both (florid) psychosis and communication about certain subjects are viewed as highly charged emotionally, and deemed to be unacceptable. Extreme emotions and expressions were avoided at Saint Anthony's because mental health workers feared them, and they were suppressed by being structured, or by medication. The importance of this 'cooling off' is not questioned, but its effect on conversations between therapists and patients is important.

If emotional expressions or reactions had to lead to situations that the therapists wished to avoid, patients would soon learn to give vent to their emotions in other ways. Goldschmidt (1976: 65–66) speaks of 'socialization for low affect'. Silence and words are both potent emotional outlets, providing both therapists and patients with a chance to cool off. In helping to keep emotional displays to a minimum, they become functional instruments for concealing, obscuring, or playing down certain matters. Silence and verbosity are the two paradoxical faces of Janus (Walker 1985). In one sense therapists think of them as normal and functional, and patients are advised to take their time to reflect when matters seem precarious. In another, they are not normal and tend to be regarded as a form of non-cooperation and inaccessibility – characteristics linked to psychotic disorders. While silence can be an attempt to hide, avoid or obscure, shared silence can also draw people closer together (cf Lehtonen and Sajavaara 1985). Verbosity can imply access and cooperation, but it can equally well lead to pseudo-cooperation. In addition to their functional value, silence and verbosity symbolize the presence or absence of specific emotions. When therapists recall the junctures at which silence and verbosity occurred they get an indication of the events, thoughts, and insights that are emotionally charged and which not.

Verbosity and emotion

Verbosity, in the form of specifying or detailing, is characteristic of conversations between therapists and patients. This occurs at specific moments, especially when emotions come into play. Hospital staff find the detailing to be ambivalent. Patients speak at length and present specific illustrations and examples, sometimes leading to the complaint that they are 'roaming too far afield' and seem to be on the run from reality. However, the detailed byways can also reveal emotional topics, as in the conversation between Mark, a schizophrenic patient, and his therapist, Louis:

Louis: How is Mark doing?
Mark: Fine. At least, I feel reasonably good. I shouldn't complain.
Louis: Uhuh
Mark: For a while now uh:: (5) these days I discover more and more uh:: things, things that help me
Louis: Hm
Mark: . . . to uh (0.5) to do something about my fears (1) for instance, I uh I fix on something, concentrate.
Louis: (0.3) Uh
Mark: For instance I go uh: at the: weekends (0.5) I walk to uh:: Patersven, close by here
Louis: Uh
Mark: . . . where the monks live, You know where that is?
Louis: No, I, I don't know that area very well. Uh
Mark: But that's a very peaceful area and when I walk there I don't need, I feel . . .
Louis: Uhuh
Mark: Yes, it is as if I feel all ten . . . all tension and fear ebbing away. A real peaceful feeling.
Louis: Uhuh
Mark: And you look down into the valley and you see the ducks swimming, on the other side you see eh::
Louis: Hm
Mark: . . . the rising reeds along the bank
Louis: Ah
Mark: It's really very uh:: (1)
Louis: It's almost like you're taking a picture, then?
Mark: (0.5) A picture of a beautiful day.
Louis: Yes? (3) Those are your secret help things against the fear that you: (0.5) but it comes back sometimes?
Mark: Yes, the fear is there in the morning uh: an irritating presence and . . .
Louis: Uhuh

Mark: (1) and every morning I have a feeling like uh: oh God, how will I get through this day? (3) But then I try, I . . . just like before our talk I was very tense

Louis: Uhuh. You did have . . .

Mark: But . . .

Louis: Yes?

Mark: I asked uh:: A. to help me. You know A.?

Louis: Ye-es.

Mark: (0.3) And uh: I asked her to give me something to do so that I would have to concentrate, keep my mind occupied.

Louis: What kind of job? What sort of work were you doing just before this?

Mark: Sorting (2)

Louis: So you start sorting just so you don't have to think about our talk. Don't need to get excited?

Mark: Yes: They have a new: you know the old way of just putting one sheet on top of the next?

Louis: Ye-es.

Mark: But now they take one sheet and then a blank and then the next sheet (0.3) because uh:: otherwise uh:: the wrong copies get mixed.

Louis: Hmm.

Mark: The blank in between prevents that.

Louis: And that helps you, or you are forced to concentrate? Not just piling one sheet on top of another, but uh:

Mark: Yes, you really have to look for uh: what color is next

Louis: Hm

Mark: uh: . . . which should horizontal, which vertical (2)

Louis: Yes. You already had two . . .

Mark: But if you . . .

Louis: Yes?

Mark: . . . if you do it for a while uh:: it becomes routine, but after half an hour of this I really have to concentrate some. Every time I start again I have to uh:: uh: (2) set myself to it.

Louis: Uhuh. So it's like you are telling yourself: you say: Come on Mark, keep your mind on the job.

Mark: Yes. Yes (2) Exactly (1)

Louis: You said that you:: uh you had more things to help you. Little secret things to uh: against fear, uh:: (2) things to keep the fear away, right?

Mark: Yes::: should I mention another one?

Mark's fear of what lay ahead was the issue, but instead he spoke almost lyric-ally of the means by which he had mastered his emotions ('the rising reeds along the bank') and reduced his fear. Louis's minimal responses showed that he was listening and the conversation should continue. He prompted Mark: 'It's almost like you're taking a picture', which can be understood as a 'sympathizer'

(Van Bijsterveld 1982). Louis wanted to change the topic to Mark's fear. Initially Mark seemed to respond but before Louis completed his question he introduced yet another evasion: sorting papers. Louis summed up. This attempt to coerce Mark into addressing the nature of his fear/tension succeeded: 'Yes. Yes. Exactly'. Another 'detailing' followed in the story about a dentist.

The emotive language in this fragment was satisfying for both. In a sense, the emotion came out in the detail and this helped the discussion partners to name and understand it. It illustrated that upsetting emotions – like extreme fear – could be controlled and concealed. In the context of the hospital, expressing negative, exceptional emotions troubled the patients, and the staff perhaps even more so. Intense detailing helped to give expression to it, and the form and nature of the detailing depended on how therapist and patient related to each other. Mark and Louis did not meet often. The detailing gives an impression of easy access, but the therapist felt this was not so. When patients and staff were in frequent contact because the patient was going through a difficult period, the detailing was more obviously intended to avoid issues. An example was Walter, an LTR psychotic patient, and his therapist Johan.

Johan: You were concerned, and that intrigued me, about a son and heir, a family heir, isn't that right?

Walter: Yes.

Johan: That kept me thinking, you know, what exactly you . . .

Walter: Hm

Johan: . . . meant by that. (2) Sure, I know what a family heir is, but – what does it mean to you?

Walter: Uh (3) Well, if it is a boy, the line goes on, doesn't it?

Johan: Yes?

Walter: None of us boys is married.

Johan: Well, that's uh:: let me say, a technical thing, isn't it? Like a pedigree, the continuation of a family, but why do you think that so important?

Walter: Why?

Johan: Yes?

Walter: Well uh:: (2) I don't know when the next edition will appear, but soon there will be another uh:: we are listed in a book, you know, the generations, and once every :::: thirty years, I think, there is a new printing.

Johan: Yes. I don't know the book, but I wouldn't doubt it.

Walter: So, that's and then uh:: yes, I am afraid it will die out.

Johan: (4)

Walter: Our branch.

Johan: Yes? (2) That's yes, I don't know how to say it. It's kind of the product of the calculation. If we reproduce, the family wouldn't die out, would it?

Walter: Yes?

Johan: A kind of arithmetic, I would almost say.
Walter: Well . . . :: (laughs)
Johan: (2) And what I'm looking for, is uh, well, to put it crudely, so what?
Walter: Yes?
Johan: Why is it so important to you?
Walter: (3) Well, it is a tradition dating back to 1541.
Johan: From 1541? A tradition?
Walter: Yes.

Walter was going to be a father. He regarded a 'son as heir' as very important and his therapist did not see why. Walter's responses to Johan's questions were socially correct, but did not satisfy his therapist. Walter's account detailed the more technical side of inheritance rather than its emotional significance. Accordingly, Johan later referred to his 'lack of emotion'. In effect, the detailing masked the emotion from Johan, who presumed it to be there but could not find it. Facial expressions, pauses during which Walter gazed through the window, shifts in his chair, pulls at his upper lip – all of these showed emotion even though its content, source and object was not obvious. They were obscured by the symbolism of lineage, which may have lost much of its value in our culture yet still remains strong enough to suggest its emotional significance. Johan said: 'I find this frightening. To me this is like the old nobility and marriages of convenience, and not something we look for in our day and age. I think it has a strong effect on me.' He tried confrontation but Walter would not be tempted. In the talk between Louis and Mark, fear was immediately linked to ways in which it could be addressed, but not in Walter's case. The details allowed him to express intense emotion, yet the form made it possible to hide its content. In part, this was due to the questions and, in part it was a case of countertransference. Allowing the debate about Walter's family lineage to intensify would have taken it into the moral realm, and therapists tend to steer clear of the moral dimension (Van Dongen 1993b).

From the sequel to the conversation between Louis and Mark it is clear that therapists do have a technique to break through resistance or to prevent patients from circumlocuting. Mark had mentioned another way to combat fear. Louis wanted to generalize ('Not knowing what is going to happen?) and tried to ask a question ('Is that convenient for you?') but Mark interrupted him. Louis listened with empathy and asked questions that gave voice to Mark's emotions. This is a common pattern in conversations when patients go into detail about emotional subjects. When the therapist is responding well and framing his questions accordingly, it generates even more detailed replies and the actual emotion is often concealed. Elaborating on specifics happens during patient–therapist conversations because of the implicit requirements of responsible self-construction and self-presentation. The patient has to give a good 'account' of his own emotional problems, yet detailed elaboration is seen as 'side-tracking' and avoiding reality. The contradiction between these aspects seems well nigh insoluble.

We learn to speak of our emotions by describing them in detail. This is emphasized in a psychiatric hospital: 'If you are emotional you must be able to talk about it'. To communicate emotion is a discursive practice and experience which is created in conversations. 'We should view emotional discourse as a form of social action that creates effects in the world, effects that are read in a culturally informed way by the audience for emotion talk' (Lutz and Abu-Lughod 1990: 12). Moreover, emotion is an experience and a learnt cultural product. In society, bodily expressions of strong emotion are replaced by words that do not seem to be immediately related to the emotion they represent.[16] Mark could only indicate what role fear played in his life by presenting specifics. In this way, he personalized the emotion (Lutz 1990: 83–87). In such situations, therapists offer minimal responses while using a pause in the talk to elaborate on the emotion, by asking questions. Louis allowed his questions to indicate that he knew that the details had special emotional significance. At the same time, he intensified the emotion. When questions interpret the emotions, therapists say that they 'move closer to the patient' and that they are after 'a deeper level' of understanding. Therapists value detailing positively because it provides room for verbalizing emotion and exploring its significance, but find it less useful if it signifies something negative or leaves out something positive.

I will try to show that when positive elements are supposedly omitted in the wider context of the conversation, it is not always the case. In the conversation between Mark and Louis the theme was 'fear of the unknown, the unexpected, the alien'. Mark sought to place this in context by referring to his experiences in a school for special education. Louis interpreted the story by way of questions. When Mark talked about a colleague in another school where a pupil threatened to use a gun, and commented that 'some people are still willing to risk their life', Louis introduced a 20-second period of silence. He considered talk of handguns and the like 'too heavy' and reverted to the here and now to ensure continuity in the conversation:

Louis: Gee, if we're talking about fear of (1) strange things, it really hit you there, didn't it?
Mark: (2)
Louis: When kids start waving guns around, well uh
Mark: Yes, that happened at that secondary school
Louis: Uhuh. That's was not for you, but
Mark: Not for me, but how about that colleague of mine (4) well, acquaintance.
Louis: Yes
Mark: Somebody I know who works there. (7)
Louis: It is hard to imagine, eh, that you'd feel at home there, eh, with that sort of thing?
Mark: Yes, that seems difficult to imagine. It seems to me you can't (9) Still, huh:: some people are still willing to risk their life, I would almost say.

Louis: Well, uh (20) I am not looking at the weather, maybe I am looking at the weather.

Mark: Yes?

Louis: What I am thinking about is feeling at home while at the same time things can seem very strange. Or, or sometimes things are very strange, aren't they?

Louis suggested that the feeling of security or insecurity and fear of the unknown were purely individual matters. He asked about unexpectedly 'pleasant' things. When Mark offered specifics about a feast given by his brother, Louis wanted him to elaborate:

Louis: Does it bother you, because you probably suppose that I know something about these things, that I still ask uh: can you say how important it is for you to come here?

Mark: (3) I don't get you.

Louis: No wait, you say, gee, I explain to my brother's friends that I nowadays I am in therapy at the (2) and how important it is for me to be at the:: (1) How is that for you? Uh:

Mark: Uh, I

Louis: What do you, can you tell me what you consider important?

Mark: (2)

Louis: It helps you to uh::

Mark: Contact with other people uh:: talking with X [another patient] about faith.

Louis: Hmm.

Mark: (3) And about praying.

Louis: Hmm.

Mark sidestepped Louis's question, but Louis did manage to make him talk: 'It helps you to uh'. In this way, Louis indicated that *he* wanted to be helped, and Mark had a chance to keep his secret. Louis explained:

> His secret is Eros and authority. He closes the door to authority. Y [a nurse] is not recognized as authority, but wrapped up and flattered. Mark cheats to keep his secret. In the past, treatment was the meaning of his life. There should be no purpose or objective . . . If the treatment were to change, Mark would make sure that the content remained the same.

Louis received only a slight hint that there was a secret. Mark placed the fear theme in wider context and again left out his private fear. But this personal feeling was therapeutically significant since it provided a point of contact for change in his life. The broader framework, entailing continuity, chaos and lack of norms, offered no map for treatment because in the short term nothing could be achieved. Therapists cannot guarantee security in a larger context. For Mark to use personal details to bring forward the problem of existence was the by-product of a chaotic world and his fear arose from the disastrous consequences of this world. But in the psychiatric hospital, there was no place for his normative problem and in this respect patients remained insecure.

Detailing is a form of concealment. In Saint Anthony's hospital, detailing is seen as an indicator of important emotions that should be discussed to enhance outpatient treatment. The definition of the emotions remains vague, since detailing is bound by certain rules. Therapists hold that there should be no exaggeration because this opens the door to excessive emotions. In this instance exaggeration is part of the psychotic reality. When it relates to a problem of norms, the detailing cannot be admitted in the conversation because a life problem cannot be part of the therapeutic process.

Silence and emotion

The potential significance of silences during talk is examined in a study of a psychotherapeutic conversation by Labov and Fanshel (1977: 313), who describe an 'eloquent silence of 13 seconds' as 'more negative than anything we have seen so far'. As in detailing, many different meanings can be ascribed to it. A patient's silence is often seen as negative, non-cooperative or a violation of the rules of discourse, but it can also hide or control an emotion. Where silence expresses emotion it is considered a discursive practice, which can imply eloquence (meaning) but also a degree of logic. Silences arise in logical ways in conversations, a common pattern that ends in silence being: *Detailing – minimal therapist response – detailing – questions – intensification – minimal patient response (silence).*

Louis:　And your position is discussed then?

Mark:　My position is discussed, yes (2) and uh, yes (1) I had – to begin with I would never wish, uh, I don't wish what I uh: have, what I felt at the time that I was overworked, what I experienced – I wouldn't wish that on my worst enemy (4) and uh:: I, it does hurt some to know that my friends are happy and married and have children (2).

Louis:　That really means something, Mark, when you say, uh, gee:: I wouldn't wish that on my enemies (2). I don't think I'm telling you anything new about fear, uh::: if we stick to that time – that horrible time when you were overworked? (2)

Mark:　Yes (6)

Louis:　Yes? (4)

Mark:　Yeah, it was uh: strange time (3)

Louis:　You still hesitate, don't you, to really (3) talk about it, that strange time?

Mark:　(2) Yes, It's not easy for me to talk about it (3)

In the above fragment there are positive and negative emotions. When deep emotion is expressed and controlled, the connotation is that 'speech is silver, silence is golden'. Conversely, silent spells are associated with the inability of patients to vocalize emotions: the 'silence of malfunction' (Scollon 1985). Significance depends largely on context, and silences gain their specific meaning in relation to vocalization. In the exchange between Mark and Louis, the silences can indicate that this has been explored before. In Mark's case, they are related to tension. The fragment below is different in this respect:

Jochem:	And this is like uh:: things in your head, say portraits or images.
Christiaan:	Yes?
Jochem:	They don't scare you so much any more? You told me before that you had devils uh:: all around you.
Christiaan:	Yes.
Jochem:	They were all after you, to hurt you and so on. But this is not as bad any more?
Christiaan:	Well. The devil still some, but uh:: he doesn't have to take cover any more.
Jochem:	Mm.
Christiaan:	(2) It happened. Nobody can do anything about it.
Jochem:	Mm.
Christiaan:	(45) [*coughs, loud breathing*]
Jochem:	But on the whole you feel calm?
Christiaan:	Calm enough.
Jochem:	For some time now?
Christiaan:	These days, yes.
Jochem:	Mm.
Christiaan:	Cause they keep me calm on the ward (3)

Christiaan's 45-second silence was unusually long and evocative and whatever he and Jochem were thinking remained unsaid.[17] The tension was strong enough to make Jochem uncomfortable. On the video we see him sinking back in his chair. The tension also seemed to increase for Christiaan, whose breathing became louder. At last, Jochem reduced the tension: 'On the whole you feel calm?' Such long silences occur when conversations touch on moral issues: feelings of guilt, death wishes, experiences of injustice, shame: a 'terrible time'. The norm for subjects that can evoke strong emotion is to 'be cool, stay calm'. Accordingly, therapists will not actively avoid silences because they are activities during which important messages are transmitted, though not necessarily verbalized. They are viewed as silent reflections on and evaluation of life events that are never discussed. Silence can signify rejection, protection of one's private interests, or refusal. In the fragment with Louis and Mark, the therapist refused to broach the intense anxiety that became evident when Mark referred to handguns, because he feared this might terminate the conversation. Sometimes patients also refused to discuss a topic:

Louis: It sounds almost poetic, it rhymes, uh:mm (4). That is as if, it is a fear
that – that order no longer exists? Traf . . . you are talking about traffic
jams – beasts instead of feasts, drinking (3) as if everything is going to
go wrong (1)

Mark: Yes (6)

Louis: You sure are a kind of uh:: yes, a prophet of doom (3). That's what
you're talking about, the end time?

Mark: [*laughs*]

Louis: The year two thousand? (3)

Louis mirrored Mark's utterances, while Mark countered with minimal
responses and ultimately ceased all reaction. In situations where therapists use
this mirror technique, patients prefer to remain silent. Defensive silence may be
ambivalent: neither wanting to break contact with Louis, nor wanting to lose
neutrality. Goffman (1967) refers to this as 'presentational rituals' and 'avoidance rituals'. It is sometimes assumed that psychotic people transgress rules
of interaction, but consciously or not they are able to restrain themselves in
interactions in order to carry on the conversation (Van Dongen 1993b). Mark
does so by way of minimal response: silence and laughter. Silence can also mean
preferring not to respond. As in the talk with Louis, Mark tried to keep his secret
while talking to his supervisor, Piet:

Mark: You could have hinted to A. that it was alright if I came along to look
at the uh:: videotapes and uh – disks for uh (4)

Piet: Yes. That's alright with me.

Mark: Yes?

Piet: (6) [*screeching of brakes*]

Mark: Gee. He sure is in a hurry (8)

Piet: H. what is it, or no, in your question I hear something of . . .

Mark: Uncertainty

Piet: Important. It is important that I give you permission for that kind of thing,
isn't it?

Mark: Yes (2) yes.

Piet: Uh (3) actually, for me too it is something that you can manage
perfectly well yourself (3) And you surely think it's a good thing that
we just check that?

Mark: Yes (1) that's nice, sure (2)

Piet: Uh (1) You think it should be that way, or uh (3)

Mark: Yes, I don't know (2) I think that – it's ni, it's nicer if my supervisor,
you are that too – that I have permission from him too.

Piet: Sure, sure (3) Yes, I feel that way too sometimes (2) I have to give it
my blessing. There is absolutely nothing wrong with it, but I still have
to uh (1) express my approval.

Mark: Yes (2)

Piet: Would it be a problem if I didn't?

Mark: (2) I think it would, yes (3)

Piet: Mm (3) What I'm thinking is, if things go wrong, can I blame Piet for it?

Mark: (4) How do you mean that?

Piet: We-ell. M: (2) It happens so casually when we run into each other. (2) You say: Piet, is it alright if? And yes, I answer quick and easy: Sure, fine (1). According to me, we did talk some about that there are things that you can manage yourself (6) I don't mean that it's all up to you, but more like, yes, some things you can figure out very well for yourself with the others here (6) There's nothing wrong with having some confidence (2)

Mark: Yes (11)

Piet: You follow me? (1)

Mark: Yes, I understand.

Piet: Uh – maybe you think I feel hurt, Mark.

Mark: [*laughs a little*] (11)

Mark and Piet looking at the videotape:

Piet: How was this for you?

Mark: I can't say much about it that makes sense.

Piet: You can't or you won't?

Mark: I'd rather not say anything about it.

At this point, Mark refused point-blank to continue. Another patient, Joris, indirectly refused to answer the therapist when asked why he was being chased by American aeroplanes. His therapist, Klaas, said 'those are not easy things to talk about' and for him, Joris's silence was an individual, internalized emotion. But silence is also contextual and in Joris's case the refusal reflected the relationship rather than an intense, inner emotion that had to be mastered. Patients used silence to express disappointment and anger. This became clear when Klaas asked Joris about his dreams: 'For some reason I have the idea that you are just not the right person to tell my dreams to. Maybe this is a case of not enough trust.'

Silences of resistance also occurred when patients felt cornered, for example, when a patient wanted permission or approval. Such episodes usually followed the pattern: *patient advances an argument – minimal therapist response – questions by therapist – brief patient replies – counter-arguments by the therapist – minimal patient response – silence.*

Body language can be eloquent during such silences of resistance: patients bow their heads, smile, raise their eyebrows, gaze outside in a demonstrative way, and drum their fingers. This behavior can be interpreted as 'being unwilling', or 'rejection'. It is viewed as a variety of psychotic expressions of discontent and tolerated as such. Therapists tend to treat it mildly and consider it a part of the stereotyped communication style of psychotic people[18] rather than part of the style in which both – therapist and patient – communicate. Silences of resistance can also be understood as a metaphor for the 'human condition' of patients, and in that context they allow the psychotic patient to resist authority without generating immediate conflict. Silences occur when there is nothing left to say:

Mark: Yes (2) I can't really uh, I can't recall how it was to uh, just blindly do things and buy.
Piet: Mm
Mark: . . . without really thinking about it (2)
Piet: It was as if you had no power over it?
Mark: Yes (2). That the power lay somewhere else. Not with me. (8)
Piet: That's beautiful, the way you say that. That the power lay somewhere else.
Mark: (14) The weather is rotten, isn't it?
Piet: Yes
Mark: [*laughs*]

In retrospect Mark said: 'I thought it was time to stop this', and Piet: 'To me it was something to stop and think about'. It was not only conversations with patients that were interspersed with silences. Often, therapists and mental health workers remained silent as well because they considered some statement by the patient to be of little direct significance (cf Ten Have 1991a). Therapists were quiet when reflecting on their next question: they retreated in order to advance more effectively. These cognitive silences (Saville-Troike 1985) indicated conscious speech acts and strategies.

I have described situations in which moral issues and reflection on the world surfaced in the conversation, but were not really pursued. Sometimes the therapist or the nurse was 'cornered' and had to find a way of handling things:

Bert: Yes (3) Can't you give me a mercy-killing injection, Marleen?
Marleen: You think that's something to laugh about?
Bert: I really want it. Yes, I can laugh about it.
Marleen: Huh (3). Bert, that is a serious thing you're saying, you know.
Bert: Yes I know.
Marleen: But your eyes, I can really tell by your eyes.
Bert: Yes.
Marleen: (3) But Bert, this is:: I can't do this. (3) I can't. When I hear you say this, I want to look, together with you, like, is this what you want.
Bert: Yes.
Marleen: And sometimes I think, sometimes you are so down and unhappy and I think, God, this is the only thing Bert wants.
Bert: Yes.

Marleen: But this is something I cannot and will not take responsibility for . . .

Bert: No?

Marleen: No. (2) It is not that I, that I have no sympathy for you. You know, for your story, for the way you feel, your situation, but even then uh::: (3) yes (2)

Bert: You wouldn't do it?

Marleen: No, I wouldn't do it, Bert. I couldn't do it and I do not want to do it. (3)

Bert: Sure, and that's why, just go on suffering, boy, right?

Marleen: Come on, I do think it is really awful, so Bert, I think maybe I can ease your suffering, by letting you regularly be the subject of our talking.

Bert: Yes, yes.

Marleen: Hmm?

Bert: It does help.

Marleen: Well, as you mentioned before like, it helps me when I can talk about it.

Bert: Yes.

Marleen: That's all I think I can do for you, Bert. About this subject. (4) Look, the way you think and feel, for me that's different and (4) well (5) I sympathize with you::, but I can't do more than listen.

Bert: Yes, you can't do more.

Marleen: No (4)

Bert: I don't know what I have to say anyway. I've really got a lot to say, an incredible lot. But it doesn't come out, I don't get my, I don't get a chance, that's all. (4)

Marleen: What do you mean, I don't get a chance. Nobody listens?

Bert: I, I don't get an opportunity, uh, people are busy around me and uh:, they are uh, right next to me and they talk together and I sit there in between and I:: nothing really (3)

Marleen: Yes

Bert: (3) And that's the end of me.

Marleen: Yes.

Bert: That's how I see it, you know.

Marleen: (4)

Bert: And then, when I'm talking to you there's a jet overhead and uh: all those things mess around in my head

Marleen: Mm. So you are not really with me, in your thinking?

Bert: No.

Marleen: You keep being distracted by all those other things going on around you?

Bert: Yes.

Marleen: And it never lets up, Bert?

Bert: It keeps going. It is chaos.
Marleen: Yes (3)
Bert: I don't need this any more. I really want uh:: should end it soon as possible.
Marleen: (3)
Bert: But that's not simple. It's out of your hands.
Marleen: No. That's right:: (4)
Bert: And cutting myself to pieces, that's not for me either.
Marleen: Yes (3) That's right, Bert.

Nurse Marleen initially tried to postpone her reply. Death wishes belonged to the symptoms of psychotic (mood) disturbances, the taboo part of the psychotic world. Marleen had empathy for this world, but she was at a loss for an immediate response. At last she presented a clear reason: 'I cannot and will not be responsible'. Her silences not only indicated moments of consideration, they also revealed incomprehension and emotion. In this instance, not knowing was in fact not being able to know: to say that life was worth living did not improve the situation for Bert. For Marleen, therefore, the solution lay in doing something: 'all I can *do* is talk about it'. The dilemma is clear. Both knew that talk was no solution: 'we cannot do more'. Marleen could not change the world for him and in this respect, she was as helpless as Bert.

The excerpts have shown that silence can be a strategy to control tense situations, help the participants to restrain their emotions and enable patients to express passive and indirect resistance without losing face. It is quite appropriate that emotions and emotional subjects should play an important role in the conversations, especially if there is no satisfactory solution. That is why silence is concealment, like a veil covering those emotions linked to personal experiences, especially illness or moral issues. Silences in the clinic were always ambivalent. They were sometimes interpreted as part of the psychotic disorder but in the context of conversations, silences were often a 'logical' consequence of earlier speech acts. Moreover, they were desirable because they prevented and regulated overheated responses where there was evidently still a 'sore spot'.

In summary, the shared reality achieved in a conversation takes shape in long question-and-answer episodes, extended detailing and long silences. This reality is fragile and easily destroyed. At Saint Anthony's psychiatric hospital both parties decided from the outset how the power relations would be constituted. To a large extent, this determined the topics to be discussed or left out. If a patient managed to ensconce himself in the therapist's position, it was unlikely that therapeutic matters would feature. At times, therapists found it difficult to penetrate the barriers that patients erected by subterfuges such as avoidance, refusal, interruption, and the like. One way to entice patients was to ask questions of a kind that may have been intended to gather information, indicate interest or convince patients. Endless questions created the impression of monotony and superficiality whereas 'mirroring' (presenting a mirror image), prying, and similar techniques marked the interactions as unusual. This begs the question: who is odd, the patient or the therapist? When a patient criticizes the therapist for prying, he is right. It is only because the patient is diagnosed as psychotic that therapists 'think' that prying is allowed. It then becomes 'a confrontation with reality', whereas in another context, prying would be rejected as an unwanted intrusion into somebody's life. For this reason, the conversations may seem odd at first glance. The problems and tensions that patients experienced with society did not fit into an individualizing, action-orientated approach. The attitude of therapists to moral and existential matters also seemed to be transparent and simple, but to patients this attitude could appear ambiguous. Patients tended to conceal their emotions and experiences relating to their personality, character and history not only through avoidance and refusal, but also by means of 'detailing' and silences. The same strategies were used by therapists when they wanted to conceal something. Therapists concealed psychotic experiences, moral issues and existential questions not because they were unwilling or lacking in understanding but for practical reasons, or because they believed that patients had 'no insight'. However, they did not discuss these questions, and took care not to impress their own world view on patients.

Chapter 6

Revealing in talk

Ha, ha! said the clown
Has the king lost his crown?

Manfred Mann, "Haha said the clown"

Christian goes on frequent walks. As he walks, he thinks about 'his healing'. He explains to his therapist: 'Because, uh, you can consider me normal, but you can also think me completely crazy. It comes to the same thing.' Therapist: 'But how do you see yourself? You say: "You can think me crazy and you can think me normal." But how do you see yourself, then?' Christian: 'I see myself as utterly crazy!' This puzzles the therapist, since nobody admits to being crazy, let alone utterly so. 'But what am I supposed to understand by this? Utterly crazy?' 'Well, it's obvious'. Christian has thought about his self-description. He thinks of things that are 'not done': 'I uh, told you that I am bothered by images, images of people. They should not be in my thoughts at all. I think of something quite different.'

The therapist cannot solve Christian's riddle, so Christian has to do so himself. Keeping within the bounds of what is permitted by convention is important to him, and he thinks constantly of things that are allowed and things that are not. Patients have to accept that 'images' and other 'unreal' things belong to the illness, and should not intrude. But when a patient freely admits to being 'crazy', therapists may feel alarmed because of the strong moral connotations attached to this term. To accept it would mean that the therapist and the patient would have to discuss it, and craziness concerns the whole being of a person. This could undermine the hospital's accepted delineation between the 'sick' and 'healthy' parts of a person. However, in her discussion of 'I am' and 'I have' illnesses, Estroff suggests that schizophrenia and psychosis 'are so closely associated with notions of the self that there may be extraordinary susceptibility to such engulfment of the person' (1993: 257). Such ambivalence creates a double bind on both therapists and patients.

In this chapter, I consider the moments in conversations during which glimpses of the psychotic world break the surface. We see how the revelation occurs and examine the types of problems created in the interaction. The psychotic world reveals itself in many characteristic shapes: in disruptions, strange tales, profanities, dabbling in the occult, patients inventing things, etc. It appears in conversations both in unusual sequences and in ways that can be understood, but are considered inappropriate and socially unacceptable. Unconventional showings of this world occur especially when the subject is interacting with others and the outside world. They also occur when explicit constructions and transformations are attached to the patient's reality. There are sequences in which therapists translate the uttering of patients into expressions they can understand, and those in which patients construct a reality through inventions and dreams. In either event, therapists regard these glimpses of the psychotic world as a negation of the treatment.

I intend to revisit the assumption that psychotic people do not conform to rules of interaction and behavior, since I feel that this conclusion does not explain transgressions such as disruption, and strange stories. As noted previously, the discourses of psychotic people follow and use conventional conversation procedures. Moreover, unusual importance is attached to conversational conventions such as taking orderly turns in speaking, although there may be frequent disruptions. My assumption is that these transgressions are intentional rather than incidental, and it is significant to note that they arise when the talk turns to a sensitive topic.

Psychiatry invariably assumes that disruptions in a conversation are caused by a lack of coherence. However, although the words can become quite unintelligible, they are not meaningless. I overheard conversations in the hospital that were incoherent and unintelligible to me, but they seemed to have a world of meaning for those involved. What I lacked at that moment was the requisite contextual knowledge. The following dialogue between two patients in a long-term residence (LTR) ward is an example:

P1: I have a child by a mayor. And one by an engineer an' a couple by a Black.
P2: You sure fucked around.
P1: Yeah, I like fucking.
P2: No wonder your guy left you.
P1: I used to grab his prick.
P2: The poor guy couldn't take it.
P1: He didn't stick it in my cunt.
P2: Pussy.
P1: I used to have a little pussy.
P2: Now you got a big one.

When taken at face value, the intention of this dialogue is not clear. Is it a joke or an attempt to shock a third party with vulgar language? Such dialogues were frequently heard in LTR wards at Saint Anthony's psychiatric hospital, and their meaning was more complicated than one would initially suppose. Sexuality is taboo in the ward, yet it is simultaneously and persistently present (Van Dongen

1989). Therapists explained such dialogues on sex in terms of sexual preoccupation, a symptom of the patient's disorder and evidence of insanity. On the other hand, Goffman (1961b) described them as 'ceremonial profanity': an intentional transgression of rules that nevertheless reveals sensitivity to those rules. I discovered in due course that there was more to such sequences than a preoccupation with sex or a transgression of rules. The speaker's history (no children of her own, divorced, a brief affair in the hospital) continued to play an important part in her life. When they surfaced in utterances like the above, it was not really meant to start a conversation; it was more like an internal monologue, a medium for expressing painful memories. The other patient (P2) knew this, and used irony to try to ease the pain somewhat. In spite of its vulgarities the dialogue was marked by a high degree of sensitivity towards the inner turmoil of the protagonist (P1).

Besides the outward meaning of the dialogue, where the emphasis is on the sense of the words and discourse as a social act, there are levels of intention, feeling and tone that underscore the subjective 'reality experience' of patients. Even if their content is not immediately intelligible, profanities, disruptions, strange tales, etc. can be given meaning in the hospital. We noted earlier that transgressing the taboo on madness is seen as a significant indicator of 'the present condition' of the patient undergoing a course of treatment, although the signifying is purely instrumental. This is readily explained: therapists often encounter problems when seeking access to the innermost feelings of patients, their subjectivity. Subjectivity can be gauged only by behavior, but behavior and intelligibility depend on the context of the conversations (Schiffrin 1987). Labov and Fanshel (1977) show how a conversation between a psychiatric patient and one of the authors contains several layers of meaning. These layers can be analyzed only because the authors know the identity of the participants, their relationship, and the views of the patient. The authors therefore make the conversation intelligible by means of 'extensions'.

To ensure that the interpretation is correct, it is important to link it to the patient's behavior. The interpretation has a normative dimension, in that patient 'interiority' is interpreted on the basis of behavior, and behavior is evaluated from the knowledge of the patients that therapists have compiled. As mentioned, this knowledge is a mixture of professional training, common sense, and experience. Interpretations always imply a value judgment: does the patient behave in a manner that would be viable outside the hospital? In a psychiatric hospital, there are certain behavioral criteria that patients must meet if their reality awareness and reality testing are to be assessed as normal. Psychotic people do not meet these expectations. Their transgressions are either viewed as symptoms of an illness, or they are 'quite understandable'. When disruptions occur, one looks for the characteristic 'disturber'. Relational aspects play a subordinate role and social rules are not taken into consideration. The interaction centers on 'what ought, or ought not to be', within the boundaries of approval and disapproval. By inference, the authority and expertise of the therapist confers on him/her the right to determine the course of a conversation. This gives rise to disruptive patient reactions, just as the nature of the conversations may contribute to the disruptions. We have seen that the conversations become odd when there is questioning, prying or 'mirroring'. Often, the patients have no other option than to respond as they do. However, their resistance is explained as a symptom of the illness, because patients are said to lack 'insight'. It introduces another dilemma: what happens when the patient's 'sick part' surfaces in a conversation? Such episodes are described and analyzed in an examination of how conversations are organized and the content of reactions. I comment on a number of aspects of social behavior and meaningful acts that are viewed as characteristically psychotic behavior, and which may give rise to interaction problems. I contend that this behavior gives form to experiences, while also taking account of the interactive situation.

Roles and disruptions

The presence and authority of the therapist contribute to the uncommon and violent reactions of psychotic people during a conversation. We noted from the outset that patients made it clear at the start of the conversations what they thought of the role and authority of therapists. But the issue is more complicated than that. Disturbances, i.e. deviations from what is normally expected in a conversation, are not merely signs of resistance to the authority of a therapist, nor do they only mean that patients want to assume power. There is another dimension to the utterances with which the conversational order is disrupted, which stems from and is bound up in the life world and experiences of psychotic people. Boundaries are crossed on both the social and the substantial level. This double abrogation makes interaction with psychotic people a complex business, as seen in the following three fragments. In each, boundaries set by the therapists are breached in different ways and for different reasons.

'You keep butting in and waffling about'

Eric: It is going, thank you. Now, uh: I believe that uh: so to speak, Jochem, my hand can wander to more romantic places?

Jochem: No, no: not in my neck you know that!

Eric: It's coming ou-out, it's coming ou-out.

Jochem: [laughs]

Eric: It's coming out, it's coming out again.

Jochem: You'd better keep your hands off me!

Eric: Everything fits that you: yes

Jochem: But we were going to talk together, weren't we?

Eric: Right. But I will really unzip my fly now. It's coming out again!

Jochem: No: no:

Eric: It's coming out again

Jochem:	No!
Eric:	No? Well, I know something anyway. Hey, now [*deep voice*]. No, I know something all right, something you say: No-ow. You think of Hitler then, right, you think: yes, yes: these were like wards. And uh: there's a fellow standing there. Golly, yes, probably, I don't really know, do I?
Jochem:	You should speak clearly; otherwise it won't get on tape.
Eric:	Yes, you go ahead and keep it intramural. You go ahead: If you say that is big eh? I sure know those barracks of X, it's a ward, isn't it? Internal section and [*unintelligible*] full of monkeys, so yes, well [*unintelligible*]. There are many places here now; it's big here, isn't it? There are many places here. Goddamned, it's all sex, my boy. A fellow like that must have a hard on. Go-oh: [*unintelligible*] that was i-i-it for today [*giggles*]
	Go-oddamn. Today came very close, but still I uh: for years we, we laughed about this before, but still I went myself uh:
Jochem:	Hey, listen to me
Eric:	Yes: this bastard is crazy anyway, yes, I know that.
Jochem:	You talk like this, I can't follow you.
Eric:	No, no, that's the point, you keep butting in and waffling on, but
Jochem:	No, no, I can't understand you very well either!
Eric:	Erlaube nur heute. Don't start off on the wrong foot. This too: yes, uh: a sensitive area, yes, yes, sensitive area.
Jochem:	Keep your hands where they belong, where they belong.
Eric:	But I, indeed
Jochem:	I have another one, I am not at all
Eric:	Sure, the whole [*unintelligible*] tungsten triloxite, you know that?
Jochem:	What? Listen. I am just a little curious about your brother.
Eric:	Just a little. Yes but, well, he just walked. Yes, he went to Australia.
Jochem:	Listen, will you
Eric:	Yes: No, he just walked.
Jochem:	Your brother, from Australia? All the way?
Eric:	No. Well he walked. He had a handful of guilders. He says, buy yourself a drink, I've seen it here. And then he went back to Australia, quick as that. Normally it is [*unintelligible*]. What?
Jochem:	Did you talk with your brother?
Eric:	Sure, I am getting daft.
Jochem:	Getting daft?
Eric:	Yes, yes, a screw loose.
Jochem:	But what did you think of it? That your brother came to visit you?
Eric:	Well, uh: I found it strange that he was gone so soon again [*laughs*].
Jochem:	You didn't talk long?
Eric:	What? Yes, five guilders, that brother.
Jochem:	Come on, tell me, what did you think of his coming here?

Eric: Well, I wanted

Jochem: How long had it been since you last saw him?

Eric: All this drivel. I'm sitting here. Doesn't fit in here. And he comes with that brother from Australia: Bullshit!

Jochem: How long since you last saw him?

Eric: What? O no: boy, you know him from the photograph. I tore that picture in pieces, those airports, uh: now they are on strike, because uh: I got aggressive. Was in the: cockpit of a Boeing 707 and uh: my brother, family, seeing each other, well, I think that's very common. Still is, but

Jochem: I'm not hearing you.

Eric: No boy, let me have my say, before the Third World War breaks out. Before Hitler [*unintelligible*] there were plenty of fugitives to Antwerp. You witnessed that, didn't you? You were born earlier than me, right?

Jochem: Just a moment. I would like to hear something about your brother.

Eric: That's whom I'm talking about, my brother.

Jochem: And, what did you think of him visiting you?

Eric: Well, I uh: God, when he arrived from E., the train stopped and I uh: I buttoned up my coat and I felt very relieved that I didn't go back to taking Valium.

Jochem: ha.

On the video, one sees how Eric harasses his therapist: his hand moves from the therapist's neck down, slowly. In a display of not very subtle clowning, Eric acts out sexual arousal and actually unzips his fly. Jochem laughs but wards him off at the same time. Eric repeats his game and uses the term 'boy' in a belittling way. Afterwards Jochem says:

At those moments, he is rather uninhibited. When I enter the ward he grabs me and kisses my neck. I fend him off. I don't want him touching me. It may be play, but I don't join the game. To forestall him becoming overactive, but also because I don't like it.

The therapist's feelings of uneasiness may well fulfill a more important role than the horseplay itself. Eric's behavior is conscious and intentional. This may be deduced from the conversation he has with a nurse the following day:

Eric: We are not going to talk about my homosexual blackmail material.

Arno: Hand me the shag, will you

Eric: We already based yesterday's tape on that.

Arno: You did?

Eric: Yesterday, I don't repeat myself that often, because uh: with Jochem it got to be a mess.

Later in this conversation, another dimension is added. Eric here more or less admits that his performance is a game meant to relieve the helplessness of his situation:

> . . . how big the problems are. Kind of towards the future. You think it strange then, that I make tapes like the last one with Jochem, should I let my hand wander to more romantic places . . .

This sort of activity occurs more often with psychiatric patients than other patients. It happened in the morning hours, while the sound system was blasting a carnival hit at full strength into the ward's sitting room, and a nurse was hopping around with one or more patients. Their views about their own futures are far from cheerful, ranging from hopelessness to coping.

In the next section, I discuss unexpected and inappropriate behavior. It must be noted that the therapists and nurses attributed Eric's overly robust game to his psychotic disorder and his 'negative approach toward others'. Obviously, this kind of behavior disrupts a conversation and upsets the plans of Jochem, the therapist: 'But we were going to talk together, weren't we?' If there is brutal overpowering by a patient, it makes it impossible for a therapist to conduct a conversation in the normal way, and it increases the likelihood of countertransference. It means that the therapist is not taken seriously. The timing was not coincidental since the surprise attack occurred immediately after the start of the conversation, when Jochem pointed out to Eric that his speech was unintelligible.

Eric's speech was indeed difficult to follow, although his non-verbal actions made it appear as if he was engaged in animated conversation with Jochem. He addressed Jochem with gestures and eye contact. One might say that he was mimicking a song with a familiar melody, but the words were not intended to engage the therapist. Unintelligibility is a problem in an interactive situation (Eric was not prepared to do anything about it). This meant that the patient was inaccessible, both on the interaction level and on the level of the conversation topic. This inaccessibility has been illustrated above, and Jochem did not get a chance to improvise the conversational situation. Inaccessibility on the level of conversation topic requires further explanation.

In Goffman's (1974) book *Frame Analysis*, he writes about the organization of experiences and contends that the way people experience whatever it is that confronts them depends on the framework they fit it into. The same event may affect people very differently, depending on the framework. Parts of reality gain significance for people because they are 'encadered' in a specific framework. Goffman speaks of 'primary frameworks' when a framework of interpretation arises directly when something occurs. Reinterpretations (with a different framework) he calls 're-encaderings'.

While Jochem and Eric talk, they do so with two frameworks, and therefore the greater part of the conversation consists of monologues, interspersed with moments of dialogue. The agenda of the conversation is, simply put, 'to talk about the life and problems of the patient'. Both discussion partners are aware of this agenda. Jochem intends to proceed in the usual manner of question and answer sequences. Evidently, he follows the basic framework used in the LTR, i.e. to focus on the here and now (Eric's brother's recent visit from Australia) and so make an opening for further conversation. Eric has a different understanding of the agenda. His framework is different. He tries to talk about his life in the hospital: 'wards', 'the barracks of X', 'full of monkeys', etc. To him, current or recent events are less important. After a number of attempts to take his leading role as therapist, Jochem moves to a current topic, Eric's brother. Eric responds, but leaves Jochem dissatisfied. 'Did you talk with your brother?' Eric supposes that this is obvious to Jochem and answers: 'Sure, I am getting daft'. But Jochem does not give up: 'What did you think of it?' 'How long since you last saw him?' The questions are primarily meant to enhance conversation in a shared framework. Eric, however, refuses to discuss his brother further, 'All this drivel!', and when Jochem repeats the question once again: 'Bullshit'. To him, his stay in the hospital and everything that goes with it is a more interesting subject. Ultimately, Jochem does manage to get some sort of dialogue going, but there is not genuine cooperation and it does not last long.

Having two distinct primary frameworks need not cause problems. After all, people can negotiate and arrive at an agreement. Jochem tries, but does not succeed in establishing such a shared framework. A major cause is Eric's unintelligible utterances, but this does not wholly explain why his jumbled words do not come through. When Jochem overlaps them, he reveals that at that moment, he finds Eric's utterances unacceptable. Eric indicates that he hears Jochem's questions all right (he replies), but at times, 'Jochem does not; he does not 'hear' [Eric's] words'. This negation can be a form of downgrading (Berenst 1986) and may give Eric the feeling that he is not taken seriously. An underlying problem is the difficulty in engaging Eric, on the level of conversation topics.

His re-encadering is at least unusual. It is quite clear that Jochem and Eric use different frames of reference (Goffman 1974: 39), when Eric talks about Hitler in relation to the LTR: 'At that point you think Hitler. That turns out to be wards'. Suppose the therapist had asked: 'Do you dislike the ward to the point that you compare it with the days of Hitler?' The incongruous frameworks would probably have persisted but the conversation certainly would have taken a totally different turn. In this regard, Jochem said:

> You cannot get the feeling of him . . . I cannot follow him as it is. He never has the same intention that others would have.

Like most other patients, Eric has displayed a number of fixed, recurring themes in his story, during his years in hospital. One of these is Hitler and the Second World War, the theme that serves to frame his discourse about the hospital and to categorize family members. In this way (the dossier says) he transforms his fear and experience of hospitalization. In the hospital, these transformations invariably evoke norms and tensions. They occur at the limits of what ought to be permissible.

Eric does not acknowledge Jochem's role and authority as therapist, and therefore keeps disrupting the order with his unintelligible utterances, assaults, and corrections. Nevertheless, one should not explain the disruptions from this perspective alone. These intentional acts are meant to evoke a clear response from the other. In one way or another this means social contact, even if it is fleeting. Jochem tries to retain a boundary between himself as therapist and Eric as patient. Eric seeks to overstep this boundary. The transgression arises in resistance, and is clearly relational in character.

Eric transgresses certain norms of propriety, but it is also revealing when in his story he uses images from a cultural domain that others may consider inappropriate ('You just should not compare your situation as psychiatric patient with Hitler and the war'). On this level, too, relationships play the most important role. In Eric's case there is a sustained inability to close the gap or find a point of confluence between patient and therapist. This factor can contribute to patients remaining imprisoned in their abnormality, because this type of conversation is experienced as a threatening offensive. It implies a lasting disruption in the precarious relationship balance (Van Dongen 1993b). In the individual experiential world of Eric, relations are a source of conflict. The madness comes out but the problem remains hidden.

'Odd, isn't it, that we live all over the world?'

Limits both social and topical are also overstepped in the conversation between Clemens, a 29-year-old chronic schizophrenic in the LTR, and therapist Gerard. But the motivation for the transgression is different from that of the above fragment, and the subject of the talk concerns Clemens's memories of the past. These memories are reproduced more or less in chronological order. The conversation is typically interspersed with breaks, silences, and short turns, with Gerard asking many questions. Typically, these questions are directly related to what Clemens has just said. In the LTR, this manner of conversing is quite common. Gerard has no preconceived plan. Consequently, the conversations as a whole consist of associations. Gerard says:

> To me the conversation was a sounding out, to orient myself about how he was doing . . . This talk, then, was orientational-informative . . . I capitalized on the familiar and the accustomed. . . . It is a mixture of psychotic memories, children's fantasy, playing with words and memories . . . Sometimes the mixture is intractable. He keeps adding things. Qua content, I leave it alone. He is unable to explain things.

One major theme of Clemens's experiential world, regularly mentioned in the dossier, is home making. The fragment below follows upon a segment of the discussion concerning the country of his birth (Indonesia), the journey (by airplane) to the Netherlands, living and going to school there, a 'previous life in America', and a visit to an entertainment park (Walibi). Clemens continues with the theme of home:

Clemens: In uh: Denmark or in uh: Sweden we burnt the light with uh: some uh:: church flower . . . church songs or something.

Gerard: I see.

Clemens: We lived there in Aartsund earth end und and uh: [*unintelligible*] of Kopenryd or something. We used to live there or something. (3)

Gerard: But I never knew that you lived in Sweden and Denmark and all.

Clemens: You didn't know?

Gerard: No (2). You never told me.

Clemens: I didn't, did I?

Gerard: No.

Clemens: Odd, isn't it, that we live all over the world?

Gerard: Yes. (2) Tell me about Walibi.

Clemens: We lived in Friesland, too.

Gerard: There too?

Clemens: Yes (3) Close to uh: Grote Kerkstraat, the Kroistriestraat.

Gerard: I see.

Clemens: Shall I tell you how come?

Gerard: Sure

Clemens: Well, on our way we really did [*unintelligible*], like uh: from Sweden we went to Brabant and from Brabant to Dordrecht, and then back to Spain, from Spain to Portugal, and from Portugal to Indonesia [*faster*], from Indonesia to-oo, oh well, H.B.H.B. it is.

Gerard: H.B.?

Clemens: Yes: well, my mother is there [*unintelligible*]

Gerard: You sure lived in many places.

Clemens: Yes.

Gerard: Mm:

Clemens: We lived in a million (?) places.

Gerard: Mm (2). According to me, uh: I think this is not quite right. You're making this up.

Clemens: No, this is really so, you know.

Gerard: It is?

Clemens: Yes (4)

Gerard: Okay, tell me something about Walibi.

Clemens: In America, right?

Gerard: In America.

Clemens: I was there too, one time. With uh: X. That's how I know what it is.

Gerard: Aha

Clemens: I went with X, took the train and the bus.

Gerard: Aha
Clemens: Long journey, by train, the night train. (5)
Gerard: Aha. And uh: (3) did you begin to think a lot about those things? Or are you just telling me this because we happen to talk about it?
Clemens: (2) Let me think a moment. I forgot to say. (9) One time I swam in canal water.
Gerard: Canal water?
Clemens: In Winschoten (6)

The excerpt clearly shows that the frames of reference used by Clemens and Gerard do not correlate. Clemens's facts do not stand up to scrutiny, i.e. the story does not correspond to objective reality. Its lack of truth is betrayed not in its symbolic significance, but simply by being implausible. Gerard interprets the statements about living here and there as a longing for closeness and security. Clemens does not divide the past into reality and fantasy, but he does acknowledge the strangeness of his story: 'Odd, isn't it, that we live(d) all over the world?' Gerard distinguishes more rigorously between these two worlds: 'Tell me about Walibi'. Some years ago, he and Clemens had been on a ward trip to this amusement park. The question that deals with this is an attempt to converse within a shared framework. Gerard takes care that the incongruity of the frameworks does not become insurmountable in the talk, but he does point out the difference: 'You are just making this up'.

The disruptions in this fragment are complicated. To a degree, the therapist acts as if it were entirely normal for Clemens to have lived in so many places. Consequently, conflict does not arise and the social order of the conversation is not disrupted. Clemens's vague and incomplete sentences are no problem either. Vague speech is not uncommon and people talk about complex problems without defining clear points of reference. Conversely, people can absorb a great deal of complex knowledge even if few words are spent on it (Gatewood 1983). This is indicated by Clemens's references, which are most likely an amalgam of geographical locations picked up in elementary school long years ago. Although his facts are not correct (Walibi is in Belgium, not in America) the fragment serves to verbalize his need for nearness and security. His statements are more like the contours and resonance of a longing. Gerard knows about this:

> Home is important to him. He depends greatly on his mother. He has a symbiotic bond with her . . . Home is a symbol for the need to be close to his mother . . . He also wants to live with his nurse and me.

Clemens can put it differently too:

> At home I feel fine. I feel the warmth surrounding me . . . I wouldn't mind being a baby forever: being carried, nice and safe and cared for.

The idiosyncratic elements in Clemens's words should not be seen as information exchange, but should rather be understood in terms of dramatic effects: subjective existence is clarified and is meant to be shared with the therapist. Clemens creates a 'phatic communion' (Malinowski 1922) with his therapist, in which the boundaries between him and Gerard should disappear. He is neither after truth nor untruth but the enjoyment of a shared game. However, the effects prove less dramatic than desired. Gerard is not about to discuss the improbability of the content. In the fragment below from the final phase of the conversation, a comparable boundary transgression occurs:

Clemens: I forgot where you live.
Gerard: Where I live?
Clemens: Yes?
Gerard: I live in B.
Clemens: In B? Where exactly?
Gerard: J. Avenue.
Clemens: J., that's right near uh: big church, that's close to the Big Church?
Gerard: No. It's near E., you went swimming there.
Clemens: Okay, right.
Gerard: It's close by there.
Clemens: In the uh: J. Avenue, right?
Gerard: Yes. Near there. You obviously know that area?
Clemens: I do, don't I?
Gerard: Yes.
Clemens: H. street, 176 actually, 'cause my mother does not live at 146.
Gerard: I see.
Clemens: 176 (3)
Gerard: But that's in the H. Street.
Clemens: That's H, right. K.?
Gerard: Yes, yes.
Clemens: We have uh: [*unintelligible*] of the refresher duty uh:: (2) and so (2) and uh: Volkskrant (a daily), mayor of uh: or the son of what's-his-name, he uh: had pipe tobacco (2) and we could always roll a cigarette.
Gerard: Aha.
Clemens: That's called V. street.
Gerard: I see.
Clemens: D. near the D.
Gerard: That's of (OFF) P.?
Clemens: I lived there, too.
Gerard: You even lived there, too?
Clemens: (3)
Gerard: Well, am I supposed to swallow all you tell me, or are you just making a lot of things up?
Clemens: You've got to make things up.

Gerard: But are you making all this up or is it all true?
Clemens: It's all true.

Initially, there is a shared framework and the therapist is drawn into the game. Clemens has in fact lived in many places, but there is also potential disruption here: it is unusual for a patient to question his therapist on the latter's private life. In a specific way, then, Clemens takes over Gerard's role. He does so successfully until he recalls an event in H. (concerning tobacco). The 'son of what's-his-name' had obviously been kind to Clemens and Clemens had lived with him. It is all part of his quest for security and closeness. Clemens will do this again later. But Gerard lets him know that from this point onwards, they will adhere to different frameworks: 'Am I supposed to swallow all you tell me?'

In the next sequence, this substantial disruption/boundary trespass is rectified. In the repair sequence, Clemens makes two remarkable statements. The first is 'You have to make things up'. This is not picked up by Gerard and one can only guess what would have ensued if he had asked 'why?' His problem is whether Clemens himself can distinguish between objective reality and fantasy: 'Sounding out how he is doing'. A remark later in the same sequence, 'You are kind of interested in what I am saying, aren't you?' is passed over as well. There is no need to pursue it, since Gerard relates this remark to the main theme of the conversation. Gerard has in fact lived and worked in many places. This is too difficult for Clemens, who reverts to asking questions. Maybe the therapist is beyond reach now. Clemens follows up by claiming that he too has lived in G., but he overreaches himself. Gerard knows the 'objective' truth. Subsequently the roles are reversed again. The disruptive action (the crossing of the boundary by Clemens) does not imply an immediate break between patient and therapist, as was the case with Eric and Jochem. With Clemens, the patient's expressions even fit the context of 'typically psychotic' action, that is, if one views them as assumptions concerning psychotic people. In effect, patients lose the usual distance between themselves and others. This is not unpleasant for the patient, but it may baffle the other person. The boundaries between reality outside the conversation and those of the reality within the conversation (that which occurs and ought to occur between discussion partners) become blurred, which could easily present a problem.

'Is that healthy? Do you know?'

The next conversation is an example of how disruptions may occur when issues such as meaning, loneliness, helplessness, and desperation surface. The fragments are taken from a conversation between a 27-year-old schizophrenic man, Bert, and therapist Sander (STR):

Sander: Sure (2). But we talked about the fact that you, say, laugh about everything.
Bert: Yes?

Sander:	Right? (2) And I don't.
Bert:	No.
Sander:	No.
Bert:	Well, that's annoying, isn't it?
Sander:	Yes.
Bert:	What do you think best?
Sander:	How can we? What is best?
Bert:	Which is better, to laugh or to be serious?
Sander:	Well. Laughing is healthy, anyway.
Bert:	Is that healthy?
Sander:	As such, laughing, yes, I think it's very healthy.
Bert:	Oh
Sander:	Not because with you there is no good feeling surfacing in you.
Bert:	Uh: Well, it isn't right then?
Sander:	I do not judge. I have no value judgment about good or bad.
Bert:	You don't?
Sander:	It is peculiar. When you ask me like, what do you think of it – that's what you mean, right?
Bert:	Yes?
Sander:	If you ask, do you think it's right; you must be a little interested in how I think about it.
Bert:	Yes.
Sander:	Exactly.
Bert:	Exactly.
Sander:	And then I think, well, it amazes me. I find it hard to put myself in a world like that.
Bert:	You can't?
Sander:	It's difficult for me, that kind of world.
Bert:	Yes.
Sander:	Because . . . yes, life gives me two reasons for smiling.
Bert:	It does?
Sander:	One is that inside of me I feel good, I think of things I enjoy, pleasant things, you know.
Bert:	Yes?
Sander:	And so I smile. You see. (2) Or else, because someone comes up to me and tells me something that makes me laugh.
Bert:	Yes, well, in my case I have some doubt about that
Sander:	The difference between you and me
Bert:	Is there a difference?
Sander:	I thought we just said that my life is not like yours.
Bert:	Yes, right. I live a little different.
Sander:	Yes. (7) and you ask, Which is better?
Bert:	Well, I don't know.
Sander:	No?

Bert:	Honestly. (5) Do you know?
Sander:	No. I know I am reasonably satisfied with my life.
Bert:	Yes?
Sander:	But whether it is better ...
Bert:	(2)
Sander:	What do you think?
Bert:	If you are satisfied, of course, that's better than when you are not satisfied.
Sander:	Mm: (4) But satisfaction also means that you have to live by the rules, of course.
Bert:	Yes.
Sander:	(2) What it comes down to is to more or less accept society the way it is, including its rules and (3) it dos and don'ts (2), and in this way feel reasonably, or at least passably happy.
Bert:	Do you feel really happy in this world?
Sander:	No. True happiness is something else again, but you can adjust to it easier.
Bert:	Yes?
Sander:	And if we look at your life (2). Suppose we go back to before you came to the hospital.
Bert:	Yes?
Sander:	(2) Yes: that was a very lonely life.
Bert:	Yes. What did we have? A loner?
Sander:	A lonely existence. (3)
Bert:	Yes: maybe it was.
Sander:	Maybe?
Bert:	Yes.
Sander:	You didn't feel it like that?
Bert:	No, I don't think so.
Sander:	No?
Bert:	No:
Sander:	You weren't lonely?
Bert:	[*sniffs*] (2)
Sander:	But how is it that those around you think so, how is that possible? Why do they think you are lonely?
Bert:	(3) Yes, how can they possibly think so? [*laughs*] (3) I am not lonely, am I?
Sander:	If you say so.
Bert:	Yes. I say so. Not lonely, just alone.
Sander:	Just alone?
Bert:	Alone (3) You are alone, too?
Sander:	(2) I am not alone, no.
Bert:	(3) No, I am not either.
Sander:	You aren't either?
Bert:	No:

The conversation between Bert and Sander differs from those quoted earlier. This can be explained in terms of the objectives of the STR staff, whose treatment is aimed at as short a stay as possible. The idea is to prepare patients for their best possible return to society, and implies among other things that their future is an important consideration. The preparation for the return usually implies a confrontation with reality, as Sander expresses it. Therapists and social workers make use of their expertise – their knowledge of patients, their lives and everything that went wrong – to convince the patients that things should be different. Persuasion takes the form of confrontation. Lakoff (1982) considers persuasion to be non-reciprocal. However, in every conversation in which the therapist seeks to persuade, patients try to bring forward their own perspectives. Therapists and psychotic people have different ideas and assumptions about life, what went wrong, and the future.

In the fragment above, the conversation turns to 'everything that went wrong'. Bert laughs while Sander sees no reason for this. Bert is also aware that his laughter is considered odd by others. With a measure of irony, he asks which is best, to laugh or to be serious. When Sander replies that laughter is healthy, he poses a second (ironic) question. He challenges Sander: laughter is healthy, but evidently bound by certain conditions. One does not laugh without cause. Sander, therefore, points to deviation. This becomes even clearer in the sequel. The lives of the therapist and the patient are opposed. To be sure, Sander does not make a value judgment when Bert asks which is better, but the meta-message is nevertheless an evaluation: the suggestion is that the therapist lives a normal life and Bert does not. Discourse about 'everything that is wrong' places the accent on the therapist's power and control. A consequence of this is that the patient will try to assume control of the conversation through disruptions: in this case, through irony.

Two frames of reference are opposed here. Sander thinks of Bert as lonely while Bert does not consider himself to be lonely, merely alone, which is different (although it is not spelt out in what way). Another difference is that for Bert, the issue is happiness, while Sander is thinking in terms of adjustment. The answer to the question as to whether Sander is all that happy is negative and gives Bert little to hope for. Sander believes that in this 'confrontation with reality' Bert avoids the true situation in which he finds himself. This avoidance behavior is a disruption of order intended to help one retain control of oneself, but it can also be related to feelings of disappointment (Rehbein 1977). The reason for Bert's negative feelings is that he does not really get answers to his questions. Although he couches them in irony, they refer to existential problems. This becomes clear in the fragment below:

Sander: When things are that bleak for you, what is it you hang on to?
Bert: Nothing.
Sander: No future at all, Bert?
Bert: No.

Sander: You sure?
Bert: Do you think there is a future?
Sander: (2) Yes, for me there is.
Bert: Is that so?
Sander: Aha. (6)
Bert: Well, I guess there probably is for me too then, if future exists. I guess there is future, alright.
Sander: (2) Yes, that's the point. You've lost the track. At one point you say, I think there is a future and (2) when I ask you point blank you say that all you see is a big black hole.

Bert reverses the roles by asking whether his therapist has something to look forward to. He expresses his doubts about the answer: 'Is that so?' In this way he avoids conflict and debate, by surrendering, and returning to the usual role pattern. Sander shows his irritation. Sequences like this are a common occurrence in conversations. Sander gets the impression that Bert is making a game of it, 'playing hide and seek'. But this may not quite be the case. If one looks at other transcripts of conversations with Bert and at his diary, one notes that whenever he poses his questions, they invariably have to do with issues of life and death, good and evil, beauty and ugliness, joy and sadness, and hope and despair. These are normal human feelings and experiences, but to Bert they are bitter, profoundly felt opposites; the 'stark reality' with which he cannot cope. His psychotic experiences on the other hand, are positive. In his diary he writes:

> A clear blue is the sky, nature a mossy green. Birds are singing and each cow has a name. You who have mastered the art of living understand all this.

It reminds one of paradise. But as he says himself, his daily life is a 'black hole', from which he cannot escape and in which he sees himself 'shrinking' and 'dying'. Bert is convinced that he has no future. Sander thinks otherwise, but in a different sense:

Sander: When you say like you have nothing to hold on to. I'm not moving or I'm not striving for this or that.
Bert: No.
Sander: Or I want to achieve this or that. You don't have that. It's not there.
Bert: No, it isn't.
Sander: No.
Bert: But nobody has that, do they?
Sander: Well, at least I act as if. [*coughs*]
Bert: Yes, me too.
Sander: (2) I know that today I have a planning, like, I have thought about it, but I, I am going to do this and I'm going to do that. 11.30, talk with

> Bert. I know that, that is a goal in itself. Part of how I fill in my day. At 12.30 I have a next appointment. At 12.00 I get a bite to eat, and so on, it's the direction I go (2) for the day as a whole.
>
> Bert: You do?

Sander is right. Bert has nothing to anchor him. He asks Sander: 'Does anybody?' The answer is a negative, 'I act as if'. This is exactly how Bert thinks he should behave. He recognizes Sander's answer and once again responds with irony which in turn evokes mixed feelings in the therapist, who is under the impression that the conversation is less a matter of cooperation than of confirmation. This is ambivalent, and the episode is reminiscent of the two stories (hope and hopelessness) in Saint Anthony's psychiatric hospital. Sander finds proof of the confirmation in Bert's questions and indicates that this is a symptom of illness:

> The questions he asks me are meant to stay on top of the conversation. He does this because he cannot cope with it. Next he adapts his communication to it so that nothing will happen. He wants to maintain a distance, and all that seems almost clownish.

Nevertheless, Bert's questions are very basic. After people have had so many problems and intense psychotic experiences, life seems empty and meaningless and they are confronted with self-imposed impossibilities. Sometimes they have literally been expelled by their families or trundled off by police. Unable to see any future for themselves, they look to the therapist to help them survive. At that point, norms are held up to them and they are introduced to specific rules that can be observed and learned by means of daily routines. What they are actually looking for are values: directives to guide their life. An opposition arises between a pragmatic–normative perspective and an existential–evaluative point of view. In conversations, this dilemma is dealt with and transformed by way of disruptions and role reversals.

Making out-of-bounds topics discussable

At the beginning of the chapter, I mentioned that psychotic expressions are frequently purposive. Goffman formulates this as follows:

> Mental symptoms are acts by an individual who openly proclaims to others that he must have assumptions about himself which the relevant bit of social organization can neither allow him nor do much about.
>
> (Goffman 1971: 412)

Mental illness not only plays a role in disruptions of the conversations due to the presence and power of the other, it is also a way of raising to the level of discourse that which cannot be discussed in other ways. Patients may lack the ability to lead others to an alternative interpretation. Often, they have insufficient verbal ability and lack social skills. Their reference to matters in other than their linguistic form leads us to suppose that the significance of these expressions is hidden in the realm of the 'unsaid' (Tyler 1978). The problem for the listener is to infer 'that which can be said' from 'that which is not said'. The expressions of psychotic people are filled with the unique meanings of the things that they carry in their mind. It is this uniqueness which must be communicated repeatedly. While the 'object' (such as seriously disturbed relations with others and with themselves) always presents itself to them in the same manner, they represent it to others in a wide variety of ways. Thus, the uniqueness of the experiences is brought out through continually differing representations. At times, therapists must have at their command almost encyclopedic knowledge if they are to make sense of all these representations. Patients tend to assume that therapists have such flexibility, but the therapist's role is without a script. In view of the ever-changing representations, therapists are left with the ambivalent situation of having to guess what they should say next.

Moreover, many psychotic people do away with mystification, i.e. giving the hearer or viewer the idea that the words harbor a secret. The secret as such would not be at issue. Rather, the point would be the stipulation of restrictions and maintenance of distance, so that a certain respect is evoked and upheld in others (Goffman 1959). Psychotic people do not seem to observe restrictions in their psychotic expressions. There seem to be no secrets. I elaborate on this in two or three excerpts.

'My vocal cords ran out'

Gerard, the therapist, asks Clemens to say something about his 'vocal cords'. Evidently, something had occurred in the ward which caused Clemens to lose his voice.

Gerard:	(3) I also want to know about the story of the vocal cords.
Clemens:	I have, oh yes, there is something wrong with my vocal cords and then I went to the hospital.
Gerard:	Yes (2). But what is it we heard this week, about your vocal cords?
Clemens:	I began to say the wrong things.
Gerard:	Wrong things?
Clemens:	I became uh.
Gerard:	And then?
Clemens:	And then all day: the whole day I said: wro-ong, wro-ong, wro-ong (2)
Gerard:	And after that?
Clemens:	It isn't so bad any more. Still wrong.
Gerard:	Yes, but what happened to your vocal cords?

Clemens:	They ran out. At one point they started to shrink and against and I can't talk any more.
Gerard:	They ran out?
Clemens:	They did, yes.
Gerard:	Oh. But yesterday you told me:
Clemens:	Because it shrinks, it was stuck to my vocal cords!
Gerard:	Oh:
Clemens:	That's why I have to go to the hospital.
Gerard:	You couldn't talk any more.

The day before the above recording, Clemens had offered a different story when he and Gerard had also talked about this episode ('Yesterday you told me that they. . . .'). He had claimed that the nurse had removed his vocal cords. Clemens later more or less admitted that what he said the day before was a strategy to talk about conflict on the ward ('it was not a real nurse'). He indicated that he knew quite well that his vocal cord story was not 'realistic', but he had no other words to express what went on inside his head. At the time of the conversations, Clemens was troubled and he wanted to go home. The only way in which he seemed able to express his dissatisfaction was by lashing out, hitting, and shouting. The dossier referred to 'increased anxiety and aggression'. Evidently, the nurse told him that he should talk about his fears ('Must talk it all out') and when this did not help, Clemens was sent to his room. Furthermore, he displayed sensitivity to his own behavior (he said 'wrong things' and 'could not talk'). His feelings were forces over which he had lost control. This was how he presented it:

Gerard:	(3) So who is boss now? You or your vocal cords?
Clemens:	The cords.
Gerard:	Is that so?
Clemens:	Yes.
Gerard:	You have no say over your vocal cords?
Clemens:	Well, I have trouble using them.
Gerard:	(3) Uhuh.
Clemens:	I don't think I know much.
Gerard:	(2) You don't know much?
Clemens:	No. I don't know a thing.
Gerard:	(2) Just like that?
Clemens:	That's why I want to go the hospital, lets me (3) sliss.
Gerard:	Okay. But what are they supposed to do there?
Clemens:	More surgery.

Clemens clearly found it difficult to express intense emotions in a way that was acceptable to others ('I don't know a thing'). He also offered a solution for the recurring conflict occasioned by his behavior: if you put a pacifier in your mouth, you cannot say the wrong things.

Clemens: Well, I can kind of talk again now. (3) But uh take a teat, keep it in my mouth (3)
Gerard: A teat? What's that for? Makes it impossible to talk.
Clemens: Right. You can't say anything at all then.
Gerard: No. You can't.
Clemens: I'm really just a baby.
Gerard: Are you?

These fragments portray situations in which psychotic experiences emerge where things cannot be verbalized or portrayed in other ways. Intense and exceptional experiences are not easily put into words (Scarry 1985). Clemens's problem is how to articulate his great anxiety and it is unique in that it seems to him to be a force beyond his control. The story of the vocal cords is an uninhibited fantasy, and an attempt to keep the problem within bounds. Clemens does not want to run the risk of a reprimand if he were to blame the nurse. Still, his strategy fails because the story is not consistent. Yesterday the nurse removed the vocal cords; today they said the wrong things and ultimately ran out. The therapist understands the story is a cover:

> As I see it there is no relation between the not knowing and the story. Clemens wants to shirk it off and avoid it, which is typically schizophrenic. He is delivered up to forces he cannot master. So he cuts off his vocal cords, which renders him innocent.

One may wonder if the instability proceeds only from Clemens's psychotic disorder or from other considerations. The vocal cords are a symbol for extreme anxiety: 'I am speechless' and simultaneously of helplessness: 'I have been silenced' (i.e. I cannot stand up to the power of staff members). Formulations of the above kind – in terms of physical disorders – are often used by patients in order to avoid greater psychological pain (Littlewood and Lipsedge 1989: 218–243). Clemens avoids Gerard's questions because Gerard is 'one of them', since he asks questions and wants to hear the story. Clemens does not stick to the therapist's script; he tells the story differently. By doing that, he avoids the risk of his behavior being interpreted as a kind of resistance against staff authority, but he does not avoid the risk of it being seen as characteristically schizophrenic. His literal representation of speechlessness and helplessness is not difficult to interpret socially, however hard it is to accept. In this way, Clemens sidesteps discussion about his participation in an event on the ward that fills him with shame. Thus, he avoids talk about relationships.

'Sometimes I ride a cow'

How does someone tell his therapist that he is a good person, even though he keeps running into conflict in the institution, people are afraid of him, and he is frequently placed in isolation? Dick, a 40-year-old, chronically schizophrenic long-term resident, developed a tactic for this. He used a rather idiosyncratic interpretation of a children's book to convey to his therapist that, in spite of less pleasant events involving him, he was a good person. The strategy is introduced during a session with his therapist, Jochem. Jochem inquires about Dick's well-being. Dick replies that he is not doing well. The therapist doubts this.

Jochem: Things are not all right, you say. But you look very fine.
Dick: Yes, I look good. But inside can be different, you know.
Jochem: Is the inside not like the outside?
Dick: Well, my heart is on this side (2). Not in the right place, I told the nurse.
Jochem: Not on the left side?
Dick: No, no on the left.
Jochem: I always have the impression that you've got your heart in the right place.
Dick: Don't know, uncle Jochem. It kind of shifts at times, I think.
Jochem: Moves around does it?
Dick: Yes, it moves around.
Jochem: That so?:: I still think you have your heart in the right place.
Dick: Right here. (3) sure.
Jochem: Because you care about other people, too. (2) Ready to help them, you are willing to help.
Dick: Yes, always did, uncle Jochem, always did.

When Dick says that his heart is on the wrong side and points to his chest, he does not intend his literal interpretation to be taken too seriously. He refers to difficult topics they have just been talking about. Jochem explains afterwards that this was an attempt by Dick to draw him out. Jochem goodnaturedly takes the bait: 'Your heart is always in the right place'. He compliments him: 'You care about other people' and so turns Dick's word play back to the metaphor. The conversation continues with examples of how Dick is always ready to lend a helping hand. Typical for this conversation are the sudden and, to Jochem, unexpected changes of topic. Halfway into a sentence, Dick inquires after the health of the therapist's father. Another surprising shift occurs in the first part of the fragment below. It follows a dialogue about medicines in which Dick remarks that he 'is cared for even under his feet'. From foot to football is a big but not inexplicable shift.

Dick: Do you ever play soccer?
Jochem: Play soccer?
Dick: Yes?
Jochem: No.

Dick:	Uh:::it's the finest sport there is. (5) Ha ha, that's good: uncle Jochem playing soccer.
Jochem:	How about you?
Dick:	Sometimes I ride a cow (3) You understand?
Jochem:	No.
Dick:	No.
Jochem:	I don't understand you.
Dick:	I said, sometimes I ride a cow.
Jochem:	Ride a cow?
Dick:	Cow.
Jochem:	Yes?
Dick:	Cows?
Jochem:	Well, okay, what do you mean?
Dick:	Well, sometimes I ride them (2) A cow ride sometimes. Cow. You never saw me ride a cow? [*laughs*]. They're fast, like, those cows.
Jochem:	Yes.
Dick:	I sit on top of one of those cows, Ride. Sometimes I ride a cow.
Jochem:	You're taking me for a ride, aren't you?
Dick:	No::
Jochem:	Yes.
Dick:	No seriously, because my father said 'It's a special boy, that's what he is', he said.
Jochem:	That's different, sure, that's something else. I believe that too, that he probably said that.
Dick:	Sure, sure.
Jochem:	(3) You really are a special boy.
Dick:	Sure. But there is nothing special about how I look, is there, uncle Jochem? Nothing, right? (2)
Jochem:	Not in that sense, no
Dick:	No. (4) well, as far as I am concerned, we're finished.

The therapist is a bit surprised about the story with the cow. Dick's remarks seem to have a purpose: 'You understand?' Nevertheless, Jochem feels cheated: 'You're taking me for a ride, aren't you?' The riddle is solved by Dick: 'That's a special boy'. The link between the cow and the father's comment ('My father said') is significant. It is a reference to a well-known boy's book, *Dik Trom*, about a boy who gets everything wrong, except in his father's eyes. In the story Dik Trom's socially unacceptable behavior culminates in a scenario in which the boy rides a donkey backwards, shocking onlookers, and in which the father coins the memorable phrase 'It's a special boy, that's what he is!' The therapist lets Dick feel that he agrees with his remarks. The utterance is placed in a known context, that of the previous fragment. Jochem said: 'I found it rather funny. Typically Dick.'

After Jochem's affirmation, Dick suddenly terminated the conversation. This was remarkable, because earlier he tended to elaborate on topics such as helping others. But in this instance, the move evokes a 'hidden' significance in Dick's use of language. Dick is not really talking about his relationship with his father or his therapist. As he said shortly afterwards:

> I came to think of Jochem as a good fellow . . . I don't want to talk about it. I know the Dik Trom book. Dik Trom, that's me, you know. It's about my father. To me, my father means loving. He was 45 when he died and I was only four. My mother was a good-looking woman and a lot younger. After my father's death my brother used to beat me.

In the fragment, Dick offers no more than an outline of the complex problem of his behavior involving his father, the therapist and being loved. He intentionally sketches only one side of the picture. In doing so, he does away with 'the rule of charity' (Grice 1975: 46, 54–56) and manages to convey more than he actually says. Jochem is forced to interpret and deduce. Initially, he does not recognize the reference to the children's book: 'It was only a little later that the donkey association came to me.' The metaphor would have been more obvious if he had made the connection, but he does realize that Dick's utterances are a way of saying that in spite of all reports, he is special. But Dick (successfully) blurs the message by exchanging the donkey for a cow. Such substitutions often occur in conversations with psychotic people. They are misleading and tend to create a loose bond rather than genuine communion. In this way, patients are still able to retain some control of a conversation because the misleading substitutions allow them to imply and then declare that the therapist's deductions are wrong.

In the discussion and analysis of exchanges between Eric and Jochem, we noted that sometimes patients exhibited impertinent behavior. The impertinence was meant to help patients achieve role reversal and to take control of a conversation. Disruptions were occasioned or exacerbated by initially incongruent frames of references between therapist and patient. If the behavior was successful it could be used for other purposes as well. This is what happened:

Jochem: Hey?
Eric: No, those girls . . .
Jochem: Can I ask you something?
Eric: I am a woman-hater, I am.
Jochem: You hate women?
Eric: I am the worst of woman-haters.
Jochem: Since when?
Eric: I would gouge out X's [*a fellow patient*] eyes, just like that. I wouldn't, not X? That serpent, talk like a witch. Piece of dirt. Wha . . . [*incomprehensible*].
Jochem: Uhuh
Eric: [*incomprehensible*]. I drank opium. Never get rid of it, I know that. But uh, can I look through your glasses?

Jochem: No.

Eric: Sure, I can look through your glasses, 'cause I, I want to look at what you see. Just let me have those glasses of yours.

Jochem: Okay, take a look.

Eric: Do you see blood? Do you see blood? (3) Yes? That's ... [*incomprehensible*]

Jochem: [*laughs*]

Eric: Oh, but now I get you. You are drunker than a corkscrew from all that coffee, right:: [*laughs*]

Jochem: [*laughs*]

Eric: Coffee gets you dead drunk [*laughs*] terrible, terri-ble!

Jochem: Awful, isn't it? What you're seeing now.

Eric: Uh::: yes [*laughs*]. If only I can find the forbidden area, 'cause I

Jochem: No!

Eric: Then I can

Jochem: I want, I want my glasses back!

Eric: I was just wondering if maybe you had something to hide.

Jochem: No, keep your hands off of me!

Eric: My hands now wander to more romantic places,

Jochem: I just let you have my glasses . . .

Eric: [*incomprehensible*]

Jochem: . . . to look through, but I didn't want you to start this 'wandering hands' business.

Eric is engaged in a long, incomprehensible monologue. Jochem butts in: 'Hey?' Perhaps Eric suspects that Jochem wants to ask further about his brother; at any rate, he does not give Jochem a chance to ask questions. He anticipates: 'I am a woman-hater'. After swearing at a female patient he continues his earlier, incomprehensible muttering. Jochem lets him know that he is being excluded: the videotape shows him raising his eyebrows. Eric mounts an attack: 'Let me have those glasses of yours.' He grabs them and Jochem has to surrender.

This impertinence is a ceremonial profanity, a situation in which people do not conform to the appropriate ritual. As such, these profanities are not unusual. When people know each other well they are less strict about observing ritual and more amenable to harmless joking, but when Eric takes Jochem's glasses and puts them on against his will, his action shows a degree of disrespect. Goffman says about this sort of action:

> These acts are exactly those calculated to convey complete disrespect and contempt through symbolic means. Whatever is in the patient's mind [. . .] it is a use of our ceremonial idiom that is as exquisite in its way as is a bow from the waist done with grace and flourish. Whether he knows it or not, the patient speaks the same ritual language as his captors.
>
> (Goffman 1967: 89)

It is an intentional act meant to indicate that he is irritated by the questions of the therapist, who keeps interrupting him. 'Now I get you,' he says. Eric's remarks are understood as an allusion to Jochem figuratively drawing blood by his insistent questioning. Throughout the exchange both the therapist and patient pursue their technique of interrupting each other. The interference, in the form of Jochem's questions and Eric's 'pinpoint bombing' responses, makes the conversation seem aggressive in character. But however offensive Eric's behavior may seem, it remains possible for Jochem not to take offense (Goffman 1967: 87). Eric has been classified as a 'defective, chronically psychotic' patient with 'serious reality disorders'. The label means that the therapist makes allowances because he ascribes this behavior to his patient's condition. Eric acts the clown and it would seem churlish to take offense against someone weak who is just trying to have fun. One can conclude that Eric's undermining of Jochem's authority is typical of the ceremonial idiom used by psychotics to convey indirect messages.

Reality transformations and reality constructions

A characteristic sequence carried out by therapists in their talks with patients was transformation, followed by the concomitant reconstruction of (patient) reality. Transformation is defined as reformulation of a person's utterances, especially those that relate to experiences. Transformations are considered to be necessary in the therapeutic process, in order to achieve change in patients.

In brief, patients were encouraged to articulate their problems, in acceptable terms, in order to remove the barriers retarding solutions. In addition, reformulation was considered necessary because of the assumed deficiencies of psychotic patients, such as their inability to describe their emotions and experiences adequately. Transformation implies the message: 'You are not saying this the way you should; let me show you how.' It is therefore a form of 'revealing' by the therapists, which helps to identify the patient's 'hang-ups', and locate distortions. As a rule in conversations, transformations of patient utterances were sequentially similar. On hearing a statement, the therapist would construct one himself and compare it with the spoken words and a given standard. Transformation, then, was the reverse of the process of producing a linguistic expression. Typically, these comparisons were tested in the openness of the conversation, and therapists checked whether their reformulations were correct. This is clear from phrases like 'Do I understand you to say that', or 'You say "sadly enough" but you mean "It hurts me"?' In this way, patients kept hearing a reworked echo of their own words. Communication returned between source and receiver, i.e. speakers and listeners who encoded and decoded messages in accordance with certain rules. One can imagine that in some ways patient experiences were attenuated and somewhat altered. In the case of attenuation or blurring, conflicts may have arisen. When a psychotic patient has been in hospital for a long time, there is transformation of his self-description and representation of experiences. The distance closes between the patient and the therapist's myths and meaning transformations, and one almost hears the patient speak as the therapist would. While running the conversation tapes, I encountered two kinds of transformation used by therapists: reformulation of patient self-representations, and ontological transformations. Ontological transformations are reformulations of utterances that refer to being in the world. They occur particularly in the STR and we have established why this is so. Each type of transformation is illustrated by a case study.

Besides therapist's transformations involving the reconstruction of reality, one also comes across patient-authored reality constructions, especially in the LTR. These constructions can be termed fabrications (Goffman 1974) or inventions, driven by hidden motives. By means of these fabrications, patients revamp part of their world, and their relationship to therapists, in a conversation. The fabrications are often seen as 'not normal'. In this section, I comment on a case in which fabrication occurs, but I first want to show how Dora illustrated that self-representation can be transformed.

'That's what makes Dora tick, right?'

Dora is a psychotic female patient in short-term residence who has for years gone through repeated cycles of psychosis and depression, and whose self-esteem and relations with others are marked by instability. From her girlhood onwards, life has been an endless chain of failed contacts, abuse by others, and wandering. Although she is an 'in–out' patient she has not given up looking for a niche of her own. According to her therapist, she is a 'fugitive' who has 'not developed a strong selfhood', and who 'invariably paints a negative picture of herself'. She feels herself delivered up to forces beyond her control, forces which take the shape of compassion with others in their misery. She feels herself abused, lonely and sucked dry 'because I put too much effort into others, I forget myself. I cease to exist'. Dora has enough inner strength to strike out on her own in new directions, but at every turn of her life's path, her choices have proved wrong.

There are attempts (in the conversations) to transform her experiences into the personality traits that she must learn to accept; i.e. her self-presentation is reformulated. It is like a trade-off in which illness is not taken away, but transformed into identity:

Dora: I let it get to me too much.
Matt: (1) Hold on, right, you let things touch you too much.
Dora: Maybe that's another reason to run – but, well, it's no joke to sit in the common room – all that bullshit.
Matt: Let me try this one, Dora. You let things get to you too much, right? (2) That's your thing, your make-up.
Dora: Yes.
Matt: That's your personal bag when you go to the women's shelter. (3)

Dora: I guess so
Matt: It's part of Dora, I think (2)
Dora: Yes, it's part of me (2)
Matt: That's what makes Dora tick, right? Very sensitive, she is.
Dora: Yes, but sometimes I don't feel that way so much, but
Matt: Right.

Therapist Matthew reformulates the words 'letting it get to me' to the concept of being 'sensitive'. This turns 'things' (other people's misery) that invade Dora from outside, into 'things' that are inside her. Such hypersensitivity could be kept in check only with outside help. After 13 hospital intakes, the decision was at last taken to place her in a women's shelter and to keep her on medication. The 'self' was initially presented in terms of 'others acting like leeches', 'being swallowed up', 'letting things affect me', and abuse and loneliness. Now, it was being represented as an intra-psychological property, a sensitive selfhood. A mirror technique was used to test if the transformation was correct:

Dora: Maybe I am too pessimistic.
Matt: Well, I don't know whether that's pessimism. That's what you say. What I'm hearing is that you are very sensitive.
Dora: Yes.
Matt: For things that demand uh: things that have to do with responsibility, right? When you see X in trouble, when X cries.
Dora: Yes.
Matt: Then you rush to her aid, even if only with your feelings.
Dora: Yes.
Matt: 'I've got to be there, there's crying there'.
Dora: Yes. I want to do something about it, right then and there.
Matt: Right. So you are really super-sensitive for it, for suffering, for (2) the serious things in life, that sort of thing.
Dora: Yes (3)
Matt: . . . to the point that sometimes you almost drown in it (3)

'Mirroring', when used in this way to manipulate a goal, leaves the patient with no alternative but to concur. Earlier in the conversation, we saw the examples of being drawn in, which were used to elaborate on the patient's hypersensitivity. The result was a form of cooperation which questioned its own authenticity. Dora has learned 'to live with it'. At a point certain point in the conversation, the psychological trait of hypersensitivity was again transformed to a handicap or disability.

Matt: Well, I see that as quite an achievement (5), to see your handicap, you know, if I can call it that, to see your handicap and:
Dora: Yes.

Matt: And really we should say, uh: I have this handicap and I have to make arrangements so that I can live with it. And that leads me to medication and the women's shelter.

Dora: Yes (2)

Matt: The prosthesis for the handicap, you might say . . .

Dora: Yes:

Matt: . . . is medication and guidance.

Dora: Yes, and not only guidance, but also being able to live together with other people.

Matt: Yes.

Dora: Living in a group, companions around you.

Matt: Yes, sure (2).

When Matt spoke to Dora here, reformulating her earlier statements, it drove home the message that she should learn to live with the situation, that her illness was not likely to disappear and so on. Dora could only respond in the affirmative. The transformation was a bridge created by the therapist. Something vague and difficult to grasp became tangible when presented as something concrete, like a handicap. One could address a handicap by providing facilities and prostheses. Handicaps were recognized by the aids used to minimize them (in this case medicines and supervision). At the same time, the transformation bridge was marked by some ambivalent news for Dora whose psychological disorder took on a permanent character. Dora commented: 'I'd still rather call it hypersensitivity. *Handicap* sounds so serious and so final.'

Matt first let his patient say that her problems would not disappear, something which Dora articulated with insight. Such an emphatic response could be seen as a successful transformation. The open reformulation showed the patient that her therapist was trying to imagine the situation. There is a chance that the reformulation, no matter how well intentioned, can become a caricature in which patients are treated as children who are not considered capable of formulating their own ideas (Van Haaster 1991: 42). The effect of reformulation is ambivalent. It may liberate, in that it is easier for someone to admit to having a handicap than being 'crazy'. While being crazy is something to be ashamed about, however, a handicap is permanent. Dora is not very strong and no one likes to admit to weakness. Nevertheless the transformation also demystifies psychological traits in terms of which patients present themselves, such as involvement and sympathy. These traits may pose serious problems for those who have them, but their social value gives them an advantage when people have to 'save face'. Using the medium of hypersensitivity to transform involvement, abuse, etc. into a handicap is a reconstruction of reality, except that the old reality of psychosis is turned into the new reality of a handicapped person with a prosthesis.

'Sad, isn't it?'

The excerpts below are examples of ontological transformation. Part of the conversation between Cor, a schizophrenic patient in STR, and his therapist, Wout, recounts how paranormal powers forced him to tear up photos of himself and to take his own life. Like Dora, he feels delivered up to outside forces: his life is 'cast in the mould of fate'. Cor feels helpless as voices urge him on, in relation to the divorce of his parents and his relationship with his girlfriend. The excerpt begins where Cor has just sketched a part of his experience, which deals with a broken relationship:

Cor: I think it's too bad that things went that way.
Wout: Yes (1) Sad?
Cor: (2) 'Cause we did have a very good time, you know (3)
Wout: Yes (2). You feel that way, just now when we are talking about it and you tell me these things (1) then, well, I feel the sadness underneath (1) You feel that yourself? Do you have that? Sadness or: that you could cry.
Cor: I never cry. I wouldn't mind to, and I did sometimes.
Wout: What?
Cor: Sometimes I howled, too.
Wout: You did? But these days it is kind of hard to cry?
Cor: Sort of, yes. (3) It has faded some.
Wout: You think that what's happening? Fading?
Cor: Yes. Sometimes I think back, but it is getting misty, vague. You start looking for other things, right?

Wout reformulates, from 'too bad' to 'sad'. He does so because this introduces empathy. Wout felt that 'the talk held emotions, but Cor was not ready for them yet'. One might ask if these were pre-existing emotions, remembered feelings, or feelings induced by the conversation. At any rate, the mirroring was suggestive: Cor replied that he was beyond sadness, and that the edges were fading. The conversation continued about present concerns, but Wout returned before long to the receding experiences that surrounded Cor's parting with his girlfriend:

Wout: But you say, it's fading. Could it be that (3) well, that maybe you are disappointed so often that you get tougher inside, and crying doesn't come that easily? That's a little different from fading, but you nod yes (3)
Cor: Maybe so, could be (3)
Wout: You don't have to agree with me. If you say maybe so I tend to think: now he is uh (7)
Cor: Yes, things turned out different, didn't they.
Wout: (4) You could not change it. It just happened, didn't it?
Cor: Yes (6) I didn't want it to go that way. It simply happened (3)

Wout: (1) So, what you're saying is, I'm looking for a place where I can finally find some quiet, where I uh:: maybe have some good times, even if I deceive myself.

Cor: Yes (4)

Wout: I feel too helpless to take on the world, or whatever you want to call it, to find a niche?

Cor: You have to make the best of it.

Wout: Yes (9) sad, isn't it (2) Or not?

Cor: I don't see it that way.

Wout: You don't?

Cor: No, uh: uh (3), well, dejected (2)

Wout formulates Cor's experience in a way that he can simply respond 'yes', but unreserved agreement is not achieved. The discrepancy in this fragment arises in the gap between the therapist's transformations and Cor's actual feelings. The message of this sort of communication is: 'The way you feel is wrong. I will tell you how you should feel', although the conversation is not as extreme as that. Wout does leave open the possibility for other ways of feeling: 'You don't have to agree with me . . .'.

For Cor, being in the world is characterized by dejection. His therapist however sees this as lack of feeling, and blunted sensitivity. 'He must regain the ability to feel; as I see it that would be the road toward healing, but I don't see it happening to him.' The dejection, which according to the therapist might well be sadness, is not pursued any further.

'I've got more children, you know. I have ten of them!'

The conversation between Truus, a chronically schizophrenic woman in the LTR, and therapist Gerard, reveals a continuous battle for reality. The two of them speak in the distinct frameworks in terms of which the struggle takes shape. The therapist would focus on the life story of the patient by going back from the here and now of the ward to her past. Truus starts from bygone events. She wants to talk about her ex-husband and the children. In this, she is successful. Repeatedly, she makes it difficult for the therapist, feigning loss of memory, or ignorance, in response to his questions. This, and sudden shifts in topic, enable her to retain control. In the sequence prior to the fragment below, Gerard reminds her of the problems with her husband. He has read about this in the dossier. Truus asks what the dossier says. Gerard hesitates: 'Well:::'. She takes advantage of the hesitation:

Truus: Why don't I ever get the children back? Is it because I won't get a house or something?

Gerard: You have one child, don't you?

Truus: I've got more children, you know. I have ten of them!

Gerard: Ten? (3) I read that you have just one.
Truus: No. I have ten children (3)
Gerard: Ten?
Truus: Yes (3) You only read about one, and that one is from way back.
Gerard: Right.
Truus: But I have nine more.
Gerard: Did they all come later?
Truus: Yes, afterwards (3)
Gerard: Nine? (3)
Truus: Yes (3)
Gerard: I can't believe it.
Truus: Yes, from uh: of my own, you see.
Gerard: Uhuh.
Truus: Of my own I have uh: eight or so (2) of my own (2) and two of his.
Gerard: What do you mean, of your own?
Truus: Can't I have children of my own?
Gerard: [*shakes his head*]
Truus: Sure I can!
Gerard: You don't get pregnant just like that?
Truus: Sure I do.
Gerard: You do?
Truus: That can happen, you know.
Gerard: It can?
Truus: Yes, not everybody. My sister got pregnant by herself, too (2) a sister of mine.
Gerard: Without going to bed with a man?
Truus: Yes.
Gerard: Is that possible?
Truus: It's possible all right.
Gerard: Oh: I never knew that.
Truus: That's new to you, isn't it?
Gerard: Yes.

Primarily the story seems to be a game that both Truus and Gerard enjoy. The therapist plays along. When he refers to the dossier again, Truus finds a way out: 'You only read about one'. Additional data are meant to make the story more plausible, and Gerard's physiological knowledge cannot detract from it. When confronted with the physical impossibility of virgin birth, she counters by indicating that perhaps Gerard does not know, and that she is giving him new insight: 'That's new to you, isn't it?' Is this in fact a game, an 'expression of childishness', as Gerard says? Perhaps it was a slip of the tongue when the woman said: 'Why don't I ever get the children back?' She makes use of the opportunity that arises to turn it into a game. The response is a blatant exaggeration that must be maintained throughout the rest of the story. Truus does so in quite inventive ways.

Gerard interprets the story as a 'a kind of game in which she takes pleasure. There is no depth to it'. As to the assumed superficiality of the game, this is an example of what Goffman (1974) calls 'fabrication':

> The intentional effort of one or more individuals to manage activity so that a party of one or more others will be induced to have a false belief about what it is that is going on. A nefarious design is involved, a plot or treacherous plan leading – when realized – to a falsification of some part of the world.
>
> (Goffman 1974: 83)

In this case, the objective of the fabrication is not nefarious. Truus presents a misleading picture of reality in order to retain control over the conversation, and Gerard allows her to do so. To understand fully why Truus wants to misrepresent reality, we need to examine the wider context of the story.

Truus has a Roman Catholic background. At the age of 15 she began a life of sexual promiscuity and wandering. She had a short-lived relation with a North African and had a child by him. The child was assigned to foster parents because Truus's way of life precluded baby care. She married another North African, but the marriage was beset with difficulties. She moved to North Africa for a period with her husband, but returned because she was 'homesick for her mother'. The marriage broke up and she took to wandering again. Finally, she was admitted to the hospital but kept running off, to loiter in the city. After contracting venereal disease, she underwent sterilization and was ultimately placed in a closed LTR ward. She is plagued by voices accusing her of being a 'whore'. Her feelings towards her ex-husband and child remain ambivalent. Sometimes she wants to go back, at other times, she does not. She would like to have her sterilization undone. 'My husband can help me to have children again.' The dossier mentions that Truus feels 'empty', an emptiness that she fills with the longing for a child, promiscuity, food and candy.

In brief, Truus's life story can be reduced to the essentials: Catholic upbringing, North Africa, children, emptiness, moral accusation (the voices), and a lingering desire for a normal way of life. The fragment about the ten children represents some of these facets of her life, albeit in an extraordinary way. Truus engages in an action as noted earlier: she refers to matters that belong in the area of that-which-can-be-signified-but-cannot-be-said. In this way she appeals to Gerard's knowledge. Simultaneously, she transforms her being in the world from a way of life that she assumes to be morally unacceptable into an acceptable one. She achieves this transformation in an extremely vague way; she creates a myth of having children without intercourse. The myth resonates with the Catholic environment and the story of the immaculate conception: a woman (Mary) who becomes pregnant without having had intercourse with a man, and who, in view of the special merit of her son (Christ) is privileged, uncontaminated by original sin and liberated from lustful desire. The myth teaches a sexual morality in which desire is sin, women are forbidden to have extra-marital sexual intercourse, and coitus is only for procreation. Motherhood is holy. The myth is a means to hold women in their place.

Truus's story rests on the myth, allowing her to avoid talking about her morally unacceptable multiple sexual lusts and liaisons. She places herself on the level of Mary, her (childhood) ideal for Catholic women. The message is: 'I am not as bad as the voices tell me'. Moreover, the children conceived immaculately ('just like that') cannot be taken away from her by others because of her past. They are born 'unblemished' as it were. In view of her experiences with North African men and her stay in the Maghreb area, it is not at all inconceivable that she became familiar with a second myth: the myth of the *ragêd*. A *ragêd* is a fetus, asleep in the womb for a long period, coming to life again after coitus. The myth is understood as a women's strategy to resist the sexual ethic and dominant norms regarding motherhood (Jansen 1982). The myth is important to North African women because it allows them to hide infertility or an abortion. The *ragêd* belief also makes it possible for women to enter into extra-marital relationships during their husband's long-term absence. It is linked also to phantom pregnancy (Jansen 1982: 102–105). Phantom pregnancy has to do with the wish to become pregnant. Pregnancy is proof of normalcy.

The story told by Truus implies a wish to be normal. Pregnancy is important to her in terms of 'filling', in relation to her sterility, and as proof of normality. Her fabrication, then, seems to have an ulterior motive. She knows of course that without coitus there can be no children. Subsequently she remarks: 'Gerard asked for it. That's why I came up with the story'. At the end of the conversation, she returned to the topic once again:

Truus: Ha (8). I want a house and I want my children back (5)
Gerard: All ten of them?
Truus: All ten of them, yes.
Gerard: You'll need a big house, then.
Truus: (2) Something like that (3)
Gerard: Ten is a lot you know.
Truus: Sure is (4) I'll manage.
Gerard: You will?
Truus: (27)
Gerard: You think about it sometimes?
Truus: About what?
Gerard: A house?
Truus: A house for me and my children.
Gerard: Uhuh (19) Uhuh (13)

This episode also refers to the intention of the earlier story. Truus shows that she knows very well what she said before and takes Gerard's ironic 'All ten of them?' in her stride. If therapists dismiss a story as a fantasy, they present no solution for the social circumstances in which psychotic people find themselves and no answer to their dreams and desires. The meaning of concepts like coherence and understanding become clear in this fragment. If the hearer's belief in the patient's intention to achieve coherence and comprehension is important, and this is not achieved, alternative explanations are impossible and the words of patients are not taken seriously. The story told by Truus stands for her longing for an ordinary life (though she knows better) and suffering under the judgment of others. It is a euphemistic idiom that opens ways to discuss delicate issues safely.

'Sure, I have much to say, but there is so little talking'

This statement by a patient reflects on conversations with therapists. It may surprise, considering that talking and conversing (still) occupy a central place in the treatment of psychiatric patients. In the hospital, there is much talk between therapists and patients, and between patients mutually. This does not refer to the quantity of 'talk', but rather to its substance. It gives us a glimpse of the dissatisfaction people may feel after a conversation. Clearly, conversations are frequently laborious and beset with difficulties and many issues remain unresolved.

For patients, a conversation with a therapist is a delicate undertaking in which the balance between openness and closure, the permitted and the non-permissible, can easily be upset. Therapists and patients go out of their way to maintain this balance, sometimes by introducing new topics into the talk, which at first may not fit. Much time and effort is invested by both parties to keep the conversation going and to achieve some kind of result, in spite of many problems. In the conversations, therapists may want to discuss topics that the patients want to avoid, and vice versa. Time and again, this is intentional. When therapeutically important issues arise, such as patient emotions and personal histories, patients tend to pull back, using a great variety of strategies to avoid them. Therapists, in turn, use tactics such as insistent questioning and repeated intimations of empathy to get these matters talked about.

If psychotic patient behavior takes forms such as disruptions, unusual utterances or imaginative reality constructions, or if patients make certain assertions about their existence and selfhood, it will usually indicate abnormality. Therapists prefer to keep these patterns out of the conversation or to transform them into something acceptable. On closer inspection such forms can be sensible strategies for the patient, for example, to remain 'tuned in' to a conversation or to make a topic fit for discussion. An evaluation of the conversations between therapists and patients reveals that their views display a remarkable similarity. If a conversation is considered laborious, both therapist and patient often feel the same way. The reactions, too, are similar: 'He [the therapist] did not understand me' – 'I did not understand him [the patient]', 'I fend him [the therapist] off' – 'I can't really reach him [the patient]'. The evaluations further show that the discussion partners interpret and evaluate strategies in similar ways:

Patient: I don't want to get in his way, but I have other things to think about.
Therapist: His tactics are to accommodate me while at the same time doing his own thing.

Patient: Drop the silences in his lap; makes him think of what to say next.
Therapist: I have to pick up the silences; I work out what to do next.

These congruencies are common in the STR, where conversations tend to be more assertive than in the LTR. In the LTR, evaluation focuses more on relational aspects. It turns out that a sympathetic understanding of patients goes with the patient's attitude. In turn, patients feel understood if nurses or therapists are willing to respond to their words, or tune in to their style. In their conversations with patients, therapists as a matter of course relate the manner in which psychotic people carry on conversations to their own specialist knowledge. As described in Chapters 8 and 9, such discourse behavior is considered symptomatic of the disorder.

Conversations between psychotic patients and therapists aim at the creation of a new reality for people with psychotic disorders, so that they can live an autonomous life, without overbearing problems. Conversations may contain hundreds of twists, turns, reformulations, questions, repairs, and so on. At first sight this form of conversing consists of an exchange of 'the banal truths of folk psychology' (Kirmayer 1993: 161). Often these are stereotypes: a therapist remarked that one should take care not to become bored during talks with patients. In the conversations, little is visible of the evocative, imaginary world of psychotic people as described by some authors. This world is also a source of fascination for many, including therapists.

But clichés abound in transformation. The words of emotion, self-description, and patient explanation are never taken as they are; instead, they are transmuted to everyday, unambiguous expressions. In this manner, therapists try to bring their patients 'back on track' whenever they present disruption, fictitious accounts, fabrication and the like. Hence, the words of patients keep being interpreted in ways other than as intended by them, which is not unusual. After all, a hearer is an interpreter. In the communication between therapists and patients, this occurs very emphatically and in a specific way. The consequences are far reaching.

In conversations, psychotic experiences are certainly not placed at center stage. The subjective perspective of psychotic people is transformed to a certain standard, which excludes any possible alternatives. The original, idiosyncratic meanings and the distinct relations between these meanings and cultural models receive too little attention. Issues of life and death, joy, pain and loneliness, etc. get little chance to germinate. Crises such as social and psychological death, sudden flashes of insight, and intense experiences, which are commonplace in ethnographies and phenomenological psychiatry, are deemed to belong more to 'armchair psychiatry' than to clinical practice. This means that in reflecting on patients and their conversations, therapists may sometimes refer to the above-mentioned crises, events, and moral issues, but that in clinical practice they are obscured. Instead of the common emotional or moral idiom that therapists believe to be normal, the only option left to patients is to 'tinker': to use images, metaphors, or stories that are interpreted by therapists. This becomes their way to relate something about their being, emotions and sense of self, without this being considered pathological.

Chapter 7

Living in two worlds

> His [the bricoleur's] universe of instruments is closed and the rules of his game are always to make do with 'whatever is at hand', that is to say with a set of tools and materials which is always finite and is also heterogeneous because what it contains bears no relation to the current project.
>
> C. Lévi-Strauss, *The Savage Mind*

The enormous impact of being labeled 'psychotic' and the taboo attached to part of the world of psychotic people can make patients at Saint Anthony's psychiatric hospital uncertain of the meaning of things. This is true in Fatima's case:

> I want you to understand how difficult it is to give everything a meaning. Because, many things which I have seen as images are just things I experienced in the past. Those things come back . . . I'll give you some examples. Really, it is so scary that I find it difficult to talk about. I have seen X [the therapist] before, before I was admitted here. When I saw X here, that image came back to me. And the little magician. There was a boy here who asked me: 'Have you seen the little magician?' I knew that boy, too, from before. I had seen him at some earlier time. And the little magician. When I was possessed I put him in a bottle. He is here in a bottle too. I'll show him . . . Also, I was given things to conjure with. Little blocks which fulfilled my wishes if I wanted. But I took them up into myself and did nothing with them. Later, on the ward, I encounter these little blocks again.

Fatima has the feeling of living in two worlds: the world-of-the-voices and the world-of-reality. They appear to be so similar that it is hard at times to draw a distinction, when she sees and hears people and things in the voice-world and also encounters them in the reality-world. This sows doubt and confusion. Did she, for example, actually put the magician in a bottle? That poster in the ward, the one with the magician in a bottle, is it real? Was it hung there especially for her? What should she do with the magician? What meaning does he have in her life? She knows that the relationship between the two worlds is significant but finds it difficult to answer these questions. Fatima and others construe a familiar symbol as a symptom of her condition.

In the next three chapters we examine the worlds of psychotic people, the ways in which they shape their experiences, and the 'things that are at hand' to give meaning and structure to their worlds. We gain insight into their evaluation of the world they must inhabit, measured against what they believe is, or ought to be. Lastly we attempt to deduce what should be done to reconcile the psychotic world with the world in which they must exist. My basis is the taped conversations between therapists and patients, my own evaluations of the aforesaid, conversations that I had with the patients, patient files, my observations and field notes.

Like the *bricoleur* whose work is discussed in relation to mythical thought by Lévi-Strauss, psychotic people have to turn back 'to an already existent set made up of tools and materials' (Lévi Strauss 1996: 18). They must discover what each of the tools and materials can signify in relation to their own experiences, but in doing so they are limited by the way in which society perceives images, stories, myths and symbols. This conventional use is restricted by virtue of its belonging to and drawing on another reality with a different meaning. Psychotic people are not able to find a way round this and go beyond the constraints imposed by others, or society. Part of the dilemma is that they have to create a bridge between the two worlds and yet maintain a satisfactory sense of 'self' in relation to others. Vincent is a chronically psychotic patient who makes this explicit distinction between 'my world' and 'your world'.

Conversations with Vincent

When we met, Vincent had been living in psychiatric hospitals for more than 20 years, virtually without a break. He shared a house in the LTR with his brother, who was also diagnosed as schizophrenic. Vincent, with his skinny frame, red hair and bad teeth, is a familiar figure inside and outside the hospital. There is no doubt that his stories and his personality charm both mental health workers and people in the city. A nurse pointed him out to me. 'He has beautiful stories; we can't follow him, but they are splendid,' said the nurse. 'You give him some money and he'll talk,' a social worker said jokingly. Initially, I did not appreciate the significance of these remarks. Vincent proved to be a man who had long before accosted me in the street to share his lucid view of the world, aeroplanes kilometres long aloft in the cosmos, the happiness to be found there and the unhappiness of this world. He agreed to a date for some talks with his therapist, a nurse and me. 'Vincent was not his usual talkative self,' said the therapist immediately after the conversation. 'It was not like other times,' the nurse agreed. There were no 'beautiful stories'. Vincent told me later, 'I wanted to make an impression of reasonableness.' The knowledge that his conversation was for research and the presence of a taperecorder had also subdued him. It was interesting to me that the staff members were amazed when he did not trot forth his usual 'beautiful stories'. These 'beautiful stories' play a dominant role in the conversations and in Vincent's life, however idiosyncratic they may have been thought by the staff.

Three types of religious conviction guided Vincent's cognitive representations: they all arose from his conflicting worlds, the world of the chronic psychiatric patient and the imaginary world ('my world'). The religious convictions differed in content, manner of representation and expression, and how effective they were in relation to their objective. Vincent's narratives about his life as chronic patient gave expression to values and norms, which in society were linked with the popular moral concepts of madness and normality (first type). These narratives were very limited. This limitation means that Vincent is certainly aware of the norms and values, but does not accept them without question. As a regulating principle in Vincent's objectives and choices, knowledge has a negative function. It belongs to the reality from which he must escape. Models of evil and badness play a role in this world, and they constitute an anti-goal in his life. His narrative about his inner world expresses a second type of religious belief in the form of a desire for social values such as harmony, peace, beauty and happiness. Compared with the first type of knowledge, they are unlimited and function as positive, regulating principles. They belong to the reality in which Vincent would like to live and hence influence his choices. Besides these two forms, there is a third category of convictions that expresses the values of success: this we can define as a conviction that with talent and the proper connections, one will move ahead successfully in society. Acting as a bridge of sorts between the first and the second echelons, the 'success model' is closely related to the second type of knowledge except that it embraces success as the ladder to heaven.

Vincent unites all of these views and types of knowledge in an unrestricted network of symbols, experiences, and ideas about himself. His distinctively woven network of meanings leads to highly personal goals and behavior. In his conversations, both the hidden and the revealed are important indications of the manner in which Vincent experiences his life in two conflicting worlds. When Victor and the health workers reveal and conceal, one finds the 'contextualization cues': intention and intonation, accentuation, feeling, tone, tempo, silences, hesitations, starting and stopping the conversation, metaphors, etc. In certain episodes of a conversation, his use of all of the above elements makes it clear that Vincent feels and expresses powerful associations.

'I am different'

Vincent as psychiatric patient

Beliefs regarding madness, together with convictions about evil, are examples of a model that serves as a forceful, negatively regulating principle. Popular models of abnormality in our society are less bound by medicine and the biomedical paradigm than one would expect on the basis of the extensive body of information available and the openness displayed towards psychiatric disorders.

People generally 'recognize' madness by character changes and unusual behavior. Often, madness is explained in terms of excessive pressure and being 'over-strained'. In the Middle Ages, lunacy dwelt in the realm of sin, and later it came to represent failure and an affront to rationality. The association for the patients was consequently shame and guilt. Although present-day psychiatric care seeks to liberate people from feelings of shame and guilt, the popular stigma still continues to link madness to personal guilt and personal failure (Goffman 1963a). To be sure, many consider the ideas entertained by psychotic people to be such sheer nonsense that they cannot possibly threaten society: behavior is the thing. People may think of psychotic behavior as embarrassing and bothersome, but as long as psychotic people behave properly and give no offence, they are tolerated, especially chronic psychotics. Evidently one must learn to be crazy in an acceptable way, and the real, shameful madness must be hidden. Some of these ideas and associations were to be found in Vincent's stories. They were introduced by the questions posed by the nurse and the therapist, while they sought to engage with the theme of Vincent's life in the hospital:

Bernard: (2) How long have you been psychiatric now?
Vincent: Let me peel this chocolate bar.
Bernard: Vincent?
Vincent: [*rustling paper*]
Bernard: How long have you been psychiatric now?
Vincent: [*rustling*]
Bernard: No, I'll put it differently. How long have you been here now?
Vincent: Twenty-one years.

Bernard evidently understands that the term 'psychiatric' has certain negative connotations for Vincent, who shows what he thinks of it by being silent or pretending to be occupied with something more worthwhile.

His way of conveying the feeling that something is amiss, Vincent's 'contextualization system' (Gumperz 1992: 238), consists of silences and deflecting maneuvers in his conversations. These indicators identify certain topics as important and provide a blueprint of how to interpret and relate them to background knowledge. From other conversations, it became clear that 'psychiatric' meant two things to Vincent: positive appreciation for the hospital because he could live, eat and sleep there, and an altogether more negative assessment where feelings of shame and inadequacy took over. Because Vincent had been in the hospital for a long time, he remembered the old institution run by nuns. He still referred to the hospital as a nunnery, a place where there is protection, where one can withdraw and find peace. Nurses turn it into an institution, he says. To the nurse, Vincent said: 'You nurses are strict'. He also feels threatened by the hospital as a place where 'odd things' happen and fighting occurs. This rather negative evaluation stems from his views about his disorder. At the time, he was overstrained and tired but there was no 'psychiatric illness'. In the early days of his residence, he had to 'come to terms with a lot of things'. He said he was unable to take care of himself, but 'maturity does not come until you are forty'. He heard about the psychiatric institution and 'went there to help. And I hung on there'. He remained because he 'took courses, to become mature, maybe'. The hospital appears to him to be a tolerant place, where he can do what he wants. His assessment was positive:

> That's allowed here, you know. Sleep as long as you want – that's healthy, they say . . . I can sleep as long as I want and eat when I want.

People do not seem to avoid Vincent, in fact they appear to be drawn to him. As Bernard, the psychiatric nurse tells him:

> But when I see you during the day, and in the evening and at night, the way you operate here on the grounds, you know, some of the cottages. Well, every-body knows Vincent and they laugh about you – I don't think that you are being ostracized.

However, he resists his position as a psychiatric patient. His strategy of trying to conceal his status suggests that he is aware that others will say that he is really a psychiatric patient, a failure. This sparks feelings of guilt and shame that arise from general beliefs regarding personal responsibility, self-help, etc. When Bernard did manage to bring the conversation round to the hospital, Vincent told me:

> I still haven't accomplished anything in the hospital . . . Society . . . I cannot get along with a single patient . . . Why not? I am too wild . . . I am different from the others.

Vincent's background can help explain his gripes. When he first arrived, he was indeed 'wild'. He would smash windows and kept breaking out of the ward to go wandering. His dossier contains a request from other patients for him to be transferred to another ward because he upset them. Vincent offered a very hazy account of his personal history. His feelings of inadequacy stemmed from his position as a patient at the time, and his financial dependence played an import-ant role. 'Five guilders per day is not much, is it?' Vincent received five guilders a day and was not allowed to control his own money. Not every patient placed such emphasis on his or her financial position, but Vincent mentioned money in each conversation. Some patients in the LTR tried to complement their pocket money with little deals; these activities could range from raising pigeons to repairing and selling second-hand bicycles. His preoccupation with his financial situation can be traced to his personal history. Once he reached adulthood, his parents pressed him to find work. He had a job and a girlfriend, but she (and her parents) felt that his job held little promise. He realized that others thought him inadequate and he blamed himself for this. When he was dismissed following problems at work, the engagement was broken and he took to wandering. Vincent sometimes offered this story as an explanation, but he had another explanation:

> I am not good at thinking. When people say: 'I don't think so', I think that I should not think. But surely, that is not normal. In my opinion this is because at one time I swallowed a penny. It still lodges in my lungs. Will it go away? 'I think so,' I said. Well, I hope so because it is not good to have a penny in your lungs.

In the above passage Vincent links his illness, his history and his special interest in money. There is another account of why money plays such an important role in Vincent's life in the last section of this chapter. His story, with variations, reflects a theme that is common among psychotic people in the hospital: failure in measuring up to certain success values, resistance to this and shame about being admitted to hospital as a psychotic patient. For most, the models of normality and abnormality have in the course of their illness become isolated as an entity which is at least superficially related to ideas about the self. This becomes clear because patients express their views in a few sentences. The ideas belong to the knowledge that Bakhtin (1981: 343) refers to as authoritative discourse: 'sharply demarcated, compact and inert . . . one must either totally affirm it, or totally reject it'. No doubt this leads to constraints in bridging the 'two worlds'. What emerged at Saint Anthony's was that for psychotic people the motivating power of the models of normality and abnormality depended on the situation. The patient texts showed that people were aware of the models, but instead of providing motivation to avoid abnormality, they seemed to have the opposite effect. There was both affirmation and rejection of ideas about normality and abnormality in the narratives of psychotic people, albeit more rejection than affirmation. Psychotics are immediately able to relate knowledge to other knowledge, as a *bricoleur* does.

The onset of psychosis and subsequent social consequences make psychotic people sensitive to inconsistencies and weakness in others, and they keenly appreciate the limitations of values and norms. Ultimately, this leads to all patients holding certain similar beliefs about the world, and their discourses show a tendency to judge not themselves, but others. Vincent:

> I wonder if I am not the devil. But in that case I am not an evil human being, and maybe God is evil. Because he died on the cross and suffered pain. That is not what life is for, to suffer pain. Life should be pleasant. Maybe I am fighting God.

This thought introduces a cognitive relationship between suffering and evil: suffering is evil; therefore God is evil. It reverses the more general view in which

God cannot be evil or be involved in evil. Other psychotic people adhere to the common view that God is good, the devil is evil: on this point Vincent's cognitive representations are unique. In the theories about life and the world advanced by psychotics, two complex concepts dominate: 'evil' as central theme and the 'evil of human beings' in the observed behavioral pattern of others. Both sets are well known, particularly in the Christian tradition that contrasts them with God and the good. Juxtaposing good and evil can help to reveal what people think about themselves and others. Holland and Quinn (1987: 11) call these complex concepts 'general-purpose models that are repeatedly incorporated into other cultural models developed for special purposes'. What is meant in both the metaphysical and the anthropological sense by 'evil' can be deduced from a conversation with the nurse, Bernard, in which Vincent emphasizes the importance of these concepts.

Vincent: Do you understand life, Bernard?
Bernard: What?
Vincent: What does life mean? Do you know?
Bernard: Well, not everything. But
Vincent: Shouldn't you know everything about life?
Vincent: I have seen so many ridiculous things. Fights and such and window smashing and such. Crazy things.

Human evil is evident to Vincent from the behavioral pattern that he encounters during his wanderings in the city and sometimes in the hospital. He is certainly well acquainted with window smashing. In excerpts from one of my conversations with him, Vincent reveals more:

They say: We only live once, and they walk around with a big jug of beer. Can you follow that? Whoever lives only once? When they die, they rot away, they say. Impossible, isn't it? Reincarnation? Nonsense, that is your world.

You see so many people and you ask yourself: Why do you see that? Why are they destroyed and not allowed to continue living? That's it, isn't it? Or do they all stay alive? No, that's not what life is, is it?

Vincent relates the random nature of destruction and carelessness of people to the theme of evil. He illustrates this in another (paraphrased) sketch where he reverses his earlier model of God and the devil, indicating how loosely the models are used. Depending on the situation in the conversation and the topic at hand, God changes from evil to good and vice versa:

God does not exist any more, because there are evil people. The devil has simply become a human. People often destroy themselves when they have been robbed blind.

He describes evil behavioral patterns in various ways in our conversation:

> I see photographs of myself from the past and I do not recognize myself. That is murder. Growing up is murder. All fathers of patients die. It is kind of childish to die. I feel the life of other people. I get a murky feeling in my body, because people creep under my thoughts. Everything I am saying now are thoughts which bad people instil in me. Sometimes my thoughts are sucked out of me. But in that way they learn nothing from me, because I know nothing. They keep saying: I do not think so, and when they say that it means for me that I do not think, that I just talk. I have been fighting bad people ever since my birth.

It is characteristic of Vincent's evil that it directs itself to him through others. He talks about it in general terms, but the appropriate behavioral patterns are personalized. This can explain his situation and his behavior. Specific experiences, like being unable to think or getting a murky feeling, become significant in this way. They are so intense that Vincent experiences the evil of others physically; it becomes part and parcel of his own body (Moyaert 1982a). In this way, the circle is closed and it can serve as a profile of an inner conflict caused by evil. In Vincent's discourse, this general model is incorporated into other models of evil. It is clear from the quotations and the paraphrase that concepts of nurture, fatherhood, sexuality and death are infused within this single model. There is another example in which evil resides in his very body:

> Nothing is dirtier than masturbating. It gives me a murky feeling; my skin disappears. Where does it go?

Vincent takes my hand, lets me feel the little bones and pretends to throw my skin away. He continues:

> All that is left is little bones. I do it three times a day. My father thrashed me when I did it the first time. But I have to keep doing it. The white stuff, you know it? You are a girl, so it doesn't bother you. But that stuff is dirty. You are not supposed to, it makes you rot, but I do it anyway.

Evil has taken a bodily form and lust is experienced as destructive, just like the people who 'creep under his thoughts'. Both induce the same murky feeling and in both cases something is shed: his thoughts, or flesh. The underlying models are greatly simplified and copied very precisely in a variety of experiences: at work, his former home situation, engagement, financial position, and his current situation as a psychiatric patient. This is a clear example of *bricolage* when the models are not used in their intended domains. Evil and human corruptions continue to reveal themselves to him even now. From our conversation:

They just say, eh, they all stand there refusing. When I enter they say 'dag' [which in Dutch can mean either 'good day' or 'goodbye']. In other words: just go away. I just come in and they say 'Dag', turn around and leave.

In his talk with Bernard, Vincent refers to the tactics of bartenders to make him feel unwelcome. He explains this in terms of his being different.

I have red hair and red people are exceptional. People say that I am crazy, maybe because of my red hair or something.

Here the concept of 'evil' human surfaces emerges again, with his body signifying abnormality. In terms of his own explanatory model, Vincent's being different provokes corruption in others. He knows that this is wrong but he cannot escape his own or other people's evil. In a sense, evil and corruption in the life of Vincent and other psychotics constitute an anti-goal (Shafer 1984), i.e. they are not objectives worth pursuing, and should if possible be avoided. At this level Vincent's masturbation could be viewed as the removal of corruption (sperm) from the body. For psychotic people, evil and corruption imply suffering, and via suffering corruption becomes a goal (Obeyesekere 1985). This can be seen in Vincent's remark that 'nothing is dirtier than masturbating' but 'I have to do it'.

The influence of others whether it is in terms of ideas, such practical matters as keeping Vincent away from the bar, or suggesting that someone is different or abnormal, impacts strongly on the lives of psychotic people, who readily assimilate these models. To Vincent and many others at Saint Anthony's, this was particularly true for concepts of abnormality: being different and evil. These were precisely the things that they noted in 'your world' and criticized most. By extension, being incorporated in a higher level objective, the 'anti-goal' helped you to see yourself as a good person, to live in a pure world.

Several models play a role in the discourse on life of a psychiatric patient, as indicated in the above description and analysis. Concepts of abnormality, evil and corruption reverberate vaguely in the conversations and are always discussed via other concepts. When concealing is indicated, possibly because the patient is feeling strong associations, these concepts tend to surface, but usually not before then.

Vincent in 'cosmos life'

In Vincent's life, abnormality, failure, evil, and the corrupt state of himself and others have an opposite effect. Therapists are surprised that this counterbalance receives very little mention. Cognitive relationships are established only by way of important verbal symbols (fame, money, death) in various passages. The fragments given below relate to fame. Together with the artist who worked on a hospital commission, Vincent has unveiled paintings. He was portrayed twice for the display and his pictures were placed on either side of a portrait of Jim Morrison, a famous rock star in the 1960s. Photographs of this event were taken for the regional newspaper. The therapist talked with Vincent about this event:

Johan: Maybe you can talk about the painting you unveiled last week? Or don't you consider that important right now?
Vincent: [*shrugs, eats a biscuit and drinks his coffee*] (27) I looked all right, didn't I?
Johan: What?
Vincent: I looked all right.
Johan: You looked fine. On the painting?
Vincent: Two times, no less.
Johan: Yes, and Jim Morrison in between?
Johan: You are used to being a public figure now, right?
Vincent: (3) Sure.
Johan: In the paper. You are going to be famous.
Vincent: (7) Sure. (7) Can I roll a cigarette, can I?

In this situation, it is the therapist who wants to discuss Vincent's world. But his unusual approach does not succeed and Vincent reverts to the behavior he displayed in the conversation with Bernard, the nurse. He remains silent, eats or rolls a cigarette. Yet, to Vincent, being famous is part of the model that bridges his two worlds, and fame is a counterpoint to evil. This becomes somewhat clearer in the following conversation, which is being videotaped. Vincent has indicated that he would not object if it were shown on television:

Vincent: Some people are ashamed to appear on their own video, aren't they?
Johan: Well: (3) yes.
Vincent: So they are given a piece of cloth to put on their face or so.
Johan: Yes. Hm.
Vincent: Just like in the Panorama or something. A murderer or something.
Johan: You do not compare yourself with that, do you?
Vincent: Not me.
Johan: No.
Vincent: I'm not like that. Thank goodness.

Here, Vincent opposes himself to evil. In texts from the dossier and during evaluation consultations, the 'other' world theme is more explicitly developed, The 'complex' of models described above is opposed by an equally involved complex of opposite models, such as normality (or even perfection), success and 'good'. This is expressed when Vincent talks with me about his life as a psychiatric patient:

Sometimes I think: I should be shorn bald and lie on the bed naked, until finally I have another shape . . . But life is not to suffer pain; it should be pleasant.

What I am striving for is to come to a standstill. Simply be myself. No other people interfering with you. That life is just pleasant.

I take care of people who show me kindness. The bad people are not allowed to see the kind persons. I have to keep them apart.

Counterbalance can be achieved in 'another shape', in pleasantness, and keeping good and bad people apart. The body, the self, and others are separated. To reach this state of apartness, according to Vincent, one should not strive for good in active ways, unlike the case with evil. Lying on a bed and standing still, lead to change. These thoughts echo a mixture of ideas current since the 1970s amongst young people which has been a goal for many: the subcultures of meditation; Bagwan, Hare Krishna, holism, pop, yoga, Zen, etc. For Vincent, the ethos of self-actualization in this subculture continues to be a motivating power:

I made myself; I created and developed myself. I come forth completely from myself and I have always been mature. But, well, you don't say things like that about yourself. You live because you are.

I live eternally. After all, you can easily become 200 years old. You say: I reincarnate. But I do not reincarnate. I disappear. The universe is infinite. Life goes on and on until the universe is full of pleasantness. My life will never end.

The goal of self-actualization is a narcissistic person, living without the restrictions of corporeality and mortality.

I want to become a cosmic man. Cosmos beings do not die. They have no anus. They are very clean and wear white clothing. They do have a pecker to pee with but they do not masturbate and they do not shit. They always stand like this [*Vincent places his hands over his genitals*]. I always stand like this [*he crosses his arms*].

Cosmos life is rough. You have to drink there until you feel good. You drink by the dram. You drink it in one gulp and it fits your mouth exactly. In life this does not happen. They drink beer and don't get to feel good.

All women should telescope together until ultimately there is just one woman.

In this part of Vincent's discourse certain aspects of good and evil are linked by comparing them and he judges himself in terms of the contrast between the two models. The body of a cosmic man is pure, devoid of corruption and devoid of excretory apparatus. It takes in just enough to feel good and what it consumes is pure, unlike beer. The white clothing is a conventional symbol of purity and ideals. Evil is in effect covered up, just as cosmic people modestly cover their genitals. The one woman remaining will be his. At the same time, Vincent compares himself to this cosmic man: 'I always stand like this', as if to indicate that he has not yet attained the state of purity. Evil still reaches out to him through the others in the pub and women, who make him aware of his body. This model, in which cognitive relationships are established between good fellowship, stillness, infinity, purity and a-sexuality creates motivation that differs substantially from the 'abnormality–evil–corruption' complex. The model is not strictly demarcated and no compact description of it occurs in any of Vincent's conversations or texts. His lofty ideals make this impossible. Vincent communicates his world piecemeal, by stopping someone in the street and pouring out his fantastic stories to him or her. Invariably, he ends with: 'Beautiful, isn't it?'

Merely excising the body's corruption cannot attain such beauty. There is a detour in the form of yet another model, partly based on the theme of fame that surfaced earlier in the conversation with the therapist. This model acts as a bridge between good and evil and is derived in part from the subculture referred to. The world of rock, its ideas and beliefs, and more specifically Jim Morrison and The Doors (Morrison's band), are a regulating principle through which to reach towards cosmic life. Intimations of this are present in the talk with his therapist:

Vincent: Do you suppose he is still alive, Jim Morrison, I mean?
Johan: No, he is dead.
Vincent: He is dead, isn't he? Yes, but I never found out that he was dead.
Johan: You didn't?
Vincent: Never. Does it hurt?
Johan: I don't know, Vincent. I never experienced it, did I?

In this fragment, death, eternity, and Jim Morrison are bound together in the text, side by side. The closeness of topics, without breaks, indicates that the topics are interrelated (Strauss 1992: 211). Vincent does not think of Jim Morrison as dead. He has not 'seen' it. He hears him, talks to him, sees him in a pub in town, and he (Vincent) is part of The Doors:

> I think that I am every one of The Doors. I am the fifth Doors. I play the saxophone, drums, guitar, everything, and my instruments travel by plane . . . Jim Morrison is a poet, a musician. Are there musicians in the world?

The ideals of Jim Morrison inspire and motivate Vincent. Fame, glitter, money, drinking, women, and music constitute for him a regulating principle, a success model that he wants to emulate:

> I dream that I own a big house, ten miles high, and I live in it with my woman. You can do anything there: play billiards, watch television, everything. I fly around the world in an aeroplane ten miles long, I go everywhere.

To Vincent, success is a condition of the good, which is in turn closely related to one's financial situation. His appreciation for money is ambivalent, yet he sees it as a prerequisite for success:

I know a girl, and if I had 5000 guilders she would come with me.

However, one should not earn money by 'the sweat of your brow'. As he sees it, working is 'pitiful':

[*Conversation with his therapist*]
Vincent: My sister has started a cafeteria.
Johan: Your sister?
Vincent: Sad, isn't it?
Johan: What do you mean?
Vincent: Sad, pitiful.
Johan: Pity, why?
Vincent: Well.
Johan: It's a way of earning money.
Vincent: Maybe. One potato is a bag full of chips, of course.
Johan: I don't know exactly, but I do know that generally those people make money. Hard work, earn a lot of money. Isn't that something for you?
Vincent: (2) Can I stay here?

Being industrious is 'pitiful', and it is also a swindle: 'One potato is a bag full of chips, of course'. Given his history, the trappings of the success model, symbolized by fame (and especially money), are important in shaping Vincent's self-respect. Financial preoccupation shapes his daily behavior.

'Isn't life too costly to get by without begging?'

The three types of models, or conditions of mind, propel Vincent to various actions. In the course of his illness, these actions have taken on a specific pattern. The pattern becomes clear in terms of his total discourse: the dossier, the conversations and consultations, his reflections. Vincent not only recounts his actions, he reflects on them and offers explanations. His success model is idiosyncratic but it includes aspects important in his society, such as being famous and having money. It is also linked to a number of symbols that are readily observed manifestations of the model. The symbols are those of the 'chauffeured limousine', a house full of servants and places of entertainment. Status symbols like these are way beyond the budget of a psychiatric patient. Nevertheless, Vincent is able to aspire to them every once in a while. He frequently 'goes to town', lets himself be driven home by taxi, and in the hospital there is a place for him where he can effortlessly eat, sleep and obtain all the medicine he needs.

In these symbols, a major part of the model complex comes together: success values, the psychiatric hospital, and his beliefs about the good in terms of 'good fellowship'. The question is: how can Vincent realize his goal? As he himself notes, his allowance is inadequate so he has to revert to cadging or overt begging to achieve his goals. He told me:

I have been begging ever since I was six. My father got angry when I once took some money from his wallet and ordered a taxi to Antwerp [costly, because it is some 40 kilometres distant]. Why did he have to get angry? He is my own father. You can't steal from your own father, can you?

I am not begging when I hold up my hand, am I? Begging means that you use a whining kind of voice: Will you give me some money? But I just ask for a quarter; I put that in the fruit machine.

At one time, I witnessed his begging first-hand. I quote from my diary:

Here comes Vincent. His red hair flashes in the wintry sun like a warning sign. Without knowing exactly why, I feel that something is about to happen. 'Hey!' Vincent shouts and with his long skinny legs he strides towards me, his hand stretched out before him. He laughs, baring his brown teeth. 'How are things? Where are you going?' he asks, shaking my hand. 'I'm going to work, Vincent.' 'Work? What are you working on? Are you going to write stories about the hospital? Well?' Vincent hops from one leg onto the other. 'Yes, that's what I am doing.' 'That's good, that's very good. Do you write all by yourself?' 'Yes, I do it by myself.' Vincent's hopping intensifies. He opens his mouth for a gulp of air. 'Hey, don't you have something for me? For a Coke? The other day you gave me something, but that's gone now. I'm not fussy: nickels, dimes, quarters. You'll get it back, you'll get it back. I will tell you another story. I pay you back. Please?' Vincent holds out his hand and looks at me, his head cocked. 'I'm thirsty, you know?' Vincent keeps talking, shifting his feet back and forth. Repeatedly, he closes his eyes, eyelids pressed together, and opens them wide again. With pursed lips he looks down at me. Feeling somewhat uncomfortable, I bring out my purse. I fall for it again. Hm, not much there. I upend my purse. 'I do not have much for you.' 'Doesn't matter, anything's all right.' And I shake out the nickels, dimes and quarters into his large hand. Why do I do it? He has me over a barrel. I am the victim of his 'Isn't-life-too-costly-to-get-by-without-begging' mentality. That's how he operates here in town. He immediately makes profuse excuses. 'You'll get it back. Did you mark down the date?' He leans into me and grins from ear to ear. That's how he operates in the city, that's how he shakes me down. 'Hey, thanks! You'll get it back!' With long strides he marches away, heading for the pub.

The taxi is an important status symbol to Vincent, rooted in his personal history. During his engagement, he and his fiancée used a taxi, with her parents footing the bill at first. Later, when the engagement was ended, Vincent's father paid the fare. When his father eventually refused to pay, Vincent resorted to begging, but people never gave him enough for a drink or a taxi ride. Vincent had to extend his resources and he did so by gambling.

[*Conversation with a nurse*]

Vincent:	(3) Five guilders per day is not much, is it.
Bernard:	Nah.
Vincent:	Four guilders just to ride the bus.
Bernard:	Right.
Vincent:	Yeah.
Bernard:	Yes, five guilders is not much. But I often see you getting into a taxicab like you own the thing. Taking a taxi. Who pays for that?
Vincent:	(2) Well, eh:::
Bernard:	Now you're laughing [*laughs*]. Don't you?
Vincent:	I guess I scrounged it together. A few guilders or something. I won them, or something.
Bernard:	Won them, how?
Vincent:	The fruit machine.
Bernard:	Oh, the fruit machine.
Vincent:	Yeah.
Bernard:	And you win something sometimes?
Vincent:	All told about 500 guilders a month, maybe.
Bernard:	Not bad.
Vincent:	Then I take a taxi or I buy cigarettes or pay for the cigarettes later.
Bernard:	I see.
Vincent:	Pay my bills in the pub.
Bernard:	Right.

Gambling and begging are not ends in themselves. They are aspects of the anti-goal. Vincent is aware of this, but emphasizes the necessity. He told me:

> My life is tough. I don't know if it exists. But life is too costly to get by without begging, isn't it?

During the period of my research, Vincent had another source of income:

Vincent:	I show my penis.
Els:	So?
Vincent:	They say I have to, and I get 40 guilders.
Els:	You don't have to if you don't want to, right?
Vincent:	Yes, I have to. Otherwise they beat me. A kind of rape when they beat me. They hit me so hard, it's like I'm inside a woman.
Vincent:	My hair is red and red people are special. So they want to see my prick with that red hair. That's something special for them. Trimmers and such do the same thing when they take a shower.
Els:	But, Vincent, that's not the same thing.
Vincent:	Yes it is. They walk around naked too.

When Vincent stresses the role of others in his helplessness, his negative tone and the reference to rape show that he knows this display of genitalia to be wrong. The proximity of topics in the conversation indicates that they are connected. Moreover, in the second quotation, he posits a cognitive relation with 'being different, being special'. Again, it is the proximity of the 'otherness' topic and exhibitionism that clarifies the relationship. Vincent shifts the accent here away from his own abnormality to the 'bad' actions of others: 'They do much the same thing'. His assertions arise from his ideas of what is abnormal and unavoidable. But money plays a role here because it permits him to achieve his ends. Whether he is begging, borrowing, gambling or colluding in exhibitionist display, Vincent is confronted by norms at work in society. His behavior is not tolerated and results in complaints by relatives, getting into fights in town, being made fun of, literally getting thrown out of pubs. This makes him aware of how others see him.

[*Suddenly, in the middle of his story during an evaluation consultation*]

Vincent: I should tell my woman all this. Are you my woman?

Els: No, I've already got somebody.

Vincent: Oh, but are you my woman?

Els: No. But I'll listen. Tell me.

Vincent: Well, when I tell my woman she falls asleep. She just sits in front of the stove with her red legs.

Els: I won't fall asleep. You have a girlfriend, then?

Vincent: Yes, X. She has a twin sister.

Els: Does she live here?

Vincent: No. I see her in town. She takes a currant gin from me and doesn't drink it. But then my money is gone and she no longer wants to. But if I had 5000 guilders she would come with me, she said. She is beautiful, one of twins. I want to tell her everything, but she won't listen.

It is not hard to surmise what happens in the pub. Vincent's dream collides painfully with abnormality, evil, and the limits others draw for him. 'Five thousand guilders' is the symbol of hope, but Vincent is quite aware that it will never materialize. However strong the motivating force of the success model, in these cases, the bridge toward the good is precarious. His is a 'tough life'. The pillars of the bridge are constructed of inadmissible behavior and taboos. If evil and being corrupt are the antithesis of desirable goals, Vincent suffers under the evil and corruption of others and despises them. At the same time, his own 'corruptness' is a repetition of his past,[1] and is explained in its terms. For more than 20 years now, Vincent has been begging and fighting. Success, if and when it comes, is temporary and short lived. It is clear from his self-deprecation that the repetitive pattern seems to have turned into an affirmation. Periodically, Vincent will sleep on the porch of some house in town.

[Conversation with the nurse]

Bernard: (3) You stay away nights sometimes, don't you?
Vincent: Eh, a day and a half or so.
Bernard: Aha. Where do you sleep then?
Vincent: In a building or something.
Bernard: In a squatter's place?
Vincent: No, no squatters. In eh . . . there's a little hall with a big mailbox for about 60 or 30 people, and then I enter and ring X. His name is X or something.
Bernard: Yes?
Vincent: And he gives me a blanket and plastic sheet or a piece of foam rubber or a piece of carton and I lie down by the mailbox.
Bernard: Yes?
Vincent: *[burps]* And they keep walking up and down. It's pretty inconvenient, but, well.

By sleeping next to the postbox of an old tenement house in the city like a garbage bag, and through socially unacceptable behavior like begging and exhibitionism, Vincent confirms what he believes others say of him. His life is filled with ambivalence, doubt, and complex opposing goals. In manifold ways, his thoughts and actions are influenced by models. Some of the models are filled with contradictions – good and evil, success and garbage; like the symbols of taxicab and tenement hallway. Nevertheless, one sees a kind of stubbornness in Vincent's attempts to attain success – his intermediate station on the way to the cosmos. Living as he does, Vincent encapsulates what is popularly expressed as chasing after success and fortune, and the battle between good and evil. He is an incarnation of modern consumer society. In studies on the motivational impact of models, it is frequently concluded that this influence derives from the conditions under which the model was learned (D'Andrade 1992: 227). These conditions can be summarized as follows:

1   The model must be linked to convincing and affect-loaded reward and punishment;
2   Attainment of a goal must be related to the self-image;
3   Successful attainment of the objective must be possible; and
4   The model renders the situation a natural and equitable one.

If these conditions are met, the motivational power is great. In Vincent's case most of these conditions are met, by and large, but the problem is that the chance of success is virtually nil. The question is why the models are such important motivators for Vincent. The ways in which the various views that he entertains are interrelated becomes clear by their close proximity in the texts. He veils with silence, sidetracks, and deflects important symbols in certain episodes in his narrative (e.g. money). The tone of his voice when he broaches a topic (e.g. his sister's cafeteria) reveals more of his thoughts than his actual words. This suggests cognitive relationships among topics. Two important elements in Vincent's persona are the motives of good and evil. During his long term of residence as a psychiatric patient, Vincent strove to attain the 'good'. This implied 'a different shape', the cosmic man, stripped of the desires that he designated as evil or a cause of evil.

Convinced of his values, he opposed them to others such as the people in the pub, the girl who does not want to go with him, the people who hit him, etc. His awareness of social judgment (I am different, I have red hair and therefore people consider me different) was a motivating force in his quest for his objective of achieving a transfiguration. His beliefs regarding success were an important stepping-stone toward good. For Vincent, these constituted the strongest motivation. In pursuing success he begged and exhibited himself, which were anathema to society. These activities showed how exceptionally important success values were to Vincent, but they also imply how corrupt people are, as he frequently asserted. Evil is an anti-goal.

Some analysts would explain the significance of models for a person in terms of a defense mechanism. This would imply that models of good and evil amount to the defense of Vincent's own feelings of inadequacy and internalized ideas of a social judgment passed on him. One could think of them as a defense against a personal, internal conflict. In that case, the objective would be to solve individual psychological problems. Begging, which has become a standard, can be understood as a ritual by means of which the need for success may be temporarily satisfied. However, it has no progressive effect, that is, it does not lead to enduring improvement of the situation. Rather, it is regressive and does not assist him to overcome his personal conflict; that conflict keeps repeating itself and keeps drawing him into difficulties.[2]

Another significant characteristic of the models, which have been incorporated into an idiosyncratic network, is their social nature. To Vincent the models are the objectives of his behavior, and they are very normal in his environment. He notes this himself with his 'we only live once' model; a conviction he shares with carnival entertainers in the province of Brabant. In that scenario Vincent can be appreciated in spite of his being different and the ill-gotten gains of begging, gambling, and exhibitionism provide him with social relationships. But he lacks alternative social institutions that can provide him with comparable satisfaction. Thus, social factors create the conditions under which models assume motivating influence and the forbidden means by which he seeks to attain his goal equally belong to the social factors. Others covertly commit what he does overtly. There is an injunction against people behaving publicly in this way because it poses a threat to society. He perceives double standards, and his visible transgressions mock this double morality, which brings him into conflict with others. His own behavior is viewed with the same sort of disdain which, judging from his discourse, he holds for some forms of behavior. Vincent exposes people's secrets and this is not the kind of thing that is likely to endear him to others.

Reality has two faces

Different types of knowledge guide the various cognitive representations. For psychotic people, knowledge arises in the distinction that they (and others) make between two worlds, referred to as 'my' world, 'your' world, or the 'sick' and 'healthy' parts. Experiences are organized around opposite poles, one being the oppositions of 'good' and 'bad'. It takes form in strongly contrasting models, as I show from Bert's texts. At the time of my study, Bert is a 37-year-old schizophrenic man, admitted for the eleventh time, for a short-term stay. His therapist describes Bert's talks with him as 'a confrontation with two worlds', and says he 'cannot understand what makes him tick'. There are clear indications in the interviews of the two worlds in which Bert lives. A fragment from a talk with therapist Sander:

Sander: (3) Can you be a little more specific about the feeling you have now?
Bert: Well, my feeling about life. How I feel now, myself, as I sit here. How I feel now with you. I experience that as nice. Next thing I've got to go down the stairs again, got to go to the commons.
Sander: Aha.
Bert: I've got to eat again, and all those things, they're too much for me really. I mean: you can really enjoy yourself quietly and I don't ever really have that. I don't know what that is (2) Being relaxed, unwind. I'm really awake day and night (7)
Sander: I'm trying to understand, you know?
Bert: Are you?

Bert's opposites are above and below, and upstairs and downstairs. Up is nice and he finds that he can talk there: 'When people talk to me, I sort of like that'. Rules apply below and he must adapt himself to the group in the ward. His tone reveals what he thinks of this 'upstairs' and 'downstairs' occur more often in Bert's texts. In his evaluation consultation he says:

> I am not lonely. My dreams, everything is perfect in them, beautiful, but when I come downstairs there is blackness.

When Bert is upstairs in his room, the world is a perfect dreamlike whole and we can gain insight into it by reading his meticulous diary. Downstairs is a negative experience, the daily humdrum, the rules, the other patients whom on one occasion he calls 'little children' and at times compares with animals at fodder. For Bert, 'upstairs' also means freedom, being alone, and surrender to the joy in nature. Downstairs means the future, a black hole.

> [*From evaluation consultation*]
> I have nothing, my future is nothing. I want to turn the gas on. I want dead; sometimes I smoke cigarettes and think: I wish I had cancer, I wouldn't care. It is nothing.

> For me, freedom is taking a bicycle, going to the woods, be one with nature. That's when I feel good, perfect. That's when I am happy. The water, lying in the sun, walking in the rain. That's perfect and happy.

Above and below gain further significance through this opposition:

> For me God is good. He always relents. People, on the one hand there is perfection in them, because they are the image of God, but on the other hand they are bad. A mess, and fights, all the time.

Above is good, and below is bad. Lakoff and Johnson (1980) call this an orienting metaphor; it gives spatial orientation to the concepts of good and bad. Here it combines the physical and social basis of Bert's experience, because the therapist's room and his own are above and the common room is below. They are social because Bert links 'above' to talks with others, or the absence of others. In the above connection, his statements must be taken at face value. Bert lives in these contrasts and his existence is an incessant seesaw between above and below, between good and bad. Every event, every encounter with others, all thought and behavior, are either good or bad, above or below. It is clear from the talks that the experiences of good and bad alternate rapidly, and there are no intermediate possibilities. This is also evident from texts in the diary. In these, Bert links to the oppositions of above – below, good – bad, which to him are models with strong motivating power. They generate the means with which he tries to attain his goals: to satisfy his longing for perfection and happiness, and to avoid evil.

> Medicines of the great country heal me of life and let me breathe freely in this room where all is love . . . the source has no name but is full of love . . . another word . . . we hit each other over the head with words . . . second-hand words and that is the end of many . . . new things are terrifying and pull the blindfold over the eyes . . . and death has two sides . . . the upward infinity and the sleep which has already taken hold of many . . . but there is still another kind of human . . . the dream human who arises and who washes himself in the light that bears him . . . this too is a bath and no human being has joined at it yet . . . it is new and always accessible for the eye that will see . . . but to reach it the little me which obviously is very weak must melt . . . dissolve like a drop in the ocean in the world of infinity . . . this world is not far away . . . you are suspended as it were in that web like a spider who also dissolves some day . . . everything dissolves itself into nothingness and all those who do not want to see this have never lived . . . every step namely is in God's works and to feel that is to glorify the true body in love . . . we need do nothing more than bathe in his light and to put on your coat lying ready for heaven is here and the door is always open for anyone who dares and wants to expose himself to the love which may be felt everywhere

... it is a poem ... a book on a journey and traveling to the end of existence ... this is serving God with heart and soul and only this provides satisfaction, knowing that you are never alone or left in the lurch ... no ... there certainly is power here but you don't see it ... but it is there and that is precisely the bliss ... knowing that you are carried in your life and that you can travel on wings through the country ready to receive all of us ... this land is called love ... or better it is nameless ... all is injunction and prohibition for the thinking and worrying member of the species ... here he is led by billboards and road markers ... but the original road has no name at all and would not want to hear it ... naming is a desire of trapped love and very confusing ... a child knows this and cries in its mother's skirts who has no time any more for the great happening a child knows ... and the expansive passion which this life has in itself is filled in and destroyed ... at least, it can go that way too ... fortunately there is a worldwide source from which all can draw and that causes relief for a deep sigh of world-weariness ... that seems almost impossible ... yet it happens ... it happened to me too ... but I pray and I will carry this prayer in my heart as long as it can still breathe ... the breath of life and not wish myself into destruction ... that is the other side of life ... the source the essence which turns itself away from the light, is the Satan who effects self-destruction and many are friends with Satan ... but even Satan may ask forgiveness ... he need not even ask it ... it will simply be given to him ... to live is to see that even ink makes an imprint impression on he who reads it ... and that words are really a symbolic understanding of life ... and that they really are thoughts of that is how it should be ... ink is a holy substance and with it you can make words out of nothing and which can lead to metaphor ... look at runic writing ... long ago there was no language ... growls and little sounds were language then ... but this human being has reached the stage that words are given back and forth because it makes for easy communication ... but it can have a blinding effect too and be dull ... that dullness now can be overcome through a self-made song ... and that is your finest task isn't it to accept your life singing ... and to know that the human who comes at you will also have to die and resign himself to this primal language ... and this is now the only exit from all problems ... and it is my weapon against impotence ... relief need not yet be relief ... if you only walk the light and do not challenge you die in your own ... no love should be shared and it is like a watering can ... that's how it works over withered flowers ... and only then you see that the garden was always barren ... at least as far as human beings are concerned ... not the true garden which grows and flowers ... and nobody can push the tree back in his seed ... you can chop him down and make cigarette paper of it and then hold the world with a box of tobacco.

This conglomeration of words, called 'free association' in the psychiatric literature, is written without punctuation to reinforce the impression that all the elements mentioned by Bert – water, love, flowers, the light, God, the nature of words, a source or spring, a book, and so on – possess the same qualities of meaning. The words are meant to keep Bert's world 'above' in check. They are magic, and generate an 'oceanic' feeling of complete submergence in the stream of the perfect. His symbolism regarding the mutual bond of these elements is quite clear, which in turn binds the world and the self together. This chain of associations is no wild product of contingent elements. The elements are cultural. Bert refers to conventional symbols used especially in the Christian tradition: the source, the water, the light, and the breath of life. Good and evil, too, are contrasted in a conventional way: God and Satan, God and man. As with other texts reflecting the thoughts of psychotic people, it is characteristic that Bert's cognitive representations have no stable structure. It appears that all knowledge that psychotic persons possess or gain is used to signify good and evil, and although the cognitive forms are related to each other they are forever changing.

As we see in the next chapter, the personal network of meaning of psychotic people is almost unrestricted, implying that all models can be linked to good or evil. All models can be the goal of action. Cognitive representations, moreover, have a double meaning. What is holy is both dull and blindingly radiant; death implies infinity but also sleep. In Bert's text, the contrast between good and evil is described as a dualistic world: the 'oceanic'/good and 'diurnal'/evil. Unlike Vincent, Bert does not perceive people as evil, but as victims of evil forces who may receive immediate forgiveness, even Satan. Like him, they are able to see the light. Bert is embroiled in a personal battle between good and evil and, as if this were not enough, he believes that he should 'witness to the light'. For this, he must go 'down':

[*Evaluation consultation*]
Bert: I have so many good things, which I could give to people, but it never comes to anything.
Els: Why is that, do you think?
Bert: Well, look, you enter somebody's private life and you have to be careful with that. When I pour somebody a cup of coffee, they take it, say nothing and drink it. I am looking for love so much, I want love, but where do you find it?

These expressions are not only a 'lament'; they also indicate that privacy can have an inhibiting effect, even though it is valued. Privacy is good and should be respected, but at the same time it prevents you from doing what you want and stands in the way of social intercourse. This illustration of the dichotomy of many cultural values is also evident in the psychotic world. That which is good can also be evil. The ambivalence of values and models redoubles the already 'doubled' world of psychotic people. The confrontations with the world as non-psychotic people know it are already rife with conflict. In the psychotic world/s, the oppositions prove to be irreconcilable. Because of his struggle for success,

Vincent is caught in a social conflict, as Bert is wrapped in inner conflict. Psychotic people experience these conflicts as proof of their theorem that the daily world is evil. This truth has its origin in the personal history and the negative image of the self that developed from it (Perry 1976). But, almost remarkably, this is not what the patients talk about. Psychotic people seldom refer to their history in terms of evil, and if they do, the text is very similar to institutional discourse. The standard by which they test their truth is how they experience the behavior of others before or during illness. This behavior repeatedly seems to affirm the veracity of the 'evil' model. The weekly experiences of Vincent, for example, in the city's entertainment center, being refused admission to pubs and coerced to exhibit his red pubic hair, constantly reaffirms his ideas about the badness of humans. Bert's views, on the other hand, are confirmed by daily life, rules, and regulations. He denies their value and experiences life below as chaos.

Psychotic people experience that they must continually mix with what they call 'the game' of evil. As Mary Douglas expresses this experience:

> Going into the world, mixing with corruption and sin, dirtying oneself with externals, have some trick with the despised forms, instead of worshipping the sacred mysteries of pure content.
>
> (Douglas 1982: 155)

The idiom used by psychotic people to describe their experiences is not only a reflection on experiences with others or perhaps a picture of an individual conflict. The text abrogates the relationship between psychotic people and others. Psychotic people play the role of observer in their own texts. Bert inwardly laughs at his fellow patients and calls them 'little children'. Another patient, Christiaan, a schizophrenic man from the long-term ward, 'looks at people passing by' and observes nothing but badness. By placing oneself in the role of observer and thus breaking the relationship between the self and others, one can evaluate the inadequacies and badness within society. The story of psychotic people becomes an ideological commentary in which inadequacies in others are unforgivable.

[*Evaluation consultation*]
Bert: Do you have children?
Els: Yes.
Bert: At least you have something to live for. Children are perfect; they are spontaneous. When I look at children it makes me happy. Do you sometimes quarrel with your children?
Els: Sometimes I do, of course. When I am very tired and irritable or if they are irritable. Then we irritate each other and that clashes, sometimes. That's natural. Or do you think it isn't?
Bert: You should not be irritated by children. They are really perfect.

The everyday world can be abhorrent to psychotic people. This dislike may be so strong that events in that world drive them to flight. Alongside this is the dreamlike 'world-of-the-good'. For Vincent this is 'cosmos life', for Bert it is 'above'. For other patients it may be paradise, nature, heaven, or eternal life. Living in this world, however, brings them into conflict with others and with themselves. As Bert told me:

> I think that my life is worse than that of for instance the therapist. Life has to be perfect and I am not perfect. That's why I am more evil.

The actions required to attain the goal of the good, unavoidably lead to disappointment. This is easy to see in Vincent's life. When he pulls down his trousers or begs, he does so in order to bask in 'success', but others find it embarrassing. Bert is equally disappointed. Others cannot understand it when he suddenly begins to laugh. The fact that he does not wash repels them. He does not wash himself because he washes 'in the light that bears [me]'.

Chapter 8

The precarious world of psychotic people

> In the widest worlds of vast wealth have I wandered,
> Caressed the most comely, least approachable breast,
> And fell soon thereafter, and sank, nearly dying
> Of sickness and sorrow, of hunger and thirst.
>
> J. Slauerhof, 'An Honest Watery Grave'[1]

Roderick has lived in an LTR apartment for some years now. Tall and skinny, he shuffles his way across the hospital grounds and quietly drinks his coffee in the coffee shop. He spends much of his time having warm baths and very rarely speaks. To the psychiatrist he says:

Roderick: Look, what I really want – maybe you know the Flash Gordon strip? Don't you?
Gerard: No.
Roderick: You don't know that one?
Gerard: No. [*laughs*]
Roderick: [*laughs*] What I want is just to live forever. That's what I want. I don't want to die; I want eternal life. And I just officially want to be an emperor. Emperor Ming. And I want my little palace here on the big lawn, on the hospital grounds.

Roderick is impressed with all the beautiful things in Emperor Ming's palace: 'At this moment I really want to be Emperor Ming.' He knows this is fantasy and complains that his fantasies 'get out of hand'. When this happens he loses control and cannot distinguish between reality and fantasy. Every one of his imaginings end badly, which leads to blind fear. 'From time to time I try to hold my fantasies in check. I try to prevent them from going bad, make them stop, you know, a fantasy like that.' When Roderick says that he wants to be Emperor Ming 'at this moment', it suggests that his identifying with the emperor is temporary and subject to change. Psychotic patients live in precarious worlds and this evanescence and vulnerability is found in most of them. In Roderick's life, Emperor Ming has replaced Baron von Munchhausen, who has in turn replaced Caligula or Tutankhamen. Roderick borrowed Emperor Ming from a comic strip he happened to see on somebody's table.

Patients incorporate things they chance on in day-to-day life into their fantasy worlds, which consist in part of incidental signifiers with a common basis. Where there is incorporation and borrowing, it is a clear example of *bricolage*. The inherent instability of this process can be explained in terms of the contradictory and irreconcilable worlds of psychotics. Opposing concepts take shape in formula-like representations, drawn from all kinds of models. For example, the opposition 'good–evil' has several derivatives, among them 'above–below', 'heaven–hell', 'God–Satan', and 'cosmos–world'. All of these generate goals that can only be achieved through action. However, the story is continually disrupted by inappropriate activities. As a consequence, a contrast emerges between the experiences of marginality/expulsion and centrality/divinity. The experience of being expelled or at best pushed out to the margins of society is encountered in social contacts; whereas in the imaginary world patients occupy a central position. This contrast is a constant source of aggravation for psychotic people. Because the psychotic world belongs to the realm of 'forbidden narratives' (Church 1995), and because these narratives fall outside the therapeutic language, they belong to the 'sick' part of the person. The effect, in turn, is that marginality and centrality contrast sharply and can never be reconciled. In this chapter I offer some of the solutions that psychotic people have conceived in order to communicate their experiences to others and to retain the credibility of their 'story'. Self-representations and presentations of relationships with others are important in this process, and for this I draw on different conversations, hospital files and my field notes.

Emperor Ming and the enemy

Self-presentations and confusing experiences

Roderick: But right now I'm Emperor Ming, you see.
Gerard: Sure.
Roderick: Life without end.
Gerard: Yes.
Roderick: Small palace on the hospital grounds.
Gerard: Right.
Roderick: I've seen the lawn, too. Every so often, I have many ideas. The lawn was marked with chalk. Our little palace would just fit there.
    Well, look. I feel nothing. I think. Look, those herbs, you know. I don't think it harms me. Eternal life? I don't think so. I sure want it. I don't think it's possible. Emperor Ming, that's utterly impossible. I think: I'll live in an institution until I die.

In Roderick's story, the self-representation – 'Now I am Emperor Ming' – ends up as makebelieve, straddling the desire and experience: 'I don't think it is possible'. 'Emperor Ming' and 'the institution' are painfully experienced oppositions. Various contexts serve to attain a psychic condition, which reaches far beyond the human (Perry 1976: 127). The theme of the king or hero is one of the most common images in a psychotic world. Roderick does not want to be only Emperor Ming; other kingly figures that transcend humanity will do as well. One encounters religious, political and mythical figures. In the idiom of religion, a psychotic may see himself as a prophet, a saint or God. In politics, this may be a king, a dictator or any other powerful personage. Mythical figures do battle with the enemy or with monsters. Often, psychotic people combine series of such personages, which change over the years. George Bush may displace the Napoleon prototype, but the basic principle remains more or less the same. The content of the image remains important because it tells others about the way people contend with their suffering.[2] In the following excerpt Roderick's observations are recorded, while Gerard simply encourages him with appropriate noises:

Roderick: I wonder if it is possible. That is really my dream, isn't it. Ming vases and Buddhas, wonderful. Because that's really life unending. I wonder about those herbs, whether it's possible. There are people who walk around with magic purses. Money comes out of them. So, I really don't know how these herbs work. Now and then I, you hear stories about magicians, about witches. I wonder if these things actually exist. I don't understand. Look, this Emperor Ming, that all very beautiful. Very Eastern. That's living in a palace on the hospital grounds. That is my ideal, isn't it?

Gerard: Yes. But are these all your fantasies, that you keep thinking up?

Roderick: Yes, I'm addicted to fantasizing. I mean, I really don't know what I want. I always have ideals. I used to imagine, for instance, that I am Caligula. With a palace. Mine, in Rome, in the city. Decadent old Rome. Sometimes I imagine I am Tutankhamen, sometimes that I am a Tsar. You understand? Other times I think of myself as a businessman, rich, living in Wassenaar. It is kind of fun. It goes on. It gave me a kick, fantasies to kick on, right? I don't really know what I want. But right now it's really Emperor Ming who I want to be.

Roderick calls himself Emperor Ming, a Chinese potentate who conquers his enemies in a comic strip. Caligula, Tutankhamen and the Tsar of Russia are political figures in whom power and divinity are combined. Each of them moves at the center of society and seems invincible. They create and maintain order, frequently by taking care of their adversaries with a flick of the wrist. A wealthy businessman from Wassenaar is less glorious, even though there are similarities with the others. The fact that most of them end up badly is essential to Roderick's story. The motive for the fantasy originates in the idea that a king or emperor is unique, endowed with the most valuable qualities a being can possess: immortality, divinity and omnipotence. The imagery helps to order and organize feelings and experiences, and it also enlivens the story. What significance this use of imagery may have in interaction with others presents more of a problem: i.e. the problem of staging the scenario. Illusions and impressions are assembled quite openly (Goffman 1967). Virtually no compromise is made. Roderick's only compromise is that he speaks of 'fantasies', indicating his awareness that his experiences are of another order. Often, such presentations are qualified by constructions[3] such as 'I think' or 'I thought' (Van Dongen 1991a). Such presentations have the effect of creating distance between the person and his mental constructions and reducing the distance between speaker and healer. However, as others could see it, outspokenly identifying with images of centrality, divinity and personages such as kings, emperors, gods and wealthy businessmen could inflate the experiences of psychotic people to unusual proportions, in which case the story loses its credibility. It is difficult to assess the emotional content of the experiences of psychotic people on the basis of these representations. The images may well function as a kind of self-identification, or compensate for perceptions of inadequacy, or a negative self-assessment. If this is the case, it is not the only significance that can be attached to the representations. Experiences always arise in a specific relationship to the surrounding world.

Feelings and emotions tell us about the world in a very vivid way. They will typically increase the activation of various schemes for action and evaluation, while still permitting delay, so that planning, goal sequencing, reappraisal and other complex procedures can occur (D'Andrade 1981: 191). 'Centrality', being at the center of the action, or omnipotence, are experiences that belong to the class of 'hypo-cognitions' (Levy 1984: 219) in Dutch society. There is a limited idiom for these emotional experiences, since Dutch people seem to have a propensity to 'act normal' (a much used saying in the Netherlands). This is a form of cognitive control in a culture of modesty and moderation, in which imagining that one is at the center of the universe and omnipotent is at most tolerated in very young children.[4] Thus, Roderick's feelings and experiences, and equally those of other psychotic patients, will be interpreted not as emotional experiences but as madness. The difficulty with Roderick's stories is not that they are told, but that they too often and too insistently predominate in his life. Roderick's stereotyped reproductions of feelings (I am Emperor Ming, Tutankhamen, Caligula) are considered impossible and exaggerated and so they can be interpreted as fantasies, symptoms of illness or compensatory mechanisms (Levy 1984: 219), rather than emotions.

Hypo-cognitions are always related to hidden and non-articulated knowledge (Sperber 1975). This knowledge plays a role in Roderick's presentations. The personages in his story meet a tragic end: the Emperor Ming is vanquished by Flash Gordon, who can fly like Superman. Caligula is murdered, as is the Tsar. Tutankhamen died when still very young. Roderick represents the universal moral of such stories, that people who wish to have superhuman powers invariably fail in the end. Roderick/Emperor Ming is indubitably headed for disaster. He told me:

> Sometimes I become afraid. That it's real, you know. That everything you think exists. Why do you think . . . if I imagine something I am afraid that it exists. And then I get scared.

Roderick's experiences illustrate the social sanctions on violating an injunction against specific emotional expressions: fear and threat. His story represents certain feelings; the cultural pressures that surround him and operate as a system of moral control influence this representation. Identifying with and personifying images of omnipotence and centrality lead to a process of paranoia. From the conversation with his therapist:

> One week, I was sitting in the common room in the hostel and it seemed as if a beam radiated from my head. As if the gods did that. Suddenly, radiation. I stopped fantasizing. And at a certain moment I nevertheless carried on with my fantasies, and a little later, well, I had hallucinations. I really thought that these people around me were gods. So, afterwards I have real fear that it . . . that it is no real hallucination. That they were real gods.

Ultimately this process, if not recognized or stopped in time, can lead to a perception of the self and the environment that is dominated by feelings of fear and being under threat. Roderick told me:

> I keep doing strange things. I wrote letters to the BVD [national security service] too. I ask them. I wrote the first letter to talk about my anxieties. The second letter, for instance I wrote them a letter, I tell them what kinds of ideas I have. The sort of thing I experience. But I know, I called them, they know of no letters of mine. At one point that was it, that was the third letter. I left it in my room for a while and it is gone. I wrote about my anxieties in that letter. And I suspect that patients in the house have stolen that letter. X, do you know X? Look, at some point X is dead, right? That gives me more of those strange ideas, that X died of fear, those letters, you know. Or that she killed herself out of fear. That's the sort of thing I think.

Fear and anxiety are not only personal experiences. The thought that they can be transmitted to others intensifies personal fear. Images that initially signify or produce feelings of desire, enjoyment and satisfaction turn into their opposites. At that point, psychotic people openly distance themselves from their stories: their experiences become 'strange', or 'odd'. Roderick says: 'I keep doing strange things'.

In the psychotic world, grandeur, centrality and omnipotence imply the irrevocable death of the patient's ego and loss of the other. When the world collapses, as frequently happens for psychotic people, feelings of anxiety, guilt, anger, shame and sorrow abound. There is a comprehensive vocabulary with which to express these feelings, which are recognized and acknowledged as genuine emotions. The emotions can be explained in terms of the Old Testament tradition, at the core of which is guilt and fear if the divine commandments are not obeyed. These representations are part of the hyper-cognitions: an elaborate system of naming, classification and dogma (Levy 1984). This is also true in psychiatric care, where anxiety is stressed as being the most threatening to psychotic people. This was one of the principal reasons for imposing a taboo on psychotic experiences at Saint Anthony's psychiatric hospital. Quelling this anxiety by means of drugs, but also by way of conversations, was invariably given priority.

Patients speak of emotional experiences such as anxiety, anger, sorrow and failure in possessive rather than active terms: 'I am' or 'I have' rather than 'I think'. Roderick told me:

> Right now too. I have medicines, but every so often I have horrible trouble. I have . . . for instance I have anxiety now. My head arches way back, completely cramped with anxiety. But I just know about myself that I am very ugly.

This use of language creates less emotional distance between the experience and the self than if the topics were desires. Remarkably, the vocabulary for these emotions and experiences was more varied than the vocabulary of centrality and omnipotence. In the latter one could discover a central theme, which was lacking in the former. Anything that presents itself in stories of social life may be used to describe and explain anxiety, shame or sorrow. Roderick described his fear of anti-psychotic drugs to the therapist, Gerard:

Gerard: And those ideas about poisoning, do you still have them? Or are they gone? You used to mention them. You thought that there might be something else in the syringe.

Roderick: Yes, I never have much pain, I have problems with my heart line. You know that, about the heart line? That has to do with health, and my heart line sits right at one of those forks. And I wonder, I used to wonder if that was full of poison. At a given, at a certain age. When it gets to where the lines fork, that I would maybe get cancer. You follow? That was because of my heart line. Sometimes I am really obsessed by my heart line. I had tetanus in my hands. Here [in the hospital] too. Because my penis just went dry. So I know it's all real. About that heart line.

In the above fragment, the source from which the signifiers were derived was palmistry. After the conversation, Roderick explained to me that he had seen signs in his hands. One of them was a broken heart line:

Two circles appeared in my heart line, and where the line forks something terrible will happen. An evil fate. I really believe that. I read a book about it and I saw it on television.

Vocabulary selections from the religious or related domains abound in the self-descriptions. When patients want to say 'I am filled with anxiety' or 'I am a failure', they revert to religious or alternative domains to find a ready-made terminology for their emotional experiences.

The self-representations of psychotic people embrace contrasting experiences. These include experiences of centrality, omnipotence and heroism, but also experiences of fear, failure and anxiety. Images and terminology from various domains are used to give linguistic expression to these contrasts. The terms must encompass both the uniqueness and divinity of people and their ephemeral nature. The mode of expression is not based on stable, fixed signifiers. Psychotic people are forever going back and forth between these experiences, which is why their self-presentations are filled with contrasts.

[From the consultation with the therapist]
Roderick: Sometimes I want to go back to society again. But I'm sure I won't make it. I want to, but I would not be able to cope. I'm all thumbs, that's how I was nurtured. People driving motorcars, I don't really understand how they do it. A miracle, really. That's really something. People do something, something simple, but for the life of me I don't see how it is possible. I'm all thumbs you see. I am truly helpless. And then I ask myself: am I just unlucky or lucky? I really don't know. I have no skills at all, yet here I am, in an institution. Society is closed to me, but you arranged for me to come here. That's lucky for me. Yet, I am not, I am here, in the institution, not in society, so I don't know if I'm lucky. Well, I know that I get treatment here. That's luck. I really don't know what I am, lucky or unlucky. Still, a lot of people help me; I don't need to do a thing. Normally, in ordinary society you have to manage everything yourself. You tell me you help me and I like that. But I don't know. Am I lucky or unlucky?

The text demonstrates the degree to which the world of psychotic people is composed of opposing dynamics. The way in which people describe themselves is strongly influenced by their moral framework,[5] and the pain to which psychotic people will be subjected by society to a considerable extent depends on what is forbidden or allowed in that society. In the final analysis, some superguy or other always manages to beat Emperor Ming. Representation of the self reveals a process that can be characterized as composing and decomposing images, of centrality and marginality. These experiences have many historical parallels. Thus, the central node of a society, as personified in kings, emperors or gods, is always witness to periods of disintegration, reconstruction and regeneration.

I want to focus on the imagery that contrasts with that of centrality and omnipotence. In 'Emperor Ming', we noted that the personifications ended dramatically: Roderick's fantasy ends in anxiety. This suggests linkage with cultural sanctions regarding feelings of centrality and omnipotence. One facet of a god or a king in society is the archetypal 'enemy', who has a corrective role when the individual's feelings of supremacy and self-adulation threaten to get out of hand. This 'correction' effected by the enemy belongs to the hidden area of culture as well as to psychotic experiences. The form that it takes is destruction. Girard (1978a) says a scapegoat mechanism is at work, and people will destroy the bearer of guilt. Where there is psychosis, however, people often destroy themselves. Thus, a psychotic person turns himself into a scapegoat. Psychoanalytic theories explain this process in terms of an unbalanced relationship with the image of omnipotence and centrality, originating in early childhood. It is said to derive from suppression of the subconscious and the patient's passivity in the mother–child relationship (cf Winnicott 1965). Patient fears of poisoning (one of the methods of dispatch in Emperor Ming), of being plotted against, of being spied upon or murdered – all of these can be related to personal histories. Since this automatically raises the question of fault or guilt attributed by some psychiatrists to patients' relatives, I will not pursue this issue here.[6] Instead, I focus on the cultural dimension of 'the enemy'.

Eric was diagnosed as schizophrenic and admitted to the hospital five years ago. He had previously resided in other psychiatric institutions, and his daily existence was ruled by two extremes: fear and euphoria. As documented in health sector reports, his life was characterized by a repetitive cycle of fear, lashing out, solitary confinement, unwinding, clowning, depression. A psychiatrist once compared Eric's stories to plays written by Ionesco. The main themes are sex, aggression and destruction. Eric differentiates and names the enemies more explicitly: spirits, voices, people, Hitler and women are full of animosity towards him. Eric does not often leave his room. He hears voices telling him not to leave because if he does, he will 'burn' out there. Even in the room, there is radiation to overcome him and murder him. People spy on him. Women seduce him and laugh at him. He is forbidden to eat, he told me:

> I eat very small portions of food which – which are given me at times. I have, under pretext of a faggot [*incomprehensible*] I have no purity at all ah . . . in dangers, you need something impure it seems.

Many psychotic people are convinced that antagonism brings impurity and blemishes into their lives and they reflect this in their stories. They often feel that someone is spying on them. Everything seems to relate to them, from the daily newspapers to programs on television. In this scenario, electrical sockets become listening devices, medicines are poison, and machines are regulating the lives of patients. It is all part of the devilish and secret actions of enemies who wish to destroy psychotic people.

Psychiatry's most important means of identifying psychotic disorders is reality testing. In psychiatric terms, a psychotic person's fear of destruction is explained in terms of loss of object relations. The loss can mean that the demands of the outside world cause cathexis and the withdrawal of the psychotic patient (Frosch 1983). The causes of the destruction are sought in the patient's history. They are not, according to Moyaert (1982b: 696), 'inscribed in the universal law of culture, which causes a breach in the immediate, natural and symbiotic mother–child relationship'.[7] This means that they do not conform to the symbolic order of language and may lack sense. Eric's expressions should be understood in terms of direct physical meaning. We may have overlooked the possibilities inherent in the ideas of psychotic people regarding the destructive activities of an enemy. These are part of a basic cultural theme that plays a role in (religious) ceremonies and modern metaphysics,[8] and helps to retain some kind of balance. As noted, centrality and omnipotence play an important role in psychotic experiences. These themes automatically evoke contrasting themes as well. God's antagonist is the devil; saintliness stands in opposition to aggression. Eric told me:

I have eternal life. And this eternal life I have is holy, too, since it surely goes together with . . . with an illness like fear of aggression.

The question is how psychotic people cope with this. Do they try to interrelate these contrasting experiences or do these forever remain irreconcilably (and unbearably) in opposition? Let us examine this briefly.

One of the themes implying reconciliation is the theme of sacrifice. Eva, a young woman with schizophrenia, constantly wrote letters to staff members in the hospital, to the people who work in the hospital's sewing shop, or to me. The excerpt below is from a letter to me:

And I think because I am Eva, that I am the smartest of all people, that I will be killed. I must die . . . I am a kind of sacrifice . . . the world has come to its end . . . Those who raised me made a kind of Christ figure of me. Abraham went to sacrifice his little boy, too, but God would not have it. Once I saw a motion picture in hot lands or of black people, and they threw their most beautiful women into the sea and they first lured the sharks with pebbles . . . (with a dog) I walked there on the beach and I wrote 'Eva' in the sand and the water washed it away again.

Eric in his conversation with a nurse confirmed that the world needed a blood sacrifice:

Eric: Yes but, according to me nowadays Christ, in these modern times, is something, um, a need . . . for a hemophil. You know what that is, a hemophil?

Nurse: Hemophil? No, I don't know what that is.
Eric: A bloodstain.

More than likely the blood he refers to is his own. A sacrifice in this sense always implies a solution to a crisis.[9] In the psychotic world it is part of a series of sacrifices that make it possible to switch from ego-centered centrality to a stance against antagonism.

A second theme is sexual transformation. A preoccupation of psychotic people, particularly schizophrenics, is their distrust of the opposite sex.[10] Whether this has to do with latent homosexual desires or not, it is clear that to a large extent this fear in psychotic people arises from experiences of being threatened by the power of the opposite sex. Eric, for instance, tells me this:

> In the profoundest misery of unravelment and anti-mystification you are in a cell and who answers you? Undoubtedly a woman . . . Or something female answers. . . . A secretive situation in which you are thrown in a cell, even by women, by female nurses . . . She makes remarks like, ah we cut his balls from his ass if he, ah, goes horny on me . . . because a woman moves towards the, ah, telltale moaning of the madman on the bed in isolation. That probably no one has experienced this, that he in the cell, when he has been slammed away, that what can be lost is stolen by women . . . For one part Holland is frog country, for another part it is fruit country [the Dutch pun contrasts kikker (frog) and flikker (fruit, homosexual)]. That's what I think. And whether they call me frog or fruit, I don't give a damn.

Transformation is both feared and desired. Eric continues:

> Then we go with all male . . . at some point from male to female . . . What it looks like? For when and at what age does a woman demystify a man? Well, hormones don't tell the story. No, for by the time you, ah, rebuild men with hormones, even if you dragged with it everything aggressive or kept it female . . . The other day I said: Suppose that in my body I have to become a woman. Well, you can request a hormone therapy to grow into a woman . . . Yes, I also think: They will fight with men again anyway.

To be sure, the inversion of the sexual identity of patients implies a frightening possibility, but it is also an emotional theme. The triad of emotion, sex and social control is inseparable in culture (Lutz 1990: 87). To speak of sex is to speak of power and emotion. This is clear from analytical and everyday concepts of emotion and its associations, as well as cultural manifestations such as transvestism[11] and recent medical techniques in the area of transsexuality (to which Eric refers). It is worth noting that psychotic patients discuss certain feelings in relation to the opposite sex. In the excerpt above, Eric talks about women in relation to aggression, while others relate misfortune to their own sexual identity without negative feelings towards the opposite sex. The man–woman theme is linked to the other oppositions of which the psychotic world is composed: it is an intrinsic part of it.

Subjectivity becomes clear in experimenting with good and evil, omnipotence and marginality. It reveals the tension between desire and the prohibited goal of desire. An important thesis of Freud was that people were always attempting to escape from time-bound and local cultural forms. Psychotic people evince this very clearly. Their self-representations are subjective, i.e. 'it is what bears the marks of the person's interaction with the world and seeks yet to erase them' (Rosenwald and Ochberg 1992: 8). As subjective accounts of experiences, self-representations imply an attempt to escape the cultural restrictions and, at the same time, a surrender to them. They imply both reduction to cultural forms and separation from them. Eva comments to the nurse:

Eva: Yes, you people are bad for me.
Nurse: Do you know something about that? About us?
Eva: Well, it's like this. You can see the world as a tower of Babel and, ah, the world has come to an end and now a new Adam and Eve come to the world.

When the nurse asked Eva why she was so afraid, she replied: 'You people are bad for me.' Pleased that Eva offered something concrete to continue the conversation, the nurse asked for more information. It turned out that when Eva said 'you people' she meant the entire world.

Apart from the opposing themes, the self-representations of psychotic people have a number of characteristic forms. These are (a) generalizations and theories, and (b) condensations or contractions. The two are closely related. The excerpt above is an example of generalization of subjective experiences, in order to protect the self. Psychotic people tend to place generalizations just before or just after expressions about themselves. Roderick does so when he tells me about his fear for his own fantasies:

At some point, I read something, you know. The fantasy of man, it begins good and ends bad. The fantasy of a woman begins good and ends bad. All fantasy is like that, really like that. Fantasies begin good, only they end bad. And once they end bad, I get fears.

Generalizations have a double effect. First, they constitute proof. Psychotic people create distance between themselves and their utterances. Subjective expressions are depersonalized. This depersonalization allows them to function as a point of reference for the experiences of people who are continually aware of their abnormality. The message to others is: 'You see, I read or heard this somewhere and hence it is true, or at least not as uncommon as you think'. Thus, they raise the truth content of the story and are meant to convince the other – the audience. Second, psychotic people place generalizations under a particular rule, because generalizations are almost immediately personalized again. The message then is: 'Look, I conform to the same laws as others do'.

Theories function in a way similar to generalizations. They create distance and raise the truth content because they provide the expression of psychotic patients with an objective character and 'objectify the subjectivity'. They differ from generalizations in that they do not fit people to a known rule; rather, a rule is created. Theories are intended to convince the hearer of the logic of the subjective world. Eric talks to me about the isolation cell in which he is harassed by women who steal from him 'that which can be lost'. To defend himself against this, he has been quite inventive:

> Only, I now have the perfect instrument, in view of my ah body temperature, which per erection rises some, you see. Locally: raise the heat ventilation a little. How to switch it on? And you switch the automatic heat control on the temperature regulator to ventilation, to make it cooler. Thus, that is to say, if the body temperature is 36.7 degrees centigrade and it would rise by one-tenth during erection, to 36.8, the fine-tuned automatic control will switch on even at these fine-tuned adjustments. And it is impossible to inseminate a woman, because the cooling begins.

Generalizations and theories are in fact representations of a score of cultural products, which generate truth regarding certain themes, and this in turn is the objective of action (cf Adams 1992). It is very much the same in the case of images of good and evil, centrality and enmity. Any cultural product that can be pressed into service to generate truth is taken up into the discourse, only to be discarded subsequently. This, by definition, is *bricolage*.

The discourse of psychotic people is also characterized by contraction. Rather than imagining, psychotic people meld events, constructions and stories together to talk about themselves. One could call this 'cultural nomadism'. A psychotic wanders from one cultural 'pasture' to another. Whatever he finds may be useful to describe his world. The excerpt below, from a man who suffered from a psychosis shortly before the conversation took place, illustrates this clearly. Events, objects, persons, natural phenomena and gods are mobilized to give expression to his story:

> I ah I made a complete picture of hist . . . , a complete scheme of how things fit together and so on . . . I saw God as sound, ah, sound and eternity and ah, sound, eternity. What's the third? . . . I had ah made a scheme and I divided it all up in eternity. I split it all into seasons, spring, summer, autumn and winter and ah, the devil dangled way below and as you looked at that way it looked like an eclipse of the sun. The moon stood between the sun, because the moon and the sun were involved, too . . . And I had made a complete scheme, but I can't recall it exactly anymore, how it all fit together. . . .

I counted: the lamps that were lit, I counted the lamps that were not lit and ah, ah, mostly I ended with three lamps. And ah, the trinity was extremely important and at some point I ended up with the number four. And then the number four became extremely important, because at that point Mary was involved with the divinities. And, and ah, I had the idea that God was in my mind and the holy spirit in my heart . . . With everything I saw, I saw the creator behind it, ah, in an ashtray for instance. I had bought an ashtray, ah, I don't remember exactly how much it cost, but I thought it very beautiful because obviously it was made by hand and I saw the Trinity in it, I saw . . . All that happened around me, it was as if all of it had to do with me. It was like a jigsaw puzzle. All I needed to do was pick up a piece and I knew exactly where it had to go . . . Space and with time and eternity and the sun and the moon and the Trinity, faith, hope and charity . . . And when I looked at the newspaper I always saw pieces that were immediately addressed to me as the feeling, I had the feeling as if . . . they were like a message to me. When I made a drawing I just drew circles. And that ah, they were ah, yes, I, kind of images of God. I, I involved a mirror in this, gravitation, Einstein . . . Without looking into them I have taken those books and I bought them and I came home with them and one, one was like a Bible to me. Everything in it, from the first page to the last say, ah, that, ah all had to do with me. And with smoking cigars. I suddenly started smoking cigars instead of cigarettes, because a, I saw a picture, a cigar picture and I saw that it was good and this and that.

The richest pastures will in time become barren flatlands, and just as a nomadic herdsman notes that he has to find new meadows, so eventually the psychotic will note from his social interaction that it is time to move on. There can be only fleeting satisfaction in a social domain where others expect nothing more than familiar models, with familiar connotations.

'I watch people passing by'

Alienation of worlds

Christiaan sits in a chair in the hall of the old building of the hospital. The large windows separate him from the outside world. He looks out over one of the busiest streets of the village. He sees the people passing by. From a conversation with a nurse:

Nurse: You often go for a walk outside, too, don't you?
Christiaan: Yes.
Nurse: Most of the time I see you sitting near the old reception desk.
Christaan: Yes, that's usually where I am.
Nurse: What do you do there?
Christiaan: Looking at the bicycles. Construction lorries drive me crazy.

Psychiatry views withdrawal from social contacts and isolation of the psychotic person as one of the most important aspects of psychotic disorders. According to DSM-IV, one of the phenomena of the early phases of schizophrenia is 'evident social separation or withdrawal' (APA 1994). The process is summed up in the term 'alienation', but this does not tell us much about the experiences of psychotic people and their social contacts. The question is whether alienation is something they feel, and how. Since patients present a range of reasons and explanations of their social behavior, I draw here on various accounts of how they experience relationships with others. Psychotic people see themselves as observers, occupying a marginal place in a world consisting of separation and involvement, an 'inside' and an 'outside'. The inside world is that of the hospital, and the outside world is society: both are very significant.

[STR, conversation with the therapist]
I often feel myself here more at home than among normal people. Yes, I don't mean to say that I am abnormal, but they don't understand that. They think it too much that I have help twice a week. They think that's laziness. They take you for a lazy woman.

People believe that due to the illness the self is placed outside of this world.[12] They feel themselves involuntarily cut off from the social environment.

[Marie, STR, conversation with therapist]
But well, just like the family, too. It seems as if they are afraid of it, I hardly ever see them. I do go with my husband, but I don't go shopping alone. I would not dare. Because I am here. Immediately people point at me, because everybody knows it. That I am here.

The exclusion results not only from the fear of being pointed at or treated as abnormal, but from fear of painful confrontation with one's personal life situation, and the desire to exclude oneself:

Ingrid: And I don't go visiting anywhere, either. For then I am always jealous. Not about the things . . . they have or things like that, but I can't stand it, I think: they are still married and they have children, and well; that's why I never go nowhere. (3)
Therapist: But you don't need to hear all those stories?
Ingrid: I don't need to hear all that and ah, (2) and they have been there and they have been there [*laughs*] and I don't have to hear those stories, then it doesn't bother me.
Therapist: Yes. (3) But you pay a price for that, of course?
Ingrid: What do you mean?
Therapist: If you don't visit there any more? You lose more people, friends?
Ingrid: Well, I don't have that many people any more.

Therapist: No. But well, there you are, you see. (3)
Ingrid: At first there was
Therapist: Your world keeps getting smaller.
Ingrid: Yes. (3)
Therapist: If you don't watch it.
Ingrid: Yes: (10), Yes, my world keeps getting smaller, yes. Sometimes I am afraid that I will be lonely (6) but actually it always goes like this, I do that nowadays, I always go to the Singles' Dance, you know. That's on Sunday evenings, I sort of like that. But Sunday afternoon, oh, then I think it's such a business, you know, before I am ready to go.
Therapist: Why?
Ingrid: (2) It's too much bother to go. But I am always happy once I have dressed. Then I think, then I always like it again.

When psychotic people withdraw from the outside world, they are often prompted by the inside world, the hospital, to try to maintain some sort of contact. In addition to their struggle to regain health in the STR, there is also the struggle to establish new contacts, since former social contacts may have been lost because of a divorce or job loss. Psychotic people invariably indicate their unwillingness and inability to do so: they are terribly tired and do not feel up to it. The relationship with the outside world is marked not only by feelings of marginality and rejection, but also by the desire for more contact and normal relationships. The desire is short-circuited by feelings of powerlessness and inability:

Therapist: Did you ever consider starting a new relationship again?
Ingrid: Now that's difficult (1). And sometimes I think that I could not cope with it, that's what I think of myself (5). Difficult (2).
Therapist: Uh, you can (2) make it come true, it's not easy of course, but the idea – you would in fact want to, I suppose?
Ingrid: The idea? Well, I think of myself that I cannot deal with it, funny, really (1) since I go to the Dancing for single people and there are plenty there, if you really want, but (3) I don't know (1). At the start you begin to compare them. Then I think: Yes.
Therapist: Aha.
Ingrid: But that's not how it works. It is all very difficult (6). So I think, what do I care about relationships? When I don't do anything, not even housekeeping?

A partner, then, is no longer something to look forward to, nor are children. Bert puts it in another way in his conversation with a nurse:

Bert: Well, in fact you walk around carrying divine seed in you. And where do you bring it?
Marleen: ??

Bert: To the grave? Sadly, yes. Well, I couldn't handle a child any more.
Marleen: Yes that's . . . a lot of responsibility. Hey, Bert, and ah, it is good to think carefully about that.
Bert: Sure is (3). No, I would not be able to, all that . . . the whole beginning again as child, becoming adult, if I had to go through all of that again. I don't think I could, the responsibility is too much.

Besides social contacts, a house and a job are important goals to patients:

Jeroen: Listen, I want to tell you something. When I can go to X [*family replacement home*], then I have to; I have to fill out applications for a house anyway. So, I . . . [*unclear*] I can't stay there forever, as I plan to.
Therapist: At the X you can live on your own, can't you?
Jeroen: Yes. As such, that is possible if I want.
Therapist: Yes
Jeroen: But I thought, ah, just, ah, take on a job as well. Seems better to me, so ah, with a job you can save for a motorcar. A lot easier than public transport to ride home to, ah, fill out applications for a house. Like, ah, well I do want to do it. Difficult to do nothing. Lot of problems, I think.

One gets the impression that for a meaningful life the house and especially a job are more important to Jeroen than social contact. Both imply the possibility of getting away from the inside world, the psychiatric hospital. In time, a job becomes increasingly less important in the life of patients, and some give up voluntary work. A year after his conversation with the therapist was recorded, Joris told me:

> All the jobs which I did at that time [when the conversations were originally taped], I no longer do. When I have set myself a goal and I come to criticize it, I attack my own goal. In the long run I found it to be a drag and that is not how I want to spend my life.

The patients in the STR, in particular, approach the inside and outside world with the same ambivalence. Inside just means a place in which a patient is one of many in a group:

Ingrid: Yes, they all have the same thing, I sometimes think. However, I guess it is also all different.
Therapist: You have something in common, say.
Ingrid: Yes (1). Yes, it is way out (2) Yes, that's the thing: (1) you don't have to feel ashamed. Not for anybody. You don't have to put on airs. (7)

In such a case the inside world compensates for the loss of contact in the outside world. The support offered by the hospital staff helps people to feel a degree of 'belonging'. Even so, social contact is often reduced to a minimum. Patients suddenly appear from nowhere and they equally suddenly disappear:

> *Diary entry:* In the common room. People are drinking coffee; staff and patients are in conversation with each other. Suddenly Eric barges in. 'Who calls me a heretic? Who calls me a heretic?' No answer, since nobody did. Eric goes back to his room.

To be taken into the hospital often implies a strengthening of feelings of marginality and a feeling of being coerced to social engagement. In that situation the hospital is part of the outside world. Joris told me:

> There is a chemist here whom I talk to and I learn something. The conversations of the others are always so inane. That bores me. Games and handicrafts, you can't fill your life with those. Things here are the death of your creativity. Every suggestion you make is shot down. The staffers are oriented to things like society, family, and rules – there is no room for anything else. But you have different brain waves at different times and, depending on that, you experience things differently too, and you are or are not active. Now then, if I want to be creative at night, because I can't sleep anyway, it is not allowed. When I was 'psychotic' I did much better really: I was no bother to anyone, I was very creative and tried to make something of my life; well, that's impossible here. If I want to develop myself or when I voice criticism I am psychotic. But that is nonsense.

Comments such as this show that psychotic people question values that are taken for granted by others. They realize how little room there is to be 'different', whether in the outside or even the inside world. Eva told the nurse:

> But you, but you ah, the staff is strict. I thought I would enter a world of love. Yes, people don't love me much any more.

Detachment is often crystallized through lack of activity. People stay in bed, withdraw to their room, listen to the radio or wander through the village for hours on end. In the common room they tend to pass the time drinking coffee and smoking in silence. But in the process, they 'work' very hard; either at their 'stillness' or the past. In the inside world psychotic people go through the motions on strict time schedules. In the STR, the therapies and household chores determine the order of the day. It is different in the LTR where therapy is not an obligation. People are at liberty to work in the garden, engage in a hobby, go to the sewing room, and so on. In the course of their stay people develop a fixed daily routine: a visit to the coffee shop, to the shopping center, a stroll through the village or dropping in at the café. These places are typically anonymous and social contact with the villagers remains restricted to a word of greeting and small talk about the weather. Often, people like Christiaan go to the outside world 'to watch people passing by'.

Dutch society values privacy, but detachment from the world still has negative connotations. This is not the case for psychotic patients. They orient themselves to the outside world or turn away from it for specific reasons and often have a very realistic 'understanding' of their marginality. Over the years the patients at Saint Anthony's have developed a particular way of life which enables them to cope with the various worlds described in this book. Christiaan is one. 'Inside' and 'outside' play an important role in his life. He said about himself:

> Imagine that I would rent an apartment to live in. Then I would, I think I would be back in the hospital in no time.

He describes himself as a timid and mild-mannered person:

> I do not talk with the staff much. You know, I find women very attractive, but I cannot approach them. If I make the effort, some other fellow beats me to it. The men here on the ward are noisy and they are always first in line. I don't ask them to move aside because it is my turn. Because if I do, they kick up a fuss or get angry and I am not looking for a quarrel.

His vulnerability is the reason why he withdraws, both 'inside' and 'outside'.

Christiaan: On the ward? Yes, well, I am sitting here and ah, X comes in, comes in dancing. (3) Sometimes starts cursing at me for no reason, and Z, she comes in, talking to herself, about me too (5). And then I sit there, and soon I go outside. It is like that, isn't it? (3)

Therapist: You go outside because you want to escape it all?

Christiaan: Yes::: (2) On the ward they all needle me. And when a nurse or an assistant comes in (2) and they, they, I don't think they do it on purpose at that moment. (10) [*drinking coffee*]. I::feel like crying. That's not hard here on the ward. O yes, just like something is moving your soul, I think that ah, I should be able to save my soul. (4)

Therapist: And, to save your soul, you go outside?

Christiaan: I go outside then, yes.

Therapist: Outside you have less difficulty than inside, on the ward?

Christiaan: Outside is less difficult, yes.

Therapist: But what difference does it make, inside or outside?

Christiaan: Outside, ah . . . I meet people at a distance, that's outside, well, you have to keep yourself in hand there too. But it gives me more room to think. (3) On the ward ah . . . yes, things are confined there.

	So, there you can't, you can't think any more. Their jabber keeps intruding.
Therapist:	Aha. But if you are alone, in your room? Does that make a difference?
Christiaan:	Yes. (3) But then P comes in and asks for a cigarette, and he hangs around and, ah, yes, I can't chase him out (4) and ah. . . . They start talking at the top of their voices downstairs, so that I can hear it upstairs. (4)
Therapist:	You hear the noise from downstairs?
Christian:	A lot of noise down below.
Therapist:	And that bothers you too?
Christiaan:	I ah . . . (3) yes, it's all about me.
Therapist:	Aha (3). They do that to needle you?
Christiaan:	It looks that way. Maybe it isn't, but it seems that way.

Christiaan has been suffering from attacks by the devil,[13] who has forbidden him to socialize for more than 20 years now. His fellow patients are the devil's accomplices and get in the way of his salvation. To save his soul Christiaan must spend his life in isolation. This loneliness he finds 'outside' in the street, where people remain at a distance from him. This evokes associations with other prophets who find solace, for example, Christ's sojourn in the desert (see Matthew 4: 1–11). However, for Christiaan 'outside' offers only detachment, no solace or salvation. When he finds the loneliness unbearable, Christiaan goes back 'inside' and seeks contact there. But this merely leads to disappointment, or it blocks his thinking. Consequently, the inside world keeps him away from that which for him signifies the good: 'They talk to me, but they say nothing that is of relevance to me.'

The movement between 'inside' and 'outside' is ritualized, and he keeps a strict timetable. He spends 24 hours in his room, where he sleeps, listens to the radio and reflects. Then, he will spend the next 24 hours in the 'outside' world. When he is outside he might stroll into the activity center to drink coffee. He has no inclination to engage in activities: 'In my opinion nobody wants to work'. Mostly he sits at the 'old reception' and looks at the world. The closed windows protect him from the sounds of traffic, especially automobiles, which are noisy on purpose 'to pester me'. Christiaan's strict regimen is of symbolic value to him: it saves his soul.

In Roderick's case, fleeting contacts outside have a magical significance, since they imply that he can manipulate the outside world. Roderick wants to visit a prostitute to overcome his propensity for non-stop walking:

Roderick:	What I think about that prostitute, I think maybe it has to do with sex, all that walking. I hope that when I go to a prostitute, first of all I just want to know what it is like, and I hope that it stops me from walking, too.

Gerard:	Aha. (3) The walking is because you are restless?
Roderick:	Yes, maybe it is sexual.
Gerard:	That it has to do with sex?
Roderick:	Yes. I wonder about that.
Gerard:	Yes. (4) But, if that turns out poorly or disappointing? How will you react to that? That's possible too, of course.
Roderick:	Yes.
Gerard:	It might be a disappointment.
Roderick:	Yes, I don't have that much trouble with my addiction to walking. It doesn't really bother me.
Gerard:	Nooo . . . but I mean going to that prostitute, if that does not measure up, if that is not what you expected of it? (2) If that turns out disappointing?
Roderick:	I know, that prostitute, that's once only. I don't suppose that in my life I would merit a prostitute. I just can't cope with it. I am addicted to walking, addicted to fantasies.

Roderick (continued):

What I know about myself is that I am horribly ugly. So I can forget about a girlfriend. But I do not really need one that much, either. So, I hope that a prostitute – you hear all kinds of stories about prostitutes; prostitutes who bore their clients, prostitutes who are terribly cynical.

I hope that I, ah, that I am not impotent, I hope so. And I just want to know how it is, you know. Look, I am just a loner. I don't really need a girlfriend.

The self-imposed spell is ritualized. His therapist calls it an 'initiation rite'. The therapist and Roderick's personal supervisor are drawn into the quest for Roderick's 'deflowering' (as he calls it). They are supposed to make the arrangements: time, place and costs. Frequently, the imaginary world and the social worlds inside and outside overlap. According to Gerard the experience with the prostitute will fit into Roderick's fantasies:

He has the feeling that he is not mature yet. He wants to be deflowered. Afterwards, sexuality will be more tangible to him and he will be able to include constructions of it in his fantasies.

This sort of overlap or intermeshing happens quite often. In Chapter 6, Vincent sought to manipulate the outside world to meet his needs. This may involve conflict: Vincent showed how imaginary (social) contacts had an important bearing on 'genuine' contacts. This is probably true of Roderick. He says:

Look, this is my plan. First I want to go to that prostitute. Then I will go to that lady, the mind reader. I will actually ask her how that works with those herbs, you know. I will ask her if it is possible. That's really my dream, isn't it?

Strong involvement with imaginary social relationships in hallucinations has important effects on actual relationships. Eric sometimes lives in a world in which Hitler, a third world war and nuclear bombs are major themes. His brother-in-law who has a Jewish background visits him periodically, but since he tends to call him Hitler these visits are reduced to a minimum. Imagined social relationships can replace existing relationships. Christiaan experiences the inside world as threatening, but the people of this world reappear in his thoughts as puppets which are exact copies of fellow patients:

> They are people whom I know [he gives names of fellow patients]. They talk to me and drink coffee with me. You know, I have no friends. I am lonely and always alone and these puppets are my company. They take walks with me and we sit together. I really see them right in front of me.

Christiaan is aware that the puppets are substitutes. He tells his therapist:

> I know very well that this is abnormal.

There are times when psychotic patients consciously withdraw, because their emotions and experiences are so strong that they sense an impending bad spell, and withdrawal is the only solution. Marian, a schizophrenic woman in the LTR, told me:

> To have thoughts of murder . . . I really thought: Now I will kill somebody. And then you keep on thinking: I'll kill you, I'll kill you, I'll kill you. I can't escape it; all I can do is lie down.

Corin (1990) calls this 'positive withdrawal', a pattern of behavior that has strong linkages with social norms. Marian fears her thoughts and finds them repulsive ('Thou shalt not kill'). Her only alternative is to lie down and 'wait for it to pass'.

Psychotic people tend to have few concrete social relationships – 'the world becomes smaller and smaller' – but they need not always feel alienated from their environment. In such cases their involvement with the world is normative. One person who experiences the world in this way is Rob, a 45-year-old schizophrenic patient who entered the hospital eight years ago. Prior to that he lived intermittently at other institutions. About himself he wrote: 'Nil volentibus arduum' (ordinary latin for 'I am no genius'). The relationship with his mother was a symbiotic *folie à deux* (APA 1987: 297, 30; shared paranoid disorder). When she died he entered a crisis and was taken in, permanently as it seems. His dossier refers to a loss of social contacts due to aggressive, explosive and unpredictable behavior. Accordingly, Rob is careful about what he does. If he has been reading too long, he will become 'chaotic' and he might react violently towards others:

But I have to take care that I do not get overwrought, in my head, or that I read too much, for then I have to rearrange too much, reorganize things and so on, and I am very poor at that. That's possible too, isn't it. You get chaotic because of all things in your head and so? Yes, on the one hand [*muttering*], I think, ah, I get it and so on and, ah::: [*sigh*] (3) it sure categorizes you.

To break the daily routine Rob goes for walks, swims and plays badminton. These activities involve few others and he does not participate in common activities in the ward. He is given to staying in his room, listening to the radio, or playing computer chess. He lives in a dream world with music, birds and the sun as his inspiration.

[*From a conversation with the therapist*]

Rob: I just experienced . . . a week ago we had fine weather, didn't we, Jochem? And I sat in the garden, bare-assed and [. . .] I got quite a tan and so. But immediately I associate a raft, a ship or so, where you are sitting with four people. And, ah, a dead fish floats by, sometimes you can lift him out, then you, then you have a hold of a fish and so, ah, just to avoid going crazy altogether, you know. Well, and . . .

Jochem: Those are the things you think about when you are sitting in the garden?

Rob: Yes, when I get hot and when I'm having a difficult time and so on.

Jochem: In the sun?

Rob: When I get very warm, I ah, I am a warm-blooded person by nature, sure, but ah . . . everything went so strange in those years and ah, I think about that when I am warm, sitting in the garden like that and I get a tan that makes me look like a nigger, so to speak, and then ah, I think that I am on a raft with the four of us [*sniffs*] and then ah, crossing the ocean, and I no longer see the grass. The grass looks blue to me then. Well, these are the things that stay with me, Jochem. It gives me a reason to struggle on.

Dreams take on great importance because in his dreams Rob seeks to work out conflicting events and sad encounters with others. When a niece of his dies he has the feeling that he is removed from this occurrence; via his dreams he seeks to heal his wounds and those of others. In this way he moves into 'a time which knows no pain':

But, because ah: (4) via another ah: another example I came back again in this newer day and age, and this is really a time, ah, of no pain and I can explain that like this: ah:: ah:: my ah:: brother-in-law and my eldest sister got a baby and that ah, after ah: it lived only a few months in an incubator and then it died. I attended there, the funeral service; I devoted a few dreams to it. And they just let it all happen, just like that. It involves me too, because it isn't there any more and so on, so it died then and ah: that's why I say, ah, I live and I live in a new age again, because I gave away music to her and ah, dreams and so on – they were mo-modern and so on.

Most psychotic people long for 'a time which knows no pain'.[14] To Rob, the world of dreams is without pain and 'a reason to struggle on'. To others, living in a dream world or some other imaginary world often implies a lack of interest in social contacts, because these contacts are likely to disrupt the world of dreams. Psychotic people do not perceive themselves as uninterested in others or as being without contacts, since their imaginary world is usually a social one. Rob describes himself as follows:

> But for myself I can tell you that I ah, ah:: ah, I am certainly a person with social feeling and so on, and ah, ah: How should I say it? I ah: am rather impulsive and so on, I am that. [. . .] I also have, I have, ah, I just can't save myself. That's very strange, I can save other people, but myself I cannot save. At the moment I believe now, now that I saved X, ah, from total::: destruction, that I come to life again myself, too. That happened this morning. X got uh very angry with me. He says: I'll bust your brains and ah::: you won't survive it, see. Then I said: X, what happened? And ah::: you won't survive or something. Well, and I told him, ah:: I gave him:: a:: good feeling inside, ah:: that he was kind of courageous to:: ah humble, ah, and that went all right and so on, and now I got that off my chest and that gives me new possibilities inside.

Social involvement plays an important role in the stories told by psychotic people. Rob is telling us that he helped a fellow patient to overcome a difficult time. He brushed his threats aside, and gave the man 'a good feeling'. By this action he creates an image of himself as popular, or a least useful. Sometimes psychotic pepole picture themselves as 'social cynosures' (Gaines and Farmer 1986); people whose suffering is a source of good for others.

Rob: Even if X or Y are sometimes angry or something. They have gone through a lot. I have gone through a lot, too. I think of them as friends and that's why I am willing to give them a part of me, and so on.

Social involvement and detachment are intermeshed in the discourse of psychotic people. They recount how they 'save' others or cheer them up; how others ask for help and how they explain the supplicant's problem. This apparent contradiction is explained by Corin (1990), who describes how a religious idiom helps people to protect their detachment from the world, how to strengthen and value it. The biblically based idiom helps them to be 'in the world but not of it', and helps to justify their distance from socially approved activities such as work.

Corin shows how 'marginal' religious groups play a role in the life of schizophrenic people, especially in the area of detachment.

In the discourse of the people in this book, the reader encounters little or no religious idiom in relation to detachment, even though almost all of the patients are of a religious (mostly Roman Catholic) background. In this setting, justification, protection, valuation and strengthening comprise mixed vocabularies. Some patients are or have been members of the Pentecostal Congregation, and in their idiom there is no attempt to defend detachment: rather, social engagement must be justified. A schizophrenic man from the STR told me:

> I had the idea that I was some kind of prophet, a Messiah, because God was within me, I felt that . . . I went there [to the Pentecostals]. Before then I never really believed that Jesus was the Son of God. I could not really call myself a Christian . . . and, ah, well, I went there and I, it was a kind of happening. I ah, that we . . . that worship service there, those people who started to sing, to sing psalms and ah with their hands raised and, yes, it was a kind of release for me, and those psalms that were projected on an overhead projector, that was projected on a screen and ah,: From that moment on I most truly believed in the existence of Christ, that Christ was the Son of God . . . I think so now that ah and, and yes, I had the feeling as if it were so. And ah, I left when the service was over. I had a cup of coffee with, and those people among themselves, yes: that was, yes very strange. They all were, seemed each other's friends, everybody talking to everybody else and the funny thing was, nobody coughed or cleared their throat during the worship service . . . And there [in Snouck's Almanac] in the back was an order form and suddenly I wanted 12 books, I wanted, ah, 12 books of each series, buy them, because ah, yes I had to, I looked for 12 apostles together. Because, ah, to witness, I wanted to spread the word of God, without, when people did, only when people asked for it. In that case I ah, was willing to talk about it; I would not begin myself, I did not want to convert people.

In this way a religious framework becomes a regulating principle. Groups such as the Pentecostals mediate a reordering of the social world of psychotic people. As a rule, this does not lead to concrete social relationships but it does encourage a feeling of 'belonging'. Moreover, the propagation of religious ideas enables people – as they experience it – to establish contacts outside of the group as such.

In summary, the presentations of social relationships in the discourse of psychotic people are characterized by themes such as 'inside' and 'outside' worlds, and by processes of detachment and involvement. The experiences in these areas are interwoven with the way in which psychotic people experience themselves. There is a close link with experiences of centrality/omnipotence and social engagement and, conversely, with marginality/fall and detachment. As with discourse about the self, relations with others are presented in ways which to others do not seem to accord with what they observe. For this reason the discourse is frequently disrupted. The words used by psychotic people are evaluative in a specific sense. They represent a valuation of their own experience of emotional response. They also represent a valuation of the values and norms in society. The apparent truth of (conventional) values and norms and their evident inadequacy in life becomes most clear in the discourse about centrality, marginality, involvement and detachment. Values such as individuality seem to promote self-realization and freedom, but in fact they imply uniformity. The tactics used by psychotic people to give meaning to their experiences are fragile, vulnerable and nomadic, shuttling back and forth between extremes.

Chapter 9

Life and death

It is Death – alas! – that consoles, and gives life
It is the aim of life, and the only hope
That, like an elixir, lifts and revives us
And gives us heart to go on until evening.[1]

It seems as if it is all empty now, all one. It seems as if I am all empty now. I hardly talk these days. I've become very quiet . . . I don't have much fun . . . There is nothing to make me laugh . . . Yes, and uh, existence is uh dreary. Each day like the next . . . Just sitting there and smoking and thoughtless staring . . . All of them lost days, really. In fact, I am a lost soul, really.

In his lament, Rob contrasts his emptiness with the fullness of before. To him, fullness meant talking, laughing and variety. His present emptiness equates with thoughtless, dreary, lost days. These experiences of a body no longer alive, of aimless wandering and silence, often come out in the discourses of psychotic people. The most compelling and emotional theme is death and the experience of the body. For psychotic people, death means emptiness and hopelessness. Sadger (1929) encapsulates the feelings of the patients when he writes that no one who has not entirely given up the hope of being loved will take his or her own life. Therapists and nurses often encounter these symptoms of the illness: feelings of desolation and a death wish. Apart from being threatening and confrontational, these experiences are filled with ambivalence for both the patient and the health team (cf Van Dongen 1998). In this chapter, I describe such experiences as related to therapists, nurses and myself.

'Every psychotic transformation is a longing, leading to death,' writes Podvoll (1990). When people emerge from a psychosis, certainly if it was a violent crisis, they feel that their life and body have fallen apart. They often encounter evidence of destruction beyond repair in their own lives and those of others. The world within and around them is fragmented and the frequent response is, as Eva said, 'I want [to be] dead, I want a happy end.' Death becomes the comforter and liberator.

Since most patients do not in fact die, a struggle ensues in which they become the arena where different sensations are locked in battle: of centrality and omnipotence, of meaninglessness, destruction and being on the periphery of life. It is a struggle between the desire to live and the longing for death. In conversation, psychotic people place life and death alongside and in opposition to each other. In their stories and waking hours, the death wish is a constant theme. Psychotic people move back and forth between experiences of life and death, just as they alternate between good and evil or omnipotence and powerlessness. It brings to mind Freud's theory that as a counterpoint to the pleasure principle, the *thanatos* instinct is intent on reverting to the original inanimate condition. The death wish expresses itself in compulsive repetition,[2] a theory that can also be applied to a life story or a discourse on self-experience. Normally, every story aims at its conclusion. Brooks (1984) interprets Freud's *thanatos* instinct theory as the dénouement of every story. The death wish moves towards the conclusion, by way of repetition, in each one. The life story has to be told time after time, and repetition only delays the ultimate ending. Accordingly, there is a homology between psychological mechanisms and stories.

Rather than elaborate on human drives and instincts, I focus in this section on models of life and of death as the *leading principles*. There need not be a contradiction between the drives and goals people set themselves. In life, the relationships between drives and goals are far more complex than would appear at first sight. Shweder (1991: 54) says concepts already contain propositions about needs, motives and desires: for example, it may be that masturbation leads to sexual arousal, rather than that the sex drive is conducive to masturbation. The parallel and oppositional placing of life and death in the stories of psychotic people is clear in the stories of some patients, who perceive the world to be shrinking, as they die a social death. But side by side with this, others experience a profound involvement in the world. At times, life and death have a quite articulated presence in the stories. There are moments when people are overcome by the senselessness of their existence, or overwhelmed by how full of meaning it is. Both moments are expressed in themes related to time, space and corporeality. They may arise in conversations when therapists want to discuss certain topics, and topics such as 'future' or 'past' events in the lives of patients may unlock a discourse on life and death, because many patients feel that they are in a hopeless situation. The usual assumption is that the story is the life of the patient, that the experience under discussion is *the* experience. However, it is possible that the story of death and emptiness is meant to convince the speaker and others of the hopelessness of a situation, or sorrow over lost time. It is also possible that stories about such experiences evoke feelings of aggression, or even suicide. For this reason, during conversations at Saint Anthony's, therapists took care that overtly violent emotions did not take precedence in the psychotic world.

Since this world belongs to the 'sick part' of people, a paradox arises: interaction with patients is not possible without empathy and contact orientation. In the process, psychotic people manage to breach the barriers. The discourse on life and death fuses together longing and fear, discourse and experience, life and death.

'You just see yourself dying, shriveling up'

The slow death

There is no wee little place on earth where I can still find peace . . . Because already I have said farewell to this world . . . And the world waves back that way at me, too . . . No, peace is death. It's a matter of death. I have felt death already . . . In that big black hole . . . a deep hole. You see yourself dying, shriveling up . . . Does life still hold any meaning, really, eh?

In his conversation with nurse Marleen, Bert describes how he as observer sees himself dying and disappearing. This emerges from discussion of the topic 'future'. When Marleen asks him what he wants in the future, Bert is overcome by the meaningless of his existence. He has no answer to this question, except death.

Most of the psychotic patients at Saint Anthony's psychiatric hospital have had an experience involving death. Some have attempted suicide more than once, others have often been at the brink. Psychotics feel themselves 'dying off' while still living, and they see the process of dying occurring in their lives. Dying is a concept with many connotations and implications. It has a spatial dimension, and one typical aspect is disappearing, which may mean that someone like Bert has the feeling of shriveling up. It may also imply that parts of the self disappear: thoughts, feelings, zest for life, pleasure, interests. A great emptiness yawns. As Joris told me:

Now there is great emptiness. I want to experience again. Now I feel nothing . . . There is nothing for me in my house. Nothing to look for, nothing to talk about.

Experiences of emptiness echo those of patients in their psychotic phases. Dying also means loss; loss of soul ('the soul is gone', 'the spirit has left'). Psychotic people feel as if they are a body without substance, without content. Emptiness, in turn, is experienced as a 'hole'. Bert to Marleen:

I see it as a black hole. Everything . . . everything: eating, sleeping, being awake, a black hole . . . It gets worse every day . . . I am caught in a dead hole.

Emptiness, or nothingness, turns to ruin. Bert to Marleen:

I am not given a chance. People around me are busy . . . they talk to each other and I sit there and, nothing really . . . That's the ruin of me. At least, that's how I see it.

Space seems to shrink, too. It is as if psychotic people require (or are left with) less and less space. Carla to her therapist:

> When I lie down peace always reigns and other than that . . . You don't really think about anything, you know. Usually I sleep a while and then, well, now and then I get up just to do what is urgently necessary . . . Not feeling like doing anything, and yet you have to. Everything is too much. I never used to have that . . . Now, I have no joy whatever . . . So, sometimes I am inclined to think: Well, I'll just sit at the window and nothing matters any more.

Experiences like this, referred to by therapists as 'inactivity', belong to the symptoms of the illness. Carla's therapist:

> The remarkable thing is the extreme lack of initiative. These people just won't get out of bed. That is typically psychotic.

Together, the 'black hole', the emptiness, lack of desire to do anything, inactivity, etc., create a point of tension in a culture in which 'activity' is a highly valued norm. Patients experience this tension, as Carla indicated to her therapist:

> And then I think: Hey, if only I could go at the house myself, you know . . . That I could do it myself. Yesterday for instance I saw a woman sweeping there again. I always sit there kind of making comparisons. I think: You have a little baby. She also has a small child, about two years old. I think: There she is, having a good time sweeping. I think: She has to keep house, she has her baby snugly in bed with her and I have nothing. You know, that's powerlessness, yes. You sure want something else, but you can't. And you are taken for garbage, because that cleaning woman . . . And for three weeks, when I came here every day. And she said: Well, I'll come and take a look how things are at your place. That's when you notice that they take you for garbage, right?

Tensions arise because psychotic people assume that they cannot meet the demands made of adults, and their discourse becomes self-effacing. The 'model' that patients hold out for a person is someone who is valuable and responsible, who takes his fate into his own hands and is able to care for himself and others. It is part of 'authoritative discourse' (Bakhtin 1981). Tensions emerge when as psychotic patients they cannot meet this norm. Devereux (1954) notes that this may not be restricted to psychotic people, but while others are familiar with it, it is more intense for psychotics. Moreover, Devereux claims that these and other symptoms are not endemic to psychotics. Rather, a culture teaches people how to be 'crazy', in this case by way of inactivity, separation and withdrawal from the world. Norms and values are seen as contrary to everyday life and the desire to be left in peace.

In addition to a spatial dimension, death has a visual dimension. Bert sees himself dying and shriveling up in a black hole. Dying evokes specific colors (gray, black, monochrome), the conventional symbols of death. Loss of the ability to see plays a role here. When I asked Rob to tell me about the time of the psychosis and the present, he answered:

> I just don't feel like doing things. I am empty inside . . . Yeah, going outside . . . I don't enjoy it much. At the time that I was psychotic it was liberating to go outside. You saw all kinds of new things, branches in the trees and beautifully colored plants . . . Right now I see nothing, nothing at all.

The process of dying also has a temporal dimension, and the way in which time is experienced changes drastically. Rob continued:

> In my psychosis I could let the clock stand still. Time was a god. Time and space were magnificent. Nowadays time is looking at your watch, time to eat, time for this or that.

Koos in his conversation with me:

> Because I wandered around through time . . . and everything that happened without my willing it . . . I long for a time that is very far back and so on . . . Then you were alive in time, weren't you? And now it is as if I live completely outside of time, almost.

The drama of death helps psychotic people to make clear that everything they ever held worthwhile or those they dreamt about or longed for was nothing but illusion. Some examples:

> *Bert*: The bottom is deep and the barrel empty. It never held anything.

> *Eva*: Sure, they sing about paradise, but paradise never is.

Dying, as described above and understood in a symbolic sense, implies that psychotic people experience themselves as external to the world. This in turn leads to a dualistic fear of death and longing for life. In the guise of Emperor Ming, Roderick longs for life, preferably eternal life. At times people attempt to stimulate a feeling of living. Dik remarked to me when we talked about what his present life meant for him:

> I drink a lot of coffee. When I drink a lot of coffee maybe I get a heart condition. In that case at least you feel something.

On the other hand, death is longed for and life is feared. Suicide attempts reflect a conscious seeking of death. Patients constantly express the wish to die and they do things that they believe may bring death sooner. After I had spoken to Bert, his therapist and the nurse, I asked him to tell me more about his ideas for the future:

> I have nothing, my future is nothing, I want to gas myself. I want [to be] dead. Sometimes I smoke cigarettes and I think: I wish I would get cancer, it wouldn't bother me. It is nothing.

If a person in Saint Anthony's has an illness such as cancer, the talk is often not of death but of fear or anxiety. Some patients already have a notion of how they want to die, and they do not necessarily choose the most dignified way of going. This reflects feelings of being human garbage, of being on the periphery of society. Koos:

> I am not the type to die in bed, really. I am more likely to die in the street, laying myself down in the gutter.

Psychotic people keep referring to death. Stories about murder, the death of children, nuclear bombs, nature dying off and the demise of the world – all of these are core moments of their discourse. These images permeate their reflections. They are analogies, and together they fuse into a drama in terms of which psychotics can clarify their own death and disappearance, as well as that of others.

In the discourses, life and death appear to be closely connected with talking about the past and the future. This is understandable, since the disorder has introduced an evident break between past and future. For psychotics there is no real longing for history because for most, the memories (especially from the time before being admitted to hospital) offer little joy. Psychotic people experience the future as something closed off from them. As far as lasting relationships, children, employment or other facets of life are concerned, this is mostly true. They consider it unlikely that they can measure up to society's benchmarks of success. Sometimes the key to the future may lie in the past, but the past has been cut off. Christiaan told me:

> I should return to a specific situation, a specific problem. I am stuck with the same thought and the same activity, so I have to go back all the way to the past . . . Everything was fine then.

Christiaan wants to 'save his soul' and for that he has to go back to the past, but his past is closed, because his 'return' to a time when everything was good is constantly being disrupted by interfering 'devils', including hospital staff and fellow patients. His vague memories of the past consist mostly of the values that (according to society) belong to very early childhood:

It is wonderful to be together with God. You sure feel [of] that in your head. I look at other people then. People adapt to my appearance. So: I adapt to your appearance and you to mine. Those people do so, too . . . That's what I want, something like that, but it keeps not happening; but if I am above, in the culture of God the father, some disturber comes along and disrupts things.

The desire to live a harmonious life is not unusual, just as disruptions in the balance between longing and being are well known in society. The phenomenology of narcissistic disruptions is familiar from writings by Winnicott (1965), Mahler (1969) and Kohut (1971) but falls outside the scope of this work. The concern, rather, is about the tensions experienced when the self relates to society. The tensions loom so large that patients are continually preoccupied with them. They become a text to live by.

Christiaan has been 'thinking back' for more than 20 years. In this time he has often been at the point where he wanted to 'throw himself under a train' and at times I saw him standing desperate and lonely on the road next to the railway line. But there is such an adamant social prohibition on killing oneself that it restrains most psychotics from suicide.[3] Christiaan confirmed this to me:

When I look at a railway track I think: I should lie down there. But I don't do it. Maybe God keeps me from doing it. I cannot put an end to my life.

According to Quinn (1992: 91), values and norms of life and death have a strong 'motivational force of self-understanding'. They prod psychotic people to life, although they can also constitute a barrier. Such quintessential values and norms demand a perfection that psychotic people are virtually unable to meet. This brings about insecurity because they cannot live and yet are not permitted to die. Christiaan suggests to me that the route to life is blocked. He is held back by 'something' inside him and 'some disturber always comes along and disrupts it'. The road to death is also cut off:

[God] says: You want to commit suicide? You can't. You cannot commit suicide. So I have to keep on living.

Christiaan externalizes and objectifies his battle between life and death. Satanic forces block the way to life. God closes the way to death. On the one hand (Quinn 1992: 91), this poses a threat to Christiaan's psychic well-being. He is forced to wander back and forth incessantly between life and death. On the other hand, it entails a certain amount of personal and social 'profit' to him (D'Andrade 1984: 98). He is able to manipulate ideas about God and the devil. In this way he can escape values and norms that seek to coerce to self-responsibility and accountability. By means of these ideas he can demonstrate that he is 'innocent terrain' on which the battle will rage; he is elected as it were both by the devil and by God, and all he can do is bear his burden.

Therapists and psychiatric staff at Saint Anthony's have never tried to hide the discourse of psychotic people about life and death. The 'cues' in the conversations – silences, brief sentences, tensions – offered a clear impression of inner suffering. Still, it seemed to me that there was no response to this discourse other than the offer to 'do something'. Perhaps the powerlessness of listeners is best illustrated at the end of the conversation between Vincent and Bernard:

Vincent: Mine is a dull life, Bernard.
Bernard: Yes? You find it boring?
Vincent: No. You can't say that. But it is not the best of its kind.
Bernard: Aha.
Vincent: No. One should simply want to join in, right?
Bernard: [*laughs*] That's, uh, true. Hey, listen Vincent. If you think the talk has been long enough, just tell me, okay?
Vincent: Yes.
Bernard: I mean, if you want to stop.
Vincent: Yes.
Bernard: I'll shut off the recorder.
Vincent: Yes, you'd better stop.
Bernard: Are you sure? Well, I'll push the button.

'I am being murdered: I have to die!'

Touch and terror

In the above section I referred to the spatial, temporal and visual dimensions of life and death. However, the most outstanding phenomenon is the tactile dimension. This refers to the awareness of psychotic people of being touched and intruded on by others. In the course of my fieldwork in Saint Anthony's I was frequently confronted with 'touch', and certain other body experiences of psychotic people, sometimes in rough, direct and immediate form. Such confrontation occurred both in the stories of patients and in interaction. The well-known anthropological method of participant observation, which is often reduced to auditory and visual observation, in this instance tended to become mostly 'tactile observation'. As a rule, I did not attempt to enter the world of people; people intruded upon me. I was embraced, kissed, scratched and almost strangled. I also heard stories about how others forced themselves upon patients, and how this was experienced.

The meaning of this penetration by others into the body and space of psychotic people is usually recounted in terms of the specific turns of phrase the patients use. A well-known example of this is Freud's person with the warped eyes (*Augenverdreher*). A woman says: 'My eyes are warped.' She explains that her love looks different every time. Therefore, she can no longer trust her eyes. She says: 'I see the world with different eyes, I have warped eyes.' That which she says and feels about her love she applies to her own body. The present section deals with this loss of distance.

In our visually biased culture 'touch'[4] seems to play a subordinate role. The tactile sense is in fact the paramount and most pervasive means of communication: touch is essential to our health, emotional well-being and development. It is necessary to convince us. The story of doubting Thomas, who wanted to touch the wounds of Jesus Christ before he would believe that He had truly risen (John 20: 25), underlines this. We feel with our entire body, and yet in our culture seeing is valued more highly than feeling (cf Synnott 1993: 156). In portraying experiences of touch, language is the mediator between our body and the world, and it creates a certain distance between them. Accordingly, in the experiences of touch, the social and physical cannot be separated. It is not surprising that language contains so many metaphors for touch: a warm person, a cold fish, a barbed remark, an untouchable person, etc. Synnott (1993: 158) writes that 'tactile metaphors are primarily concerned with our feelings, sensitivities and emotions, and our interactions with other people'. While this may seem self-evident, it soon becomes clear what significance these sensory perceptions have when the experience of touch changes drastically, for instance because of a disorder. If people can no longer be touched or no longer want to be touched, it has far-reaching consequences in social and personal relationships and experiences. At that moment it also becomes clear to the subject how society views these things.

Our senses are instruments whereby we enter the world, but sometimes the order is reversed. In psychotic disorders people do not enter the world; the world enters people. Uninvited and often unwanted auditory and visual hallucinations enter the body of the psychotic person. However horrid they may be, these sense perceptions often foretell the surfacing of something repressed (Moyaert 1982a). A more destructive and inexplicable process than hallucination occurs when psychotic people feel 'touched' by others. This touch implies the destruction of their own body. It occurs in psychotic bodies because certain things that happen or are said are no longer kept at a distance from the body by the medium of language. They become part of the body and hence it feels as if they cut directly into it. 'Word' and sense of touch fuse into one, and the relationship between psychotic people and others becomes lifeless.

Clearly, the tactile sense plays a special role in a psychotic disorder. By virtue of the distinction between the word and the thing signified by it, people normally maintain a distance between word and touch. Psychotic people sometimes seemed to feel the word as immediate sensation, and one could say that things or words were characterized by immediacy or non-mediation. At one moment there was a surplus of feeling or touch, a vulnerability to touch by others, and the next, the psychotic was untouchable or without feeling.

The world within the body

Eva wrote in a letter:

> My mother lives inside my head. She gives me bad thoughts. I even feel
> it cracking in my brains. My mother is a mad clairvoyant. She can pester
> people, give them needs and take them away. Then something rises from
> her stomach and I have to breathe it in.

This fragment shows how someone else can be felt inside the body. Maybe Eva's
words 'My mother lives inside my head' are reminiscent of dreams or intense
experiences, like Frank Sinatra singing 'I've got you under my skin'. Usually
there is distance between the body and an object: nobody will seriously claim
that intense love leads one to swallow the lover. Language mediates.

But for Eva the distance between her body and her mother has fallen away.
Everything she says about the mother is tied to the body or a part of it. The mother
not only got into her head, but also into her vagina, her belly, her stomach.
Everything her mother does or says has become a physical sensation. The body
and others are being intertwined. She continues:

> My mother rapes me . . . She gives me sexual feelings . . . She poisons
> me . . . She wants to see me dead . . . I am getting murdered.

One cannot merely dismiss these statements as figures of speech. In two articles on language, corporeality and effect, philosopher and therapist Moyaert
(1982a, 1982b) describes representations and effects in schizophrenia. Moyaert's
insights will guide me in this section, and may be summed up as follows: the
signified is reduced to a part of the body and the psychotic person relates every
experience of the other to his or her own body. This involvement is not the
feelings of pleasure which Sinatra sings about; it is, rather, feelings of hypo-
chondria. The body and the object signified are not kept apart; they become one.
In this sense we can understand what Eva feels: everything her mother says
about her becomes her body. She has sexual feelings, her body is raped and
that which she feels was not hers originally has now become part of her body.

In this sense we can also understand why Christiaan came very close to
beating a nurse, because he felt that her words had touched his penis. Words
were immediate contact with his body. They were deeply felt or entered deeply
into the body. Such fusion or intertwinement becomes especially clear in relation to negative experiences, such as when a daughter is abused by a parent. The
lack of a separation between the word and the sense of touch has to do with the
blurring of the boundary between the 'I' of psychotic persons and others. Word
and touch flow together and the relation between psychotic people and others
becomes thing-like (Lacan 1966; Mooy 1987).

What psychotic people say about 'touch' hardly contains possible solutions
to the conflicting physical sensations. On the contrary, it often implies more

physical sensation and destruction: they touch their own bodies. By way of language, the psychotic destroys his own body. Language ceases to be a mediator capable of realizing the required distance between body and world. In the most literal sense language becomes the 'toucher'. Says Vincent: 'We talk ourselves completely empty.' With every word he utters, his body becomes that much emptier, its content disappears and the body is destroyed.

The way in which psychotic people express their body and other's touch is not symbolic. The signified merges with the body (Moyaert 1982a: 52), and the utterance of words is experienced as the body falling apart or being emptied. Moyaert describes a woman who, during therapy, continually has to look at her reflection to make sure that her facial features remain intact during her conversation with the therapist. She says that talking to her therapist disintegrates her body. Empty, disintegrated – the body is destroyed by words spoken by others, or by psychotics themselves.

The sense, or meaning, of what patients say about touch is, unlike the case of delusions and hallucinations, not at all obscure. It is what people say it is. With delusions, therapists need not overcome resistance in order to let the meaning emerge. In that respect there is also no tension here. Moyaert notes in his patients that a second process indicates the loss of symbolic meanings: the reduction of meaning. He demonstrates this with a case of a woman to whom all bodily orifices produce the same sensation, as does the anus. Sensation spreads to all orifices. Everything that passes through them, whether words or faeces, all is the same 'stinking filth'. In this context Moyaert speaks of 'demetaphorization', since only stereotyped similarities remain of the bodily orifices, rather than (symbolic) differences. All over, the body is a hole; it is rape, filth or evil. Each part feels like any other.

Eva, raped by her mother, is not raped only in her vagina, but also in her head, her belly, in short, wherever her body contains spaces. Nor is her mother the only one to rape her. She is abused by her brother or by men who approach her bed. It is brutal and painful sexual experiencing felt by the woman as the endless destruction of her body. The things her mother says about her, her thoughts and words, incidental minor discomforts like menstruation, the superficial brush of a nurse's arm, all of them, always evoke the same painful sexual awareness. Every part of the body is familiar with it.

According to Moyaert, demetaphorization occurs mostly in signifying one's own body. This means that a person is, or identifies with, his words. Eric, for example, talking with his therapist, suddenly exclaims that there is a knife pointed at him. The knife will cut off part of his penis. He cries: 'Whoa! Dammit, hey! I feel nothing, man!' He says that his prick is gone, which does not keep him a moment later from saying that someone called him a prick. Somebody says that his heart is not in the right place and the man points to the right side of his chest. When the therapist takes this in the metaphorical sense: 'I think your heart *is* in the right place, you want to help, don't you?', the man responds: 'I don't know, sometimes it shifts'. For psychotic people metaphorical statements become 'literal inscriptions' whenever they refer to the body. That which others say about them or to them is, as far as the body is concerned, painful and destructive. It enters the body unbidden. The patient's body is not securely delimited, as ours is. It lies open and vulnerable to threatening actions and objects. Eva told me:

> I am a sacrifice. I must die. My mother wants to kill me . . . You all want to kill me . . . They murder me with a red-hot screwdriver stuck in my navel . . . I start to scream and [that] the police should finish me off, because I keep screaming.

A nurse's superficial touch is an attempt at murder. When the ward nurse asked Eva what her problem with the ward's people was, she answered:

> You want to kill me, I say . . . Yes, and X, she shouted at me and so, they all shout at me and T, the male nurse, he shoves me sometimes. Then he says: You are spilling your coffee again . . . Sure, he can chide me for that, but he doesn't have to shove me.

The body structure is broken up, crumbled, says Moyaert (1982b: 698). This means that it can be dismembered, pieces can be hacked off, hands can be given away, heads can lie on windowsills, and an eye can be lost or mislaid. 'I took old medicine and because of that I lost an eye.' The other (or the words of the other) can be felt with various parts of the body: the eyes, the mouth, the genitals, and the skin. One of the patients stopped saying anything at all at one point. His explanation, later, was that a staff member had taken out his vocal cords because he had raised a rather loud protest against ward procedures. 'I said the wrong things.' He wanted to be transferred to a hospital to be operated on so that he would never again say wrong things.

All of this implies feelings of distaste in the body of psychotic people. These feelings cannot be avoided; they can only be hated. One popular view is that everything that gives rise to feelings of displeasure in human beings should if possible be banned or cast off and everything that induces pleasure should be treated lovingly. This originally Freudian theory makes it clear that people will try to do away with objects that cause displeasure. As a rule these are objects outside the body. In psychotic people, however, it is one's own body which is the source of displeasure; hence, it becomes an object to get rid of or to destroy.

Self-mutilation, suicide attempts and also masturbation can be understood in this sense. It is the destruction of one's own (evil) body or an attempt to purify the body. Eric says: 'Masturbate in the institute: rid yourself of the impure, the unclean'. Another patient compares his cutting himself with the medieval practice of bloodletting. The 'disease' has to go. Eva punishes her body. She shaves her head partially bald; cuts a cactus plant to drink the poisonous milk; jumps out of the window 'for her mother'. In her letters she describes her scatological peculiarities.

I stayed in my room once. And I drank shit and piss. In D. I was in an institution. I got rid of my alcohol problem there by putting sand in my arse.

Oey (1990) says activities like these are in fact signs of life, or would be if they could lead to physical restoration. Sadly, this is often not the case. These actions are repeated time and again, in a regressive process (Obeyesekere 1990). Moyaert says they are not symbolic expressions because they accomplish that which any practical being would want to avoid: the destruction of one's own body.

The immediacy of touch is also expressed in statements such as those by Eva: 'I have AIDS doctor, because I have to masturbate so often.' The initially pleasurable feeling is felt as something bad, placing it in the same context as rape, and also leading to destruction of the body.

Psychotic people are continually enmeshed in a battle with their own body and the feelings its produces. To Vincent his body is nothing but an organ producing unclean secretions: 'that white stuff is filthy'. That which is capable of destroying the body is within the body. For others, destruction usually comes from the outside, or if like a tumor it resides in the body, it is destroyed in order to save the body. This is not the case with psychotic people. They do not dwell in their body; they reject it. Their desire is not to touch and not to be touched. 'I am a rock,' says Rob. A rock is without feeling.

The occasionally observed condition of apathy and its flat and dull affect is not only negative; it is a 'condition of complete rest, without any tension or displeasure (suspended animation)' (Moyaert 1982a: 67). As such, it is a defense against the destructive drives of one's own body and the intrusion of others into it.

The world and the body

The process above describes the terrible suffering an individual can endure. Moyaert has sought to provide relief for these experiences in his therapies. He tried to 'direct and bind' the destructive impulses 'to a part of the therapist's body', in order that 'the destruction of the body [. . .] no longer arises and comes to fruition directly and immediately in the body of the patient himself' (Moyaert 1982b: 706). In this way he creates a ritual in which experiences are denuded of their immediacy and become less terrifying for the patients and for others. This mediation on the part of the therapist is in fact an attempt to subsume something that is experienced as threatening into the social order. Of necessity, in this order there has to be distance between the body and the world.

Psychotic people suffer greatly. Partly because it calls attention to their own helplessness, others cannot countenance it. The suffering confronts us with an unconscious knowledge that in our culture sympathy can evidently be transformed into aid, but only if we have a degree of mastery over the other. It may be that we recognize the longing for death in a psychotic person, or the Buddhist longing to leave the body, but in these cases we are aware that we lose control over the body of the other. The body can neither be touched physically nor approached in language. It is like talking to a rock wall. In this case the psychiatric staff live in constant fear of the suicidal tendencies that some patients nurture, or the fear that they will drink themselves to death. For the staff, there is no option but to detain such persons in the ward. In such situations there is helplessness and a keen awareness of the shortcomings of psychiatry. Responses in this environment repeatedly emphasize that it is precisely the direct, open and physical experiences that shame and shock. While the language that patients use in relation to touch and the body is no longer symbolic, it is not the accidental product of a sick mind. Rather, it is part of a cultural idiom. We noted earlier that people have nothing else at their disposal (although some psychotics invent completely new systems of language). People who deal with psychotics are influenced when confronted with this cultural mirror. Even when psychotics reject their own body or display cruelty in self-mutilation or death wishes, they are referring to values and ideals (cf Feder 1980), and the ambiguity thereof. Cultural idiom gives others a degree of understanding of their behavior, while religious values and norms of the body are obvious models for this. Mental or spiritual and physical suffering is usually caused by a catastrophic event. Adam's fall is an example of this. The restraints imposed upon Eve in the creation story are visually recognized in her nakedness. The eye of the other is almost a touching, and Eve hurriedly covers her shame. The wrath of God falling upon those who transgress the rule results in an immediate physical experience. At the root of the catastrophe there is always an error, a trespass, a sin.

Sensations in the body of being touched by others are a consequence of transgressions of laws and rules that others have imposed. When Adam and Eve were disobedient, God's wrath drove them from paradise. In this sense, touch is an expression of the power which others (or the Other) have over people (cf Synott 1992: 167). It is physical punishment, always involving the destruction of part of the body. This is a form of punishment in many societies: whipping, torture, laceration and more. It may be prohibited, but the law is ignored by many, as is evident from cases of child abuse and the abuse of women.

Other catastrophes may not relate so much to prohibitions being broken, but they do occasion physical punishment. Political unrest, social wrongs and unfulfilled expectation about individual well-being, lead to negative assessments of individual behavior. In the mythical world (Lévi-Strauss 1962) a guilty person is burned to death by his family. Collective violence is valued positively, and individual behavior is judged negatively. But this mechanism is also found outside the world of myth. The theme of the scapegoat lives on in occasional eruptions of xenophobia, from the lynching of police officers in Ireland, to throwing *amakwerekweres* (foreign Black Africans: literally, 'queer speakers') off moving trains in Johannesburg. According to Girard (1990), these outbreaks of physical violence originate in the scapegoat mechanism, where one is sacrificed for all. At the margins of every society there are sadistic and masochistic practices associated with crime and punishment, or with purification, desire or even health. Sometimes these take on extreme forms of torture, sometimes less forbidding, as in sadomasochistic (SM) circles or fitness centers.

Sin, scapegoat, sacrifice, lynching, sadism and masochism are recurring themes among psychotic people. There is a constant sense of impending catastrophe: of attacks by the devil, or others invading the body. The catastrophe ensues when laws decreed by the invaders are broken. Lacan (1966) explains subjugation to others in terms of data indicating that psychotic people do not enter into the symbolic order of language. For this reason they lack means of identification and simply remain whatever others say about them. Eva writes in her letters:

> My mother gives me evil thoughts . . . I think my mother is inside my head and she can sometimes make me do strange things, like fighting . . . My mother is evil . . . My mother encourages bad feelings about me . . . There is something in my head, you know. And they blame me for everything . . . I used to draw pictures, but my mother and my brother did not let me. My mother said: Keep your hands off the paper . . . When I was 28, I had a friend. We had sex, but we broke up because my mother forbade it . . . I am in an institution now because my mother and I have quarrels. She poisons me and gives me sexual feelings . . . Once I was thinking that I would take a stepladder and crawl under a bull. Then I went to the isolation ward . . . When I slept at my mother's, boys came to my bed, I think, and they were murdered by my mother and my brother . . . Now I guess I have to die too . . . The world has come to an end and now Adam and Eve are coming into the world and I think, because I am Eva I am the smartest of all people and now I will be killed. I must die . . . I am a kind of sacrifice . . . I also think that girls cannot have sex; they are built all wrong.

Eva's mother forbids 'sexual feelings' – just one of the many things she forbids – but she also causes them to assert themselves. Eva is punished when she has them, and like the transgression, punishment is in the area of sexuality. However, it has become rape, which in turn leads to more defiling of the body. To avert this repeating catastrophe, Eva makes a wish:

> I now want to be dead. I would like to die. I would like a happy end.

Before psychotics arrive at the point where they express a death wish, they will have attempted to remove the evil defilement injected into their bodies by others, or by virtue of their own transgressions. This takes the form of self-laceration, burning, going hungry, vomiting, staying awake, etc., in the hope that if they appear to be dead, it will open paradise or heaven to them. The powerful stories told by patients evoke associations with related cultural events. In the late Middle Ages, itinerant groups of crucifers went about singing psalms and publicly flagellating themselves. Public self-castigation is a form of asceticism that was first recorded in Italy in 1260. It emerged from political unrest, social injustice and overwrought eschatological expectations. Many medieval citizens greatly feared this fanatical movement,[5] whose adherents hoped that bruised and broken bodies would evoke divine mercy.

The principle of self-castigation is present in the Biblical injunction:

> If your hand or your foot causes you to sin, cut it off and throw it from you; it is better for you to enter life maimed or lame than with two hands or two feet to be thrown into the eternal fire. And if your eye causes you to sin, pluck it out and throw it from you; it is better for you to enter life with one eye than with two eyes to be thrown into the hell of fire.
>
> (Matthew 18: 8, 9)

Most Christians do not take this literally, but the message is clear: sin must be avoided even at the cost of great sacrifice. Moreover, in the Christian tradition, touch is ambiguous. Touching can heal or restore; it can also defile and destroy. Christ's touch brought life, but the body of Christ had to be broken to save the world. Not long ago touching one's own body and that of others for purposes other than procreation, cleaning and hygiene was believed and proclaimed by many to be a sinful act, and liable to attract death by stoning in some instances. The duality of the meaning of the body, good and evil, still has great impact in opposition to the sanctity of the mystical body of Christ in which all Christians participate, even if today there are many constructions of corporeality (Synnott 1993).

Psychotic people aim these norms and values at themselves, and allow them to play a role as models and motivators of mutilation and self-destruction. The stories told by psychotic people, and their behavior, indicate strong preoccupation with oppositions such as good and evil, God and the devil, centrality and marginality. These stories are formulaic representations, rigid repetitions of conventional models, because it is so difficult for psychotic people to cope with ambiguities.

On the basis of the above considerations, one can make sense of psychotic self-destructiveness: bad and evil reside in the body; the body must be punished or cut loose in order to attain something better; the injured or broken body might evoke the pity of others. In this sense, psychotic people reflect culture, or confront others with a mirror. This does not imply that they are innovators, because inspection will reveal a familiar image, urging that we embrace the good and avoid the bad. If we heed this, the world will improve: nothing can be more familiar. In a way, this is reassuring for the rest, and psychotic people can be kept within the borders of a (cultural) paradise because the experiences of touch and the subsequent destruction of the body can be explained. But in the process, psychotic people are referred back to themselves: *their* feelings of guilt and *their* inability to achieve distance from sources of irritation have the potential to destroy the body. However, what psychotics show in their stories about this sort of experience and what they show by the rituals of punishment and purification they visit upon their own bodies is that some find it impossible to live with the ambiguities in our culture.

The body in the world

In the section above I have tried to demonstrate that 'touch' could be associated with cultural (religious) models that – certainly in the discourse of patients – constitute a regulating principle for behavior.[6]

Association with religious models, such as those of good and evil, or myths, is not enough to explain the reactions of others to what psychotics do, or how they act. The meanings are too far removed from the immediate, manifest significance of touching. They serve first and foremost to give meaning to our observations, in order to make some sense of their destructive behavior.

The links with existing cultural frameworks indicate that psychotic people have not invented anything new. Perhaps the description does explain the origin and bring out hidden meanings of touch and its concomitant destruction, but it does not provide clarity on how the experiences of being relate to the moral system and, hence, relate to others. Touch and the experience of touch constitute a drama that has sometimes tragic and sometimes comical effects on others. Stories and behavior arising from experiences of touch render psychotic people into tragicomic personages. In the light of the dramatic accounts quoted above, it may seem out of place to speak of the comic aspects in the life of a suffering human being. Therapists sometimes refer to the discourse concerning these experiences as 'play'. This is an important insight. But it should not be looked upon as play only, for this would 'bracket out' human activities that are important in that sense: thinking and talking about values, norms and beliefs. Ricoeur (1969: 219) remarked that comic persons indeed amuse others, but that ethical indictments are at the root of comedy. Ricoeur holds that the tragic person is safeguarded against moral judgments by others and is presented as an 'object' of pity. The psychotic is both a clown and a tragic human being, both a challenger and someone to be pitied.

The clownishness in psychotic people comes to expression in bizarre linkages of all sorts of cultural elements that normally have little to do with each other. Eva, for example, says that she has AIDS. She believes this is because she has to masturbate frequently (Van Dongen 2002). The causal link between AIDS and masturbation is absurd, and others (such as the therapist) experience such talk as play, expressive of a preoccupation with sex and intended to shock others or to gain their attention. In the common room of the ward a patient shouts: 'Come carnival I will hang myself! That will make me a carnival child!' Here again, there is a linkage between two extremes that do not normally occur together. Stories about rape, cutting off the genitals, a mother cracking into one's brain, 'feeling' the thoughts of others and the like are often told in a manner that can be associated with folklore, Chaucer's *Canterbury Tales* or the works of

Rabelais (1980). Like those of Rabelais, the psychotic stories are satiric and in a way make others laugh. Such laughter is not only about what psychotic people say, but also about that which people recognize as their own thoughts. The discourse reveals a kind of 'grotesque realism' (Bakhtin 1981) and is the expression of an 'ideology that opposes the official and authoritarian languages that dominate our surface' (Booth 1983: 67).

A major characteristic of psychotics' discourse is their openness in discussing their experiences. Patient expressions not only aim at reversal of the ascetic body, the 'beauty of the body' (Synnott 1993: 21), but also to bring that which is normally hidden onto the public stage. Psychotic people are clever enough to understand that these linkages have a powerful effect on others. This is expressed also in the involvement of others in physical experiences. The way in which others are drawn into immediate touching is a conscious trespass upon every norm in social intercourse. Eric, for example, assaults his therapist. Touching his therapist he 'lets his hand wander to more romantic places', unzips his fly and shouts: 'Here it comes, here it comes again!', suggesting that his meeting with the therapist is an extremely pleasurable event. Goffman (1961b) suggests that such 'ceremonial profanities' display sensitivity to rules, values and norms. By 'acting the clown', psychotic people generate concern in others about their amorality and their fate, and as a consequence their behavior is functional and invites discussion.

Involving others, however, goes beyond the clownish assaults on a therapist who knows the patient's antics. When public masturbation, aggression, public self-mutilation and exhibitionism occur as well, these acts destroy the psychotic just as surely as private self-mutilation in the psychiatric hospital. The comedy turns into tragedy. This behavior confronts psychotics with the norms and (double) moral standards of society. 'They' now adopt precisely the stance that psychotic people are most critical of in the world. It constitutes an anti-goal for behavior. Because our society prohibits public engagement in this sort of behavior, Vincent exhibits his penis in the city. Eva masturbates in a telephone booth. Prohibitions are transgressed but one can ask who is really transgressing, Vincent, or those who go 'slumming' in the city? Who feels soiled by this? Not Vincent. Walking about naked is permitted in certain places, but not in town, not in the entertainment district, and Vincent cannot understand this. 'Sports people do that too, don't they?' To his mind, naked is just naked, wherever it occurs. This makes Vincent a tragic person, because he becomes an object of ridicule. There are complaints about his exhibitionism, there are fistfights and he is thrown out of pubs. To others, the way in which these prohibitions are publicly ignored makes social morality something to be ridiculed. His behavior reveals the secrets, or, rather the secretiveness of people: 'They tell me to do this.' When Vincent does 'this' he is punished. Who is behaving bizarrely here?

The psychotic's behavior constitutes attempts to escape the restraints of the (social) body via self-destruction. Together with the desire to destroy their own body, the longing for a new body emerges. Attempts to escape from the old (evil) body can be illustrated with Vincent's words, quoted earlier:

> Sometimes I think: I should be shorn bald and laid on the bed naked, until finally I have another shape . . . I will not die . . . I will not reincarnate . . . I disappear . . . I want to be a cosmos man. Cosmos humans do not die. They have no anus. They are very clean and wear white clothing. They do have a pecker to pee with but they do not masturbate.

Others may understand the longing for a different body, but the simple disappearance of the old one is not acceptable in our society. The body may be hurt to make it stronger or more beautiful. It may be denied to attain a higher goal, it may even be altered, but it remains the basis for anything new[7] and has to be nurtured. It cannot just disappear together with all the feelings in it, because emptiness is an unbearable gaze into the abyss.[8] Moyaert (1982c) formulates the fear of others for the emptiness of the body (and of psychotic discourse) as follows: 'The schizophrenic confronts us with the [. . .] yawning gap of a radical *not-knowing*. Faced with this not-knowing we are powerless and no longer able to defend ourselves.'

Given their stories about touch, physical experiences and behavior, psychotic people evince a kind of freedom from control by others. By reason of the emptiness and the 'disappearance' of the body, the 'political' control over the individual body is lost. Non-feeling and non-being imply that others no longer have a hold. The fact that psychotic people are well-nigh untouchable renders others powerless. It is perhaps the most threatening process of all that can occur in human beings.

We have seen that therapists consider inactivity to be a symptom of psychosis, but the life of psychotic people is not marked by inactivity. This seems to be a paradox, but therapists refer to specific inactivity, which means not being employed or working, not attending social events, not being able to do housework, etc. Even if psychotic patients are not active in socially 'normal' ways, they work hard at making sense of experiences that they know to belong to their 'sick' parts. They have to deal with 'power [which] reaches into the very grain of individuals [which] touches their bodies and inserts itself into their actions and attitudes, their discourses [. . .] and everyday lives' (Foucault 1964). According to Csordas (1994: 6), anthropology's concern with embodiment is the problematization of interrelated conceptual realities: the pre-objective and objectified; mind and body; mental and material. In the lives of psychotic people, it appears that there is a blurring of these dualities. Psychotic people call into question the distinction between experience and ontology, between subject and object. Their bodies are the source of their subjectivity and their minds are the source of their objectification (Csordas 1994: 9).

In summary, the basic experiences of the psychotic body are emptiness, loss and disappearance. Psychotic people describe the process of dying, which involves spatial, temporal, visual and tactile dimensions. Much of what is said in their discourse must be understood symbolically. There is distance between what people say and what is signified by their words. Everyday, conventional metaphors such as 'at loose ends' or 'a black hole' mediate between experiences of death and the body. This discourse enables psychotic people to indicate the field of tension between experiences of selfhood and cultural values and norms. By recounting what they have lost (in the body), they also clarify what they believe the life of ordinary people to be like. In the normal body there is no emptiness: it has a soul, or a mind, and it initiatives activities, and so on. All of this adds up to 'life'.

These norms and values have sufficient power as models to encourage patients to keep up their attempts to comply with them. At the same time, however, they constitute a threshold and a hindrance. Values and norms tend to envisage a 'healthy' perfection, which is unattainable. 'Life' cannot be realized and neither can death. A discourse on life and death that relies on metaphors and stories of murder and manslaughter highlights the dramatic content in the life of psychotic people. Their speech invariably relates to the past and the future. Patients sometimes indicate that their future – their life – lies hidden in the past, and the past is blocked. This indicates the tenacity of the cultural belief that a person's history largely determines that individual's future. It is a strongly held conviction, so much so that the psychiatric health team finds it difficult to deal with people who can no longer remember the concept of their future, along with their present and past life, and those of others.[9]

Besides discourse about death in the symbolic sense, there is also a discourse in terms of immediate physical experiences. The words spoken by others are experienced as destroying the body, and one's own speech causes the body to disintegrate further or become empty. These experiences lead to acts intent on removing the object that produces the feelings of displeasure. This 'object' is the body. The way in which this removal is enacted and repeated by psychotic people evokes associations with religious models, in particular. However, the myths and tales are nothing but the attempts of others (including myself) to mediate experiences such as the direct touch of words leading to self-destruction, and to create distance between the body and the world in this way. They are constructions; they could have been different.

Chapter 10

Conclusion
Psychotic discourse revisited

In retrospect

The stories and subjective experiences of patients are given little space in interactions between patients and therapists. This is a hindrance to psychiatric healing, because it excludes the possibility of reflection on the multiple ways in which society and culture affect the lives of psychotic people.

It is commonly held in psychiatry that psychotic experiences are germane to the ways in which patients shape their lives, but their experiences are also viewed as an obstacle to the therapeutic process. Health professionals tend to undervalue these experiences because they belong to the 'sick' part of patients, the part that should not be discussed. I contend that since psychotic experiences have a profound meaning for patients, they could be a catalyst for an in-depth exploration of the lives of people who suffer deeply from mental problems.

In spite of ever-increasing specialization in psychiatry as well as exciting developments in medical treatment and increasingly refined communication techniques, patients' stories of psychotic experiences remain 'forbidden territory'. But there has been a shift within the prohibition: a morally normative control mechanism has been replaced by a pragmatically normative control mechanism.

At present, there is a widespread belief in Dutch society that the most important issue is the danger or threat occasioned by the behavior of psychotic people. This orientation leads to the isolation of psychotic persons, since there is a tendency to equate madness with wandering, threat, and the possibility of violence. The ship of fools (Foucault 1972) is in port and the psychotic passengers are about to disembark.

Therapists believe that psychiatry is under increasing pressure to seek multiple, quick and easily dispensable solutions. Developments in psychiatric science tend toward the view that a psychological disorder is analogous to a biomedical disease, and therefore the emphasis is on individual disorders associated with disturbances of thought, speech, personality and development. There appears to be a tacit agreement that serious mental disorders such as psychosis and schizophrenia have in all respects been well enough scrutinized to justify a biomedical approach, which offers pharmaceutical and medical treatment combined with a refined and persuasive 'resocialization discourse', and stresses rules and techniques of interaction, but tends to overlook the meaning and value of the experience of being psychotic (Van Dongen 1993a). As a result, psychotic people are locked away in 'excluded discourse'. The meaning of their experiences is reduced to disorders of perception, cognition and speech.

The dilemma for psychiatric practice is to find a balance between psychiatry as a branch of biomedicine and psychiatry as human healing. As long as the stories and voices of psychotic people continue to be ignored, this dilemma cannot be resolved by ongoing refinement of diagnosis or improved insights into processes of communication for mental health professionals. My research at Saint Anthony's psychiatric hospital indicates that the current regimen merely increases the likelihood of conflict between psychotic people and therapists. Therapists may, in fact, interpret such conflicts as confirmation of a disorder in the patient's reality awareness and reality testing. I have described this as a consolidation of countertransference, in which case psychiatry can be viewed as an institution that reproduces cultural value, norms and rules but does not offer new possibilities for people's lives, a representation of the story of abnormality in a different guise, like old wine in new bottles.

The process whereby patients give meaning to psychotic disorders and resist the control of others is often expressed in awkward behavioral patterns such as upsetting daily routines, creating a nuisance, presenting a threat, disrupting public order, etc., or it can lead to disorders in thinking, acting, speaking, and reality testing. For the patients, it is clear that in spite of its supposed neutrality, psychiatry functions as a moral subsystem. But by definition the use of reality testing in psychiatry to determine whether and to what extent a person is psychotic is in itself a point of contention because it involves imposing a version of reality that can serve as a moral yardstick. We have seen that although therapists and staff try to maintain a 'neutral' position, they have a moral vision of how life should be lived. Try as they might to avoid imposing their own ideas on the world or patients' views of it, psychiatrists end up doing precisely this. It is reassuring, because the therapeutic ritual is oriented to the reproduction and renewed acceptance of cultural values and norms over subjective experience or personal renewal. It is clear from the hospital careers of psychotic people that change and progress mean resocialization. They remain for some time in a liminal condition, straddling the divide between daily life and a condition mostly chaotic and disharmonious, which implies temporary isolation and exclusion from the fullness of everyday life.

Therapists and nurses alike maintain that psychotic patients cannot cope with transitions and crises in their lives, but in spite of this they must ultimately be led back to everyday order through inclusion in the psychiatric perspective. I argue that the liminality of psychotic patients may also, at least potentially, mean that in their marginal position, they have the freedom to present cultural criticism and to renew their social life through communitas, defined by Turner (1975: 21) as 'relationships which are undifferentiated, egalitarian, direct, extant, non-rational, existential'. Without exception, psychotic persons speak of the abuse and injustices they encounter in society. They tell us that their problems result from the evil intentions or the indifference of others, and they comment on the unwholesome aspects of society. Psychotic people convey meaning by way of cultural rhetoric and images. Mostly they make use of well-known imagery to construct explanations that provide them with an anchor amid the uncertainties that attend the disorder. To this end they utilize terms familiar to others in Dutch society (for example, environmental issues, the restrictive force of rules and regulations, xenophobia, racism, good and evil) in evocative and culturally authentic ways. Their idiom displays evidence of intention, resistance, and comment on the values, norms and rules of Dutch culture, and expresses a deeply felt desire for freedom, happiness, and peace.

However, the 'idiom of distress' used by psychotics does not usually give rise to exploration of their problems in relation to cultural concepts and categories, as has been the case with other cultural phenomena and in some other cultural settings. Nichter (1981), for example, describes how menstruation complaints provide Ayurvedic healers with an occasion to discuss cleanliness, control of emotions, sexuality, etc. In Dutch culture no such discussions arise between therapists and patients about the unfairness or the negative effects of certain social rules and norms on vulnerable groups. The psychotic 'idiom of distress' does not lead to an exploration of intersubjective experience; it is read only as a sign of abnormality, and it leads only to hospitalization.

I have shown that psychiatric practice is characterized by fragmentation and disintegration. It adapts to the individual patient and is not based on a particular world view, at least not openly so. The effect is that the meanings which psychotic people give to their experiences cannot be reconciled with the cultural meanings embedded in Dutch society. Fragmentation is evident in the specialization of tasks among the staff members in the institution. From the moment that professional help becomes operative, the world of psychotic people is characterized by atomization and discontinuity. There are continual disruptions all along the chain of care as patients are referred to a RIAGG (Regional Ambulatory Mental Health Care Service), to general practitioners, to different types of sheltered housing, and the like. At every transfer to a different institution or unit, patients have to become accustomed to different therapists and nurses. Within the ward, too, there are disruptions: patients must interact with different staff members in different kinds of therapies.

Psychotics, like everyone else, construct a world in which they try to organize their experiences into meaningful categories that become models, or schemes, to live by. Contradictions in these constructions are experienced as contradictions in the cultural system. Patients cannot find satisfying explanations for these contradictions. The discontinuity of a psychiatric career disrupts the 'illusion of wholeness' (Ewing 1990) and feelings of belonging created in their stories. A deep-seated doubt arises. Psychotic people cannot find their own answers to questions such as 'What should I do?', 'Why me?', and 'Why am I being ostracized?', and the answers offered by mental health professionals are not satisfactory.

We have observed that from the outset, resistance, struggle and a lack of congruency in how the disorder is portrayed and understood characterize relationships between mental health professionals and psychotic patients. For the most part, therapists measure the seriousness of the disorder in terms of patient behavior. The world views of mental health professionals remain implicit and are not up for discussion. However, patients form an idea of the views of therapists by interpreting their silences, minimal responses and reinterpretations of patients' words, which, taken together, add up to 'meta-messages'. Those views are derived from the results of scientific research, but they also reveal the day-to-day relationships of patients with individual therapists, hospital management, and others in the various clinics. Psychotic problems are evaluated in terms of the degree to which they influence or obstruct the therapeutic process. When such obstructions arise, therapists may interpret them as expressions of the 'sick part' of the patient, and this, in turn, reinforces patient insecurity. In the process, therapists' notions about psychosis are reaffirmed, and countertransference may be consolidated.

Psychotic patients complain that therapy is an alienating experience, exemplified by the distinction between short-term treatment and long-term residence in the hospital. The normal and optimistic therapeutic story of progress – that is, enhanced patient insight and a return to social competence – is adjusted downward in the case of psychotic patients. For the therapist treating psychotic patients, this means that psychiatric practice is not a 'repair service industry' (Goffman 1961a), but more closely resembles an attempt to 'recycle' people who, because of their disorder, have moved to the periphery of society. The recycling analogy is based on an assumption that psychotic people suffer from an inner vacuum which results in a partial or total absence of insight into their own life, capacity for autonomous action, or any real chance of complete healing. Psychotic people confirm this analogy, not because they agree with it, but because they continually face crises occasioned by their living conditions and the discontinuity wrought by their long trek through the wilderness of mental health care.

The illness is often viewed as a 'handicap' by therapists and nurses, and an already minimal expectation of complete recovery is further diminished by lack of continuity in the mental health care system. If patients are 'bricoleurs' engaged in 'cultural wandering', it is because the psychiatric system forces them to wander in a fruitless search for meaning and wholeness. When the psychotic disorder has become chronic, the emphasis shifts from recycling to care. In care, the focus is on regulation and management of the psychosis and the practical problems of patients' daily lives. Here too, patients seem to confirm assumptions about themselves. The question is whether this self-fulfilling prophecy arises from the disorder, or from the social situation of the patient. Comparison with marginalized groups elsewhere in the world shows that behavior seriously at odds with prevailing cultural norms and values originates in a hopeless life situation (cf Turnbull 1972) in which those values and norms do not help people to survive. Psychotic patients, whether in units for short-term treatment or in long-term residency, confirm and reinforce the psychiatric story about them because they have no other choice. As Eva said when she was admitted to the LTR: 'I thought I came to a world of love, but . . .'.

Open resistance to the therapeutic myth carries the risk of total isolation. In this way the truth of the story is reinforced. The spiral of confirming and reinforcing has already led to a situation in which solutions for the psychiatric disorder are increasingly sought in orthodox medical treatment. As a consequence, the patient's subjective experiences and existential questions about being and meaning are pushed into the background, and psychotic people become increasingly isolated from the world.

This is a form of symbolic violence, because possible meanings of the patient's experiences and lifeworld are disgraced. Psychotic people never completely accept their isolation. They will always try to present themselves as whole, or as a part of the greater whole, and so they will go in search of whatever culture may have to offer in this respect. The consequence is 'cultural wandering' or 'bricolage'.

In the hospital, the locus assigned to subjective and psychotic experiences becomes clear in how these experiences are managed. Because the psychotic world is an obstacle to the therapeutic process, this world is placed under control. An important aspect of this control is the response to threat or danger, not as related to the normal order of society but to the disruption of order in the hospital. Psychotic experiences upset the order and regularity of the wards, and they also interfere with the relations between patients and staff. Something is always under threat, whether it is the well-being of patients, staff members' access to patients, communication, or interaction. Until now, the best ways to deflect aggression and danger seemed to lie in ad hoc measures such as isolating people or drawing up non-suicide contracts with them, but these measures do not alter the increasing level of aggression both inside and outside hospitals.

In this respect, an important task awaits psychiatry: to become a catalyst for social change, or at least not to shy away from public discussion of the issues involved. This idea is not entirely new. Kleinman argues:

> The professionalization of human problems as psychiatric disorders, undeciphered anthropological codes or class warfare, causes sufferers (and their communities) to lose a world, the local context that organizes experience through the moral reverberations and reinforcement of popular cultural categories about what life means and what is at stake in living.
>
> (Kleinman 1995: 117)

Kleinman (1995: 95–120) pleads for 'an ethnography of interpersonal suffering'. Although he refers to suffering caused by violence and trauma rather than by mental illness, I believe that the forms of human suffering caused by psychosis must also be 'constituted out of . . . shared forms of resistance' (Kleinman 1995: 119). However, mental health professionals give meaning to the subjective experiences of psychotic people in rational terms of causality and individual history, with the result that the world of psychotics appears to be generally chaotic and unstructured. The idea of loss of structure is based on the assumption that structure is the opposite of chaos, and that structure must emerge from chaos. By extension, chaos means lack of order. This supposition is not specifically psychiatric; it is a cultural construction. However, I have shown that the psychotic world does have structure. The world of psychotic imaginings and hallucinations displays amazing similarities to the 'normal' world: there are social relationships, rules establishing hierarchical relations between human and non-human beings, and so on (Van Dongen 1991a).

A psychotic world always implies uncertainty. The selfhood of patients is divided into a forbidden 'sick' part consisting of such expressions of psychotic reality as aggression, chaos, lack of insight, wildness and 'wild' associations of thought and speech; and a 'healthy' part, which participates in the therapeutic process. In the process of interaction between therapists and patients, psychotic reality is subjected to the negative compulsion of the taboo and the patient's lack of reality awareness is pointed out. Those elements that assist the therapeutic process are strongly promoted. Control and management are core concepts in this process and reinforce the authority of the therapist. The problem facing therapists, however, is that personal freedom and the questioning of authority have been highly valued in Dutch culture for the past 50 years and, and this makes it difficult for therapists to tell their patients how they should behave in order to live a 'good, moral life'. The consequence is that 'adapting to society' is most evident in mundane and practical areas such as housing, hygiene, and inter-action with others, whereas mental health implies autonomy and a capacity for independent action to achieve a specific goal. This is exactly what is denied to psychotic persons, and the paradox gnaws at the power of psychiatry. A strong belief in control and management of mental disorders hampers the therapeutic process and blocks the way to a more fruitful path to mental health for both therapists and patients.

Inconsistencies and dilemmas in the therapeutic relation

From the above it appears that in interaction between mental health profes-sionals and psychotic people problems arise that lead ineluctably to a struggle, both overt and covert, over the nature and definition of reality. As they construct the psychotic's reality through conversation, the discussion partners alternate between tactics of revealing and concealing. This generates disorder, which on the surface of the interaction seems to stem from the patient's illness. Therapists transform the meaning of what the patient says, and place a taboo on part of the patient's selfhood. Their assessment of psychotic imaginings and tinkering is largely negative, and the net effect is to reinforce the tendency of psychotic people to use deviant imagery and words to describe their life, their experiences and their self-image.

In the hospital, the behavior, actions and speech of psychotic people are couched in a specifically instrumental framework of interpretation (Goffman 1974). This framework determines the 'how' of the interpretation. Accordingly, disruptions that express the patient's psychotic state are important because they 'tell' the therapist how serious the illness is. The source of the command to which the patient responds – the devil, Hitler, a computer – is of lesser diagnostic value (Hoenig 1983: 396). Patients experience this intrusion as a suppression of meaningful 'messages' and they can barely cope with it. They feel like a book judged only by its cover, and this makes the style of the exchange all the more important, because the therapist represents the reality to which patients must conform in order to become acceptable members of society again. It is the presence of the other – in this case, the therapist, who imposes structure, rules and restrictions on the topics and content of the conversation – that gives rise to problems. For psychotic people, the rules of conversation – taking turns, repairs, overlaps, and so on – are not problematic. The problem is that these rules are imposed by mental health care professionals, who represent the abstract power of the state. The elevated status of therapists automatically confers on them the right to assume authority in the consultation room, to break off topics and otherwise define the interaction.

These characteristics of conversational power are a determining factor when psychotic people respond with 'insanity' or insert surprising turns in the conversation. Patients share with therapists cultural presuppositions about the abnormality and deviance of psychotic experiences, and they are generally aware that hallucinations and delusions are inappropriate and cannot be a leitmotif of daily life because they lead invariably to conflict with others. This awareness indicates that they have not lost touch with reality, but owing to their experiences they have come to know a world they cannot forget, no matter how badly they might want to. The psychotic's life-world and perspective on the outside world undergo profound change after an episode of psychosis.

Problems in conversations between patients and therapists stem from differences in ideas about the place and meaning of psychotic experiences in the lives of patients. The world views of psychotic people are reduced to the status of individually determined pathological peculiarities. For the patient, the disorder and its consequences not only change daily life in basic ways but also alter their views and perception of existence. I found that patients' revelations in the conversations were intentional and always related to specific topics, which turned on existential problems. If therapists think of these revelations as 'bizarre', 'incomprehensible', or 'a game', they are assuming that psychotic people employ a personal symbolism unrelated to cultural meanings.[1] From this point of view, experiences signified by this personal symbolism cannot be a basic theme underlying the actions of psychotic people. But it becomes clear in the course of the conversations that they do constitute the non-thematic knowledge that produces specific forms of communication between psychotic people and therapists. Differences concerning the position and meaning of psychotic experiences need not always mean confrontation. They even constitute a condition for conversations between therapists and patients. However, the differences in the interaction consist of paradox, ambivalence, inconsistency and contradiction. This pattern persists throughout the entire interaction of therapists and psychotic people and shapes the stories they tell about themselves and each other. When a patient complained of feeling afraid at night, some therapists treated her fear as a symptom of psychosis, while others would say that she was just 'overly concerned'. Consider Roderick, who tells his therapist that he does not know whether he is lucky or unlucky to be in the hospital, and receives no response to his uncertainty even though the therapist is supposed to engage in empathic conversation. Mental health professionals also have problems intervening in the lives of psychotic persons, even when they see their patients deteriorating. This can at times present severe dilemmas, since it casts doubt on both the power of therapy and on the legitimacy of cultural values and norms.

Therapists and nurses are confronted with the ambivalence of their own discipline. Is it medical science or social science? This indeterminacy gives rise to a series of dilemmas that quickly become apparent in interaction with psychotic people. An important consideration in the helping professions is empathy versus professional distance. Both are considered necessary in interaction with patients and both can have positive and negative effects on the relationship between therapist and patient.

Distance implies coercion, authority, respect for personal autonomy and privacy, control, and inequality. Empathy implies cooperation, understanding, taking patients' feelings into account, intimacy, an atmosphere of trust, contact orientation, and some form of equality. The professional attitudes of empathy and distance collide with the subjectivity of mental health professionals. Therapists and nurses are not cool rationalists who show nothing but professional compassion to their patients. They feel involved in the suffering of people and feel by turns irritated, tried, tested and bored, but professionally their emotions must appear neutral. The process of consolidation and countertransference demonstrates that emotions do play a role below the surface. Patient emotion is allowed to play a role in the interaction, although its expression is bound to certain conditions.

When people speak of emotions, they must do so without expressing them too intensely. In the domain of emotionality, psychiatry sends an ambivalent message. Patients must learn to discuss their emotions and relate them to their disorder, but not to display intense feeling. Emotions that become too intense can be curbed medically, but it is more desirable to say 'If you are emotional, come and talk about it'. Communication of emotion is thus a discursive practice.

Emotion is also a social construct giving rise to certain effects that are interpreted according to cultural standards (cf Abu-Lughod and Lutz 1990: 12). Psychotic people talk about their emotions, sometimes by means of detail ('verbosity'). Detailing can also be interpreted as subterfuge and an attempt to conceal emotion, which is said to be characteristic of psychotic discourse. Besides being a discursive practice, emotion is also an experience and a cultural product because emotion contains an interpretation linked to certain behavior (cf Solomon 1984: 249). It seems that in psychiatry bodily expression of strong emotions is largely replaced by words. These words are not always specifically terms of emotion, nor do they seem to have a direct relation with the emotions they stand for. Dutch culture offers few specific terms for intense emotions, although one frequently hears the wry expression 'Act normally, that is crazy enough.'[2]

The dilemma of 'empathy versus distance' carries other double messages for patients. We have seen that the 'sick' part cannot be permitted to play a prominent role in patient–therapist interactions because it is considered a barrier to the therapeutic process. However, the 'sick' part invariably comes to the fore in these interactions because one of the principles of psychiatric communication is that patients must learn to see the links between their circumstances, symptoms and emotions. Therapists adopt an ambivalent attitude with respect to the position which psychotic experiences could be accorded in interaction. A tolerant view of what is, what is allowed, and what is possible (often expressed as 'Everyone is equal' or 'Who am I to say what I think of it?') does not diminish the essential hierarchy of the therapist–patient relation, for although 'everyone is equal', some are more equal than others.

Another conundrum arises in the response of therapists when patients touch on moral issues, social injustices or certain existential questions. Therapists do not state this openly, but since they use the speech of patients to determine how serious their disorders are, they also diagnose these moral issues. This confronts mental health professionals with a paradox concerning the separation of problems into different categories: those for which the individual is supposedly responsible, and those that arise out of the tension between individual and society. There are, evidently, cultural issues that certain groups of especially vulnerable people cannot countenance. The neglect of the social causes of affliction transmutes resistance into a medical problem and denies weak people whatever power they might otherwise have. The consequence is an attenuated form of resistance that is played out in interactions with the therapist.

There is a fine line between meeting patients' needs and the requirements of personal autonomy. Whenever mental health professionals must decide whether to intervene in the lives of psychotic people, they also encounter contradictory social values and mutually incompatible norms. On the one hand, there are the values of self-responsibility, autonomy, uniqueness, privacy and individuality; on the other, there is the need to adapt to normative restrictions on behavior. But in this dilemma, compassion for human suffering also plays a role. In the matter of intervention versus non-intervention, mental health professionals are

vulnerable, because their decisions – for example, extending a patient's hospitalization – are supervised by outside agencies, and they cannot predict whether
their choice will lead to disruption of a hard-won good relationship with a patient.
An entire spectrum of considerations sustains this complex effect of vulnerability: risk to the therapist's relationship with the patient, certain beliefs concerning the person as a social being, and the scope of external oversight. Further
complicating these matters is the existence of two more or less distinct therapeutic perspectives. The first implies progress, increased insight on the part of
patients into their own problems, and the restoration of social identity and social
skills, based on an idealistic view of people as capable, autonomous, active,
self-developing and self-controlling beings possessed of a clear and unique identity. The other perspective, which holds specifically for many psychotic people,
implies adaptation, acceptance of the disorder, and lasting dependence on health
care. It emerges from a view of people as dependent, more or less passive beings
who are in need of help. The message psychotic people receive from mental health
professionals is ambivalent. They will have to accept that they will never again
be like others, yet at the same time they must learn again to live like others.

Like mental health professionals, and probably in much more emphatic ways,
psychotics are confronted with inconsistency, ambivalence and contradiction.
Their world is doubled and precarious, filled with oppositions. I have described
how patients at Saint Anthony's who sought to interrelate things were constantly
confronted with hindrances and obstacles both within themselves and in the
outside world. Psychotic people seem to have no choice other than to become
tinkers who must struggle against a world they experience as disorderly; a world
they must seek to control with improvised tools scavenged from everything
culture can offer for this purpose.[3] Although psychotic people use conventional
cultural models, these are seldom elaborated to any extent. Their models remain
at the level of rudimentary images that leave much to guesswork. This requires
therapists and nurses to employ a frame of reference other than medical and
psychiatric knowledge if they wish to interpret patients' messages with a measure of accuracy. The central question here, according to Estroff (1993), is whether
they fail to do so because they are unable, or because they are unwilling.

Sometimes, out of sheer need, psychotic people experiment with the limits of
acceptable discourse, and this intensifies the subjectivity of their story. But this
discrepancy in meaning between representations and expected effects arises
from their intense experience of the strong ambivalence in cultural models,
values and norms. Therapists fear that raising the issue of ambiguity might all
too easily become a Sisyphean task because psychotic people evidently do not
accept such ambivalence. To them, oppositions such as good and evil are irreconcilable and compromise is impossible. Psychotic people speak of the world as
it could be and as it should not be. Their narratives are moral commentaries that
reveal attempts to attain valuable goals, and make it clear what patients consider
immoral, especially since they anticipate the terrible consequences that the evil
of others will visit on the hapless psychotic. Moreover, models of good and evil

have great directive impact on self-actualization, and psychotics seek to translate them 'literally' and uncompromisingly.

The problem is that their narratives are undermined by their behavior. In this sense, psychotic people court their own fate, because the emotional consequences of psychotic experiences are considerable for everyone, and worst of all for psychotics themselves. As they feel themselves sinking deeper into a 'black hole', their otherness is emphasized all the more. From experience they know that they must of necessity play along in the game of life. To this end, they must develop a strategy that can explain their experiences and lend credibility to their story. This strategy consists of devising formulaic representations of norms and values, so that personal experiences are concealed in impersonal, generalizing and theorizing models. Models of centrality and marginality clarify how people should deal with these models. Being the center of the world, or being a hero, is not acceptable, and these experiences should not be communicated. Stories about heroes or emperors are 'punished', usually by psychotic persons themselves. Concepts of centrality are hypo-cognitions; they should be (re)presented neither too much nor too often. But concepts of marginality are hyper-cognitions. Evidently, in Dutch culture everyone agrees on this score.

Some researchers have compared psychotic experience and the psychotic world with revitalization movements as described by Wallace (1956). Caughey (1984) refers to a study by the anthropologist and psychiatrist, Faulk, who concludes that the hallucinations of schizophrenics are the same as the visions of revitalization movement leaders. But psychotic people are not social reformers and offer no blueprints for a new cultural system. They will never be leaders and their suffering is enough for them. They have only the 'weapons of the weak' (Scott 1985). Their world is not exclusively bizarre, pathological or marginal, and their stories about their world inform us about the contradictory realities people must live with. I agree with Caughey's statement (1984: 240) quoted at the outset of this book: ' "Schizophrenic" is perhaps best kept in its traditional . . . sense, as a pejorative label for deviants whose visions we do not like.' Even if we do not like their visions, they can reveal to us the ambivalence and paradoxes in our culture, and they may extend our notion of what 'reality' involves.

Psychiatry, however, does not interpret symbols from the psychotic world in terms of a cultural perspective. As a rule, no link is established between psychotic experiences and culture, especially not in a relationship in which both the therapist and the patient have similar cultural backgrounds. Non-rational or mythical experiences, for instance, are excluded; but alien forces, fate, powerlessness and subsequent despair constitute an ontological reality that is not unusual to psychotic people. It is an ontology that recalls Socrates, the Greek and Egyptian temples of dreams, shamans, and Eastern religions. In the Netherlands, there is a growing realization that this ontological reality has meaning and significance (Mooy 1988; Romme and Escher 1990), although traditional psychiatric care has yet to accept it. This mode of being, seen as a more or less unmanageable deviation, is transformed into a manageable process of mourning for things that went wrong. Sorrow can be dealt with, and the process of 'recycling' can begin to take its course.

Probably the most telling example of cultural commentary can be found in the embodiment of those experiences of psychotic people that relate to death. Psychotic people show that the body is not necessarily the safe haven we tend to think; it is not only sticks and stones that can break our bones, because words *can* hurt us. They demonstrate that the self can be broken and the pieces manipulated, and that the body is a political entity subject to control by others. If it eludes their grasp, the consequences are severe, and psychotics' experiences of being touched clarify how terrible they are. If the laws of the body are transgressed, 'evil punishes itself'.

Psychosis, psychiatry and culture

In this final section, I argue that in the microcosm of the conversations between therapists and psychotic people, ambivalence, paradox, irreconcilable contradictions and double messages merge. Both parties experience them fully and unceasingly, and they are, in fact, unavoidable. Therapists and patients are caught in a 'double bind' (Bateson 1972) that cannot easily be unbound.

Interactions between therapists and psychotic people are essentially a battle for truth. Therapists judge the speech acts of psychotic persons as untrue on three counts: with respect to their existential presuppositions, with respect to their normative content, and with respect to the intentions of the discussion partners (cf Habermas 1990). Hallucinations and delusions are evaluated as untrue and the psychotic world is denied the right to exist within the normal social order. Psychotic speech is forbidden speech, and a new reality must be worked out in interaction between patient and therapist, ideally through consensus, although, given the powerful truth claims of psychiatric discourse, this is unlikely. Both therapist and patient proceed tentatively. Uncertainty arises from the ambivalence, contradiction and paradox inherent in the cultural system of meanings, and the risk of disagreement is always present. Because of this, the conversation is in a sense 'chronic'; that is, a potentially interminable recycling process in which the pragmatically normative discourse of therapists opposes the existentially evaluative discourse of patients. When patients' values and experiences are excluded from consideration, intersubjective space shrinks, and what ensues are 'costly discourses' (Habermas 1990): lengthy negotiations, cultural tinkering, and sudden strategic moves by both therapists and patients.

Patients' psychotic experiences threaten to defamiliarize the self-evident and unquestioned truths of the cultural order. Such experiences always prove to be exhausting battles in which patients are caught between, and defeated by, irreconcilable meanings. In order to shield them from this fate, it is necessary for therapists to maintain close relationships with them. This does not mean that therapists should accept their patients' realities at their face value, but it does suggest that psychotic speech, grounded as it is in familiar cultural models, is intentional and goal directed. The stories psychotic people tell testify to serious doubts about cultural discourses of identity and of personal responsibility and autonomy. They are a mediating device, a way of avoiding direct confrontation with 'normal' life and the painful changes that would be necessary in order to rejoin it. It is possible to negotiate this passage progressively, if psychotic people's stories are not categorically judged to be false representations, and as a rule psychotic people themselves indicate how this could take place (Van Dongen 1993d). The generalizing theories and elaborate ritualized safety measures they invent for themselves as a defense against irreconcilable cultural contradictions point to culturally institutionalized forms of injustice and hypocrisy that affect all members of society. Recognition of this might serve as a starting point for a psychiatric discourse on cultural change.

If we could concede that the experience of psychotic people is given form and inscribed in the body through the agency of culture, we would be far less inclined to isolate them. This notion is implicit in studies of psychosis in non-Western cultures (Van den Bosch 1993). It appears to be the case that the prognosis of psychotic disorders in these societies is more favorable,[4] partly because the sufferers' social bonds are not severed and partly because treatment by traditional healers rests on explication of psychotic experiences aided by culturally specific ceremonies (Ward 1989). We should, however, resist the temptation to conclude that non-Western societies always offer more acceptance, shelter and care to those whose behavior transgresses socially accepted boundaries. Rejection, ridicule and social exclusion can also be found in these societies. Some have claimed that this is a consequence of urbanization and its associated problems (Gernaat 1993). Others see no reason to include traditional therapies in the treatment of psychotic people in non-Western societies because they do not yield better results; nor do they target improved social functioning or reduce the negative reactions that psychotic people encounter from others (Assen 1990). A detailed analysis of this literature is beyond the scope of this book, but I would suggest that we should neither adopt uncritically the practices of non-Western cultures nor dismiss their cultural achievements out of hand.

Anthropologists have described rituals of healing whose significance far transcends simple recovery (Katz 1989; Devisch 1993). These rituals induce feelings of solidarity between healing spirits, healers, society and the stricken person, emphasizing processes of transformation as shared experience. The healer is a 'moral explorer' (Katz 1989) interacting with cultural mysteries and delivering a moral judgment. Transformations are effected by working with culture as a form of mediation, a potential space between feelings, thoughts and experiences, and the social world (Devisch 1993). Such therapeutic rituals offer alternatives to the fragmentation characteristic of current psychiatric practice because their efficacy rests on experiences of interpersonal solidarity that are essential to survival (Rappaport 1978).

Much more is possible in conversations between therapists and psychotic people than some believe. In this book, interaction between therapists and patients has been frozen by inscription, so that it can be examined for possible opportunities. Even in the most immediate and terrible moments of hallucination, psychotic people always prove able to articulate their suffering and to countenance it. They seek to build their own bridges across the gulf created by irreconcilable cultural contradictions in order to restore their feeling of wholeness. They create a space by externalizing their feelings in the form of unusual stories, and by their actions they show that they know these to be mental constructs. This, in turn, gives therapists space to work with them. Against the background of cultural contradictions intensely experienced in the interaction between patients and therapists, new areas of experience can be explored and questions posed concerning moral issues and the nature of reality. This is possible because these contradictions not only point to the loneliness and pain, evil and death that are the consequences of transgression, but also offer stories of joy and comfort that can lead to change and thence to healing.

I argue that the stories of psychotic people are not simple metaphors for something else; they are part of the very fabric of culture. In psychotic disorders, suffering is given a symbolic form shaped by pre-existing cultural concepts and categories, and at the same time it shapes a part of the afflicted person. The effect of this is that the psychotic person becomes an 'intermediary' who is likely to evoke shame and aversion both in himself and in others (Schutz 1971).

I suggest that therapists could direct and bind to themselves the experiences of psychotic patients, so that their suffering is no longer restricted to their inner lives. In this way, the necessary transformations brought about by the therapeutic process are not restricted to the patient. If the boundaries of the individual were less sharply drawn, psychotic people could stop struggling and recognize that their discourse, like that of therapists, contains essential truths where it relates to cultural indeterminacy and contradiction.

In the conversations I observed between therapists and psychotic people, there were occasional moments when they became very close. These poignant and touching moments were a joy to both. Perhaps this joy was partly inspired by the idea that after this conversation treatment had been 'completed'. What is certain is that when the therapist did not set out with the intention of conveying a message, no battle ensued. When struggle was eliminated, the joy of the performance came to the fore and the intersubjective space of this enjoyment was filled with an exploration of the thoughts and ideas of both parties, a cooperative 'wandering' without falling, sinking, or getting lost. Perhaps it is possible to begin a therapeutic relationship in this way, by listening and working with the dialectics of good and evil, omnipotence and enmity, life and death in order to discover there 'islands of clarity' (Podvoll 1990). This, in turn, may move us to reflect on the ambiguities and double moralities present in our culture, which evidently occasion so much pain in the experience of vulnerable people.

A psychiatry that limits itself to the identification and treatment of psychotic disorders is metonymic; the self is fragmented, and the 'sick' part is made to stand for the entire 'sick person'. But if the psychotic person is viewed in the context of ill-making aspects of a cultural system, psychiatry can become metaphoric; that is, the link between the disorder and the individual can yield, on the symbolic level, important knowledge about the world in which we all live. The resulting conversation would be a vehicle for shared human concerns in a therapy that does not cling stubbornly to notions of personal responsibility, self-realization and individuality, but accepts dependence, moral exploration of the world, and 'bricolage' as indispensable elements of healing.

Notes

I Introduction

1 Research was subsidised by the Stichting Sociaal Culturele Wetenschappen (Foundation for Social and Cultural Sciences), renamed Stichting voor Economische, Sociaal-culturele en Ruimtelijke Wetenschappen (Foundation for Economic, Social-cultural and Planological Sciences), part of the Nederlandse Wetenschappelijke Organisatie NWO (Netherlands Scientific Organisation). Dossier number 510-76-306.

2 At the time of the research the third version of the DSM was in use. In the Dutch version of the manual of diagnostic criteria (DSM-III-R 1987: 301) 'psychotic' is described as serious shortcomings in reality testing and the creation of a new reality. The concept is also used to designate seriously disoriented behavior. In DSM, schizophrenia, delusion disorders, psychotic disorders not described elsewhere in the manual, a number of psycho-organic disorders and some mood disturbances are listed as psychotic disorders. Since the time of my research this version of the DSM has been supplanted by a fourth version, which is now used in Dutch psychiatry.

3 The Evaluation Committee of the Hospital Board declared the inquiry 'ethically permissible'. This committee evaluates all research projects carried out in hospitals. Specific requirements which must be met include proper advance patient information, signed participant declarations of willingness to participate, guarantees for the protection of the privacy and anonymity and guarantees for appropriate measures in case of negative effects of the research.

4 Anthropology lectures are part of the curriculum of training for nursing staff in this hospital.

5 The 'intellectual *habitus*' (Richters 1991: 33) of psychiatrists to listen to anthropological accounts which imply critical reflection on their own history and relevance is less rare than reported among somatic doctors.

2 The quest for reality and the work with culture

1 The patient could have referred to a subdiscipline of anthropology: primatology. Works of Goodall and the Leakeys in Africa are well known, as is Morris's book *The Naked Ape* (Susan DiGiacomo, personal communication). I will never know.

2 This view is described by both Foucault (1972) and Porter (1987). In Foucault's *L'Histoire de la folie à l'âge classique* the psychotic person presents society with a mirror in which to discover the truth that culture lacks reason and that humanity is ridiculous. This view is found also in anti-psychiatry (Thomas Szasz 1976; Laing 1971) in this case with the objective of world improvement by way of insights supplied by psychotic people. This image of lunatics as potential world improvers or culture critics also emerged in anthropological writings during the 1970s (Crapanzano 1977).

3 This view resulted from the growing awareness during the 1950s and 1960s that dull-wittedness, apathy and aggression might well be the consequence of confinement. Researchers like Goffman (1961a) and in the Netherlands Loois (1964), Trimbos (1957) and Romme (1967) point to psychological change in people who are continually confined and to the negative effects of institutions. First, the near-impregnable institutions were rebuilt into hospitals where busy daily programmes and patient-oriented therapies were meant to promote healing and curtail the negative effects of admission. Therapeutic communities with multidisciplinary teams came somewhat later and extramural care replaced hospitalization. In recent years mental health care has concentrated increasingly on home care. A large number, among others the mentally handicapped who up to then had remained in psychiatric establishments, left the institution and moved to specially designed clinics. Elderly long-term residents have since died. The number of long-term residential mentally ill has dwindled and comprehensive extramural mental health care has been established. Nevertheless many whose psychotic disorder was chronic or severe enough to require continuous supervision remained behind. The hospitals are converted into more or less 'open' houses, where patients live together in small groups, supervised by nurses and therapists. Other forms of sheltered housing have been established, but the intramural facilities cannot cope with the number of patients that are eligible for long-term residence, and society is not ready for communal care (cf Giel 1984).

4 In anthropology the assumed value-free character of the system is questioned. Attempts are made to demonstrate that the classification system entails (American) values, norms and cultural articulations of madness (Richters 1988 and others). Kleinman (1988: 14) speaks of 'category fallacy' when 'one culture's diagnostic categories and their projection onto patients in another culture, where those categories lack coherence and their validity has not been established' is reified.

5 To try to cope with these problems psychiatry developed a biopsychosocial concept of illness (Pols 1984: 178ff) which includes not only biological aspects, but also intrapsychic, relational and socio-cultural aspects. Mental illnesses are now called psychiatric disorders: 'disorders which come to expression in experience and behaviour regardless of their cause' (Pols 1984: 167). This designation distinguishes them clearly from physical illness.

6 'What is the most typical characteristic of psychiatry? It is its dual structure, its position as human science and as natural science' (Rümke 1948).

7 For example, see Vos and Van Berkesteijn (1993) on the history of psychiatric training in the Netherlands. The authors document the shifts in emphasis in the training programmes over the past 150 years. Up to the 1960s training tended to be medical, after that more psychosocial and psychotherapeutic while scientific research gained greater prominence. Currently it is to be expected that, under the pressure of social opinion (cf recent discussions concerning psychotherapy as task of the psychiatrist), the task of the psychiatrist will become increasingly more 'technical' and medical.

8 Impaired reality testing is a consequence of disturbances in reality awareness. These come forward in the relation one has with reality. The disturbances are characterized, among other things, by animism, intolerance towards changes in the environment, heightened sensitivity to stimuli, inability to distinguish between self and environment, depersonalization, increased perceptive sensitivity, dismemberment of the sick part as a defence against and denial of the problem (Frosch 1983).

9 'In the proper manner' here means: in accordance with conventional social knowledge.

10 It can be said that psychiatry defines the limits of culture very precisely. It describes with increasing accuracy people who transgress cultural prohibitions and so indicates what is still permitted. In this, psychiatry is firmly tied to culture.

11 These approaches are based on 'the new cybernetics' (Heylighen et al. 1991) of constructivists such as Maturana, Varela, Von Glasersfeld, Von Förster, Pask. The

constructivist approach in psychiatry, particularly in reflection on system therapy, was introduced by Kenny, Dell, Goolishian, Hoffman and Watzlawick.

12 Psychiatry is, system theoretically speaking, a matter of 'sharing the knowledge in a conversation' (Rosseel 1990).

13 See also Rosseel's comment on the basic aspects of constructivism (1990: 27–29).

14 Most research aimed at the refinement of diagnostics takes place outside of the clinical or social context. In it, distinctions are typically made between disorders in form, structural and relational aspects of language and semantic disturbance, in relation to disorders in the nervous system. The disorders become visible, for example, in disorders in linguistic perception, incoherence, loss of memory, restricted use of language and restricted language content.

15 The conclusion is that the perspective on linguistic disorders is clouded due to the ambiguity of the concept of thought disorders and the lack of standardized measurements (Andreasen 1979a, 1979b). It appears that linguistic disorders occur in schizophrenic discourse, but also in manic and depressive psychotic conditions (Andreasen 1979b; Harvey 1983; LeCours and Varnier-Clement 1976), and that these deviations are not universally or equally prevalent (Brown 1973; Harvey 1983). As a consequence of these findings, a formal language based on empirical research and statistical analysis has been developed for the accurate description of patient behavior (Andreasen 1979a, 1979b; Andreasen and Olsen 1982; Johnston and Holzman 1979). Concepts such as tangentiality, echolalia, neologism, sound association, blockage, derailment, poverty of content, and poverty of language, are listed in order of importance and standardized as instruments of measurements. Andreasen (1979a: 474–481) distinguishes 20 categories into which psychotic discourse and thought can be divided.

16 Various inquiries show that psychotics cannot properly survey the context and hence cannot give words the correct meaning (Chapman 1965 and others). This disorder, usually referred to as decontextualizing, is explained in further research in successively different ways and is confirmed or adjusted on the basis of different results. Salzinger et al. (1970), for example, says that psychotic people react to words immediately preceding, rather than to words used earlier. Maher (1972) finds that the context is not used to correct associative, semantic and responsive errors; he confirms this in later research (Maher et al. 1980). Another group of studies (Smith 1970 and others) relates decontextualizing to problems in the ability to concentrate.

17 This presupposition, in turn, is the starting point for research in the area of 'expressed emotions' (Brown 1973; Goldstein et al. 1989; Kuipers et al. 1983; Leff and Vaughn 1981), which shows that in family relations where relatives reveal their emotions towards the psychotic member, there is increased risk of decompensation or psychotic crisis. Such research helps to explain the need for caution and restraint relative to psychotic patients in a clinic, but I doubt whether extreme reserve is always indicated.

18 Preferably, the literature of outstanding authors in the field (Freud, Arieti, Sullivan, Moyaert). Experience and subjectivity are core concepts; meaning is attributed on the basis of the text as a whole, and the context but meaning is understood as an individual, intentional category which is a more or less cryptic representation of hidden individual meanings and a problematic individual history. It is assumed that in psychotic people symbolic processes are disturbed (Kubie 1953; Moyaert 1982a, 1982b) and that an idiosyncratic system of significations came into being.

19 Many are gloomy about the application of psychotherapies (McGlashan 1984; Gunderson et al. 1984; Van den Bosch 1990). Psychoanalysis is seen as impossible. The general opinion is that one should be reserved and cautious (Cullberg 1989), avoid emotions and protect the patients.

20 Chaika (1981), for example, describes how a psychotic woman was forced into a monologue because of the minimal reactions of the other. Van Bijsterveld (1982) specifies

Chaika's observation that rules of discourse are not applied correctly by relating psychiatric views on schizophrenia to use of language. The author asks to what extent people have recourse to strategies to protect or uphold themselves *vis-à-vis* their environment and to what extent these strategies occasion special interaction patterns which, as such, are not unusual. Hoffman (1986a) points to the importance of the listener (the normal discussion partner): if he cannot successfully structure the text he will consider it incoherent, vague and difficult to follow. The speech of psychotic people is understood as intentional speech acts to establish identity (Van Belle 1987).

21 My approach has certain similarities to linguistic pragmatics (cf Austin 1960; Leech 1983), but differs in that not only speech acts are considered; I take pragmatics in a broader sense, and relate speech acts to the situation, to reality constructions and to 'culture'.

22 In *Sein und Zeit*, M. Heidegger calls this meaning in the daily practice of people 'interpretation', and the method by which an interpretation is interpreted is 'hermeneutics'. Richters (1991) calls this form of hermeneutics 'objective hermeneutics' because, since the goal is a detailed study of how people understand their life world, the subjectivity of a researcher plays a negligible role. In addition, Richters distinguishes two other forms of hermeneutics: dialogical hermeneutics, which aims at maximum intersubjectivity between researcher and subjects, and reconstructive hermeneutics, in which dialogical hermeneutics is linked to causal explanations in the attempt to treat themes like ideology, criticism of ideology, power and emancipation in terms of a critical theory.

23 The models function as regulating principles (D'Andrade and Strauss 1992) which influence choices, objectives and behavior. Models give shape to interpretations and experiences. Their contours become clear in communicative processes (Holland and Quinn 1987; White 1992).

24 I do not discuss the concept of subjectivity as understood in dialogical anthropology. Others have done so in the context of their research (cf Pool 1989; Krumeich 1994). Although I agree that the subjectivity of the researcher can contribute importantly to scientific knowledge (Krumeich 1994), I also believe, as does Richters (1991), that at some point one must distance oneself. This distance is needed, for example, when one seeks to trace the effect of certain dominant values and norms in a society for groups of people and when the question arises whether such values and norms should be reconsidered.

25 Foucault refers to this position as 'knowledge': 'knowledge is also the space in which the subject may take up a position and speak of the objects with which he deals in his discourse' (Foucault 1972: 182).

26 Cf Bock (1980: 17): 'The study of motivation is concerned with biological needs and psychological drives that influence the behavior of organisms.'

27 From this perspective, psychiatry interprets the symbols in the speech of psychotics as (linguistic) behavior arising from certain normal needs. Since a psychotic person has distorted the process of internalization of values and norms, his linguistic behavior is different from that of non-psychotics. It is said that psychotic people are not properly integrated into the cultural order (cf Lacan 1966; Moyaert 1982b) and that for this reason they denude language of its normal symbolic meanings. In this view, culture is seen as steering people's needs and drives, although in 'erroneous' ways. This mode of contextualizing (i.e. in line with traditional motivation theory) reduces culture to mental phenomena and behavioral patterns (cf Geertz 1973), but does not explain the great diversity in expression of needs and drives of patients. It also obscures or hides the manipulative aspects of culture. Articulation in all its diversity does not pertain to content only, but also to the situation in which the utterances are made (I discuss this point in Chapter 7). Furthermore, this theoretical perspective provides no room to study how people fit their experiences of madness into

frameworks and models. Knowledge of how experiences of madness are given form (and internalized) is required to understand the implications of psychosis (cf Richters 1991: 391). An alternative to traditional motivation theory is the recent approach in cognitive anthropology, which investigates how various models are mutually inter-related (D'Andrade 1992; Holland and Quinn 1987). According to this approach cultural models not only describe the world, but they also explicate people's purposes and clarify their desires. Cognitive anthropology brings out an important property of models (which are also referred to as schemas, frameworks or scenarios): the hierarchic organization, in which interpretations that are given form in a model are passed on to higher level models to achieve more generalized interpretations. By way of the hierarchical relations among models the situational variation in model use can be clarified and explained. An important function of the highest level is that it represents an objective. As D'Andrade (1992: 30f) formulates: 'A person's most general interpretations of what is going on will function as important goals for that person . . . to understand people one needs to understand what leads them to act as they do, and to understand what leads them to act as they do one needs to know their goals, and to understand their goals one must understand their overall interpretive system . . . and to understand their interpretive system – their schemas – one must understand something about the hierarchical relations among these schemas.'

28 The comparison is from cybernetics (cf Bateson 1972).
29 Nevertheless, substitution in the sense of detachment and distancing from the origin of for instance fear, sorrow or conflicts is important to psychotic people. Also, it is a basic function of 'doing' culture (Obeyesekere 1990: 63): 'unconscious ideas, themselves unacceptable to consciousness, can obviously become acceptable to the conscience . . . when they are transformed into public culture'. I return to this in Chapters 7 and 8.
30 There are two traditions in anthropology: one which analyses the socio-cultural dimensions of texts and one which views texts as 'performances'. These two approaches need not be mutually exclusive; they can be complementary. The significance of experiences of psychotic people resides in the events spoken of in the conversations and in the relations of those events with different worlds, as well as the way in which complex and culture-specific knowledge is evoked or used (Durantt and Goodwin 1992).
31 For example, learning to recognize that one's feeling of being a victim is part of ridding oneself of feelings of guilt.
32 Rhodes (1991), for example, shows the nature and limitations of power in a psychiatric institution. She asserts that power is not external and autonomous, but often linked to a specific situation. According to her, power has its impact on both patients and therapists.

3 Shaping the context of speech events

1 See Sullivan (1974) on the beginnings of schizophrenia. The period preceding psychosis is called the pre-psychotic period. The author notes: 'Not family physicians alone, but specialists in rhinology, laryngology, gastrointestinal maladies, in urology and in gynaecology, all these see the incipient schizophrenic and all too often let things ride' (1974: 106).
2 The idiom used is connected to symbolic and affective associations which get their meaning in relation to specific stressors, the availability and the social implications of the use of a given idiom, its communicative power and the willingness of others to react to it (Nichter 1981: 379).
3 In an explorative study in the field, Jongerius et al. (1991) conclude that, although relatives of psychiatric patients feel that they are doing all they can for their relative,

they are continually confronted with the impossibility of having any influence at all on the problem. Relatives say that ambulant help by the RIAGG (regional ambulatory psychiatry) is inadequate: because it extends home treatment far too long.

4 The social network of patients is restricted to the parents, a brother or sister or a few acquaintances. Of the 26 patients in this study, for example, there were six whose parents were directly involved in the hospital admission.

5 In this context intentions are not argued or considered objectives. They are understood as psychological conditions containing a number of assumptions which people would make clear to others (Sperber and Wilson 1986).

6 In this study 21 out of 26.

7 Not all vagrants, however, suffer from psychotic disorders (Baasher et al. 1983).

8 The reference is to Jerzy Kosinsky's novel (1965).

9 An intermediate level school.

10 See Price (1987: 319, 325) on counter-examples in illness histories.

4 Hope and hopelessness, healthy and sick parts

1 According to an internal hospital report from the time of the research the figures are as given below. Of a total population of 343 patients in the STR 41 are diagnosed as schizophrenic, 26 as delusional and 35 as psychotic NOS. The number of persons admitted via a court order or warrant is increasing, both in terms of percentage and in absolute terms. Between 16 and 20 per cent of the patients were either taken into custody or admitted via a court order.

2 In psychiatry this concept is well known. It implies maximum self-responsibility and autonomy on the part of patients. Care to measure is further linked to outreaching, that is to say, home care of psychiatric patients.

3 See Van Dongen (1989), which describes how, in the course of a discussion with a group of patients during creative therapy a new meaning is given to a certain type of behavior. The term arrived at is subsequently taken over in daily conversations.

4 Creative therapy, gymnastics and gardening therapy, hobby activities and working outside of the hospital.

5 In this they reveal a similarity with culture critics. Foucault, for example, analyzes in 'L'absence de l'oeuvre' (1964) how new developments in medicine will cause mental illness to disappear. Foucault holds that these disorders will be allocated increasingly more controllable space, as a result of which madness will become invisible.

6 Patients who keep being admitted and dismissed are called *draaideurpatienten* (revolving door patients).

7 This is a form of sheltered housing: Regionale Instelling Beschermd Wonen (regional institute for sheltered housing).

8 Handbooks on nursing and the treatment of psychotic people habitually emphasize that mental health workers should remain well attuned to their own psychic traits – it is presupposed that all humans have them – without letting them become frightening. The emphasis is on the need of stability for the mental health worker as counterweight to the instability of psychotics (Cook 1971; Cullberg 1989; Searles 1961).

9 See also Kernberg (1975) for an all-inclusive definition of countertransference.

10 It is assumed that psychotic expressions fall under a culture's linguistic prohibitions (Foucault 1964). I take the view that in present culture this is no longer the case (Van Dongen 1993b). Moral prohibitions in many cases no longer relate 'offensive' thinking or speech; they relate to behavior, aggressiveness especially.

11 See Van Dongen (1989, 1991b).

12 In this connection De Swaan (1979) remarks that the patient is educated to become his own therapist.

13 The conditions of the principle of cooperation are: that people should provide as much information as required, but no more; all their statements should be true; lack of clarity and equivocation should be avoided; the information should be brief and clear. The conditions of the principle of politeness are: tactfulness, generosity, approval, humility, agreeability and sympathy.

14 Van Haaster (1991) calls the rules for intercourse with psychotic people 'tips by careful therapists'. In his doctoral dissertation he presents a number of suggestions by Searles (1961) that show similarities with the general rules of discourse, though related here to confusion, fear and uncertainty.

15 *Binnenhof* refers to an old pavilion, demolished when the hospital was renovated.

16 These traits and abilities are in agreement with cultural views on the scope of personality. See for example Richters (1988). This is not the place to expand on the agreement between self-images in psychiatry and in society.

17 See, for instance, Kerkhof (1985) concerning suicide and mental health care. Aggressiveness of psychiatric patients evoked a heated discussion on the occasion of the murder of a young girl in Amsterdam in March 1993. The issue was closing or reducing the number of psychiatric hospitals.

18 Oderwald (1985: 163–164) posits that in medicine the original identity of patients is restored via the exchange of diagnosis for therapy. Identity is restored because the ailment is removed, or rather the causes of the ailment are removed. Identity and illness are in this case strictly distinguished entities. In the case of psychotic people the trade is dissimilar. Here the exchange does not imply removal of the illness; a negative diagnosis is presupposed. The causes cannot be taken away; at best they can be given a new meaning. This exchange is generally based on acceptance of life as a psychotic person. The illness, then, is not overcome, but is redefined as an entity that is part of the individual.

19 Freud's interpretation of President Schreber's religious megalomania is an example of this (see Mooy 1987).

5 Hiding in talk

1 In psychiatric treatment 'meaning is not created at random; what happens is that new meaning is given to the patient's history' (cf Moyaert 1982a: 143).

2 See Van Haaster (1991). In the first chapters of *Wartaal* (gibberish) the author presents a discussion of ways in which therapists deal with psychotics, especially schizophrenics.

3 The instant that the psychiatrist presses the button of the taperecorder it marks the formal start of the conversation.

4 The coffee ceremony applies especially in the LTR. It has a double significance: on the one hand it is meant to put patients at ease in an unusual situation, since therapists and patients do not converse regularly. On the other hand it is an announcement that the therapist means to tempt the patients to be cooperative and open.

5 According to Hall (1973) territoriality is the personal space one desires around himself. It is a very important aspect of human behavior although not usually experienced consciously.

6 Earlier, René had refused the session, but eventually he agreed to come.

7 The patient did volunteer work in the municipality where he lived.

8 In this connection, Goffman (1974) refers to 'framing': placing the conversation in a framework with the intention that the discussion partners know what kind of conversation is expected. Goffman refers to the clarification of positions and roles as alignment.

9 'Face': the status and value of either actor before an (imaginary) audience.

10 Paraphrasing Sperber and Wilson (1986: 125): 'An assessment is relevant in a context to the extent that its contextual effects in this context are large. [. . .] an assessment is relevant in a context to the extent that the effort required to process it in this context is small.'

11 Restriction on the part of therapists is much more evident in ontological transforma- tions, when emotional expressions by patients are translated into therapeutically suitable language.

12 In this connection Levy (1984: 219) speaks of 'hypocognized emotions' – emotions for the expression of which in a particular culture few words are available.

13 In the STR, one of the most important objectives is 'productivity', that is, the intention is to treat and discharge as many patients as possible in the shortest time possible. In this process people 'learn' to engage independently in certain activities, such as handling money, taking care of oneself, cooking, and going shopping.

14 For many years now, government effort has been directed at reducing the number of beds in psychiatric hospitals.

15 Saville-Troike (1985) reviews the complex nature of silence. She discusses the many types of silence and their function and differentiates between silence as a structur- ing principle and a communicative principle. She shows how silence can take over the function of most speech acts. Saville-Troike further argues that the symbolic meaning of silence renders it ambiguous and prone to serious communication mis- understandings. A comparable argument can be made for verbosity. Maltz (1985) for instance shows that 'noise' in an American Pentecostal church has an important religious function and that the very same function is fulfilled among Quakers by silence.

16 However, showing emotion – crying, loud laughing, etc. – is almost obligatory in current television shows. Emotions are presented because viewers demand them.

17 See Van Dongen (1993c). In this article I describe how Christiaan and others are continually plagued by devils which command them to approach others aggressively.

18 Gilmore (1985) terms this behavior 'stylized sulking'.

6 Revealing in talk (No notes)

7 Living in two worlds

1 Compare Obeyesekere (1990: 19): 'The symbols do not help to overcome his troubled past, but repeat that past' (the author is referring to a Muslim ecstatic who regularly executes the ritual of hanging from a hook).

2 Compare Obeyesekere (1990: 4–28), the dynamics of regression/progression.

8 The precarious world of psychotic people

1 In de wijdste wereldsche weelden heb ik gezworven,
Gerust aan de schoonste ongenaakbaarste borst,
En ben kort daarna, gevallen, gezonken, bijna gestorven
Van kommer en heimwee, van honger en dorst. ('Een Eerlijk Zeemansgraf'. The translation is by John Kraay.)

2 To deal with variations in the symptoms between persons, clinical psychiatry makes a distinction between pathogenic and pathoplastic determinants of a mental illness. The pathogenic determinants are the biological causes of the illness (form). The patho- plastic determinants are the personal and cultural varations (content). Treatment is directed to the underlying cause of the illness, and content has less bearing on the cause (cf Littlewood 2000: 69–73).

3 Performative terms establish a relation with reality as experienced: 'they bring the communicative dimension into the open by referring to the speaker–hearer's acts of saying, cogitating and doing' (Tyler 1978: 382).

4 Compare Miller (1989), who describes the drama of people's lost feelings.

5 Compare Shweder (1991). In this work the author gives an exposition of his theory of social construction.

6 Recent biological and technical advances in psychiatric treatment make it easier to avoid the question of guilt.

7 Here, Moyaert paraphrases Lacan (1966).

8 I am thinking, for example, of 'urban myths'. In these new myths, unsavoury persons use modern medical techniques, or human capacities are ascribed to computers. The myths can be understood as a warning against life in the city, where uncontrollable and powerful agents engage in dark practices. An example of such new myths is the story of the man in Marrakesh (or some other city) awaking on a bench and discovering that he has lost one of his kidneys. He is a victim of a criminal gang dealing in human organs, stolen of course by the 'strangers' (Moroccans).

9 Compare Girard (1978a: 36–44); Freud (1913, *Totem und Tabu*).

10 A well-known example is that of President Schreber, a case in which Freud comments on this problem.

11 In the southern Dutch culture this occurs during carnival celebrations, which can be traced to the Saturnalia. As in other parts of the world, these festivals are characterized by masquerades and exchanges of clothing. Transvestism is frequently associated with the worship of the Great Mother Goddess, whereby men dramatize their loyalty to her by wearing her clothing. This meaning is less clearly present in contemporary carnival transvestism. It is true, however, that at carnival time many men still dress as women.

12 My findings are similar to those of Corin (1990), who shows that detachment from the world has positive aspects and that cultural frameworks serve the expression of personal experiences. One of the most important frameworks serving to express detachment is religion.

13 Elsewhere (Van Dongen 1993d) I have written about Christiaan's self-diagnosis.

14 This longing for a life without pain can ultimately lead to apparent apathy and lack of interest. This should not be seen as entirely negative. For psychotic people it often means a condition of complete serenity and the complete absence of unease. Compare also Moyaert (1982a, 1982b: Chapter 8).

9 Life and death

1 The translation of Baudelaire's poem is by Susan DiGiacomo.

> C'est la Mort qui console, hélas!, et qui fait vivre
> C'est le but de la vie, et c'est le seul espoir
> Qui, comme un élixir, nous monte et nous enivie
> Et nous donne le coeur de marcher jusqu'au soir.
> (Baudelaire, *La mort des pauvres*)

2 Freud (1920) *Jenseits des Lustprinzips*. Freud claimed that the purpose of all life is death, and developed this theory to explain the continually repeated experiencing of traumas.

3 Approximately 10 per cent of the 150,000 schizophrenics in the Netherlands actually end their lives (*Volkskrant*, 16 November 1993).

4 With this term I mean to cover both the physical and inner awareness of touch or feeling.

5 The flagellant movement receded towards the end of the 14th century, but revived when all Europe was scourged by the plague. The flagellants turned against the then dominant hierarchy and participated in the holocaust. The movement was finally condemned by the Council of Konstanz (1417). In point of fact, self-castigation occurred in monasteries: the discipline of the *flagellum*, a knotted rope. I recall that as a child I saw remnants of the *flagellum* tied around the waist of monks of certain orders.

6 In a specific type of psychiatric aid these cultural models play a role. This is the case, for example, in the Jungian tradition, which works with archetypes and myths (cf Perry 1976).

7 At the time of the research, a feature in the *Volkskrant* and the *NRC* (major Dutch daily newspapers) reported that the Parisian artist Orlan composed a computer model from paintings depicting five mythical women in order to create a self-portrait by means of surgery. This gives most of us pause; chimeras are concretized here in the 'strange' way Orlan treats her body. But her art is based on creation and bricolage with existing shapes. Psychotic people, by contrast, destroy their own body.

8 This is true for Western culture. In Buddhist cultures the inability to realize emptiness implies ignorance.

9 Psychotic people resemble the seer Cassandra in Christa Wolf's novel *Cassandra*: a Greek woman sometimes said to be mad, who wishes to let go of 'reality' and free herself from the world.

10 Conclusion

1 In the announcement of a symposium on psychotic people organized by Saint Anthony's, I read this telling assertion: 'The symbolism of a psychotic has no metaphoric properties; there is no transmission of meaning.'

2 Translation of 'Doe maar gewoon, dan doe je al gek genoeg.'

3 See Podvoll (1990). The author calls these 'psychotically transformative experiences', occurring when direct contact is established with forces beyond human control, some of which have benevolent effects while others have evil effects. Shamans, who assume that they are harmful to health, know these forces.

4 International Pilot Study of Schizophrenia and Collaborative Study on Determinants of Outcome of Severe Mental Disorders (World Health Organization). For a review see Jablensky *et al.* (1992) and Leff *et al.* (1992).

References

Abu-Lughod, L. and C. Lutz (1990) 'Introduction: emotion, discourse, and the politics of everyday life', in: C. Lutz and L. Abu-Lughod (eds), *Language and the politics of emotion*, Cambridge: Cambridge University Press, 1–24.

Adams, V. (1992) 'The production of self and body in Sherpa–Tibetan society', in: M. Nichter (ed.), *Anthropological approaches to the study of ethnomedicine*, Philadelphia: Gordon and Breach, 149–191.

Alverson, H. and S. Rosenberg (1990) 'Discourse analysis of schizophrenic speech: a critique and proposal, *Applied Psycholinguistics 11*: 167–184.

American Psychiatric Association (APA) (1987) *Quick reference to the diagnostic criteria from DSM-III-R*, Washington, DC: APA.

—— (1994) *Diagnostic and statistical manual of mental disorders*, 4th edn, Washington, DC: APA.

Anderson, H., H. Goolishian and L. Winderman (1986) 'Problem determined systems: toward transformation in family therapy', *Journal of Strategic and Systemic Therapies 5*: 14–19.

Andreasen, N. (1979a) 'The clinical assessment of thought, language, and communication disorders', *Archives of General Psychiatry 36*: 1325–1321.

—— (1979b) 'The diagnostic significance of disorders in thought, language and communication', *Archives of General Psychiatry 36*: 1325–1330.

Assen, G. (1990) *Lilalu. Psychose in Kenya*, dissertation, Groningen: Universiteit van Groningen.

Austin, J. (1960) *How to do things with words*, Oxford: Clarendon Press.

Baasher, T., A. Elhakim, E. Fawal, K. Giel, R. Harding and T. Wankiiri (1983) 'On vagrancy and psychosis', *Community Mental Health Journal 19/1*: 27–41.

Bakhtin, M. M. (1981) 'Discourse in the novel', in: M. Holquist (ed.), *The dialogic imagination: Four essays by M. M. Bakhtin*, Austin: University of Texas Press.

Basso, E. B. (1992) 'Contextualization in Kalapalo narratives', in: A. Duranti and C. Goodwin (eds), *Rethinking context. Language as an interactive phenomenon*, Cambridge: Cambridge University Press, 253–271.

Bateson, G. (1972) *Steps to an ecology of mind*, New York: Ballentine.

Belle, W. van (1987) 'Assertive speech acts in psychotic discourse', in: R. Wodak and P. van de Craen (eds), *Neurotic and psychotic language behaviour*, Clevedon: Multilingual Matters Ltd: 332–346.

Berenst, J. (1986) 'Conversation control in doctor patient interaction', in: T. Ensink, A. van Essen and T. van der Geest (eds), *Discourse analysis and public life*, Dordrecht: Foris, 123–147.

Berger, P. L. and T. Luckmann (1966) *The social construction of reality*, New York: Doubleday and Company.

Bernstein, B. (1964) 'Elaborated and restricted codes: Their origins and some consequences', in: D. Hymes and J. Gumperz (eds), *The ethnography of communication, American Anthropologist 66*: 55–69.

Bijsterveld, D. van (1982) 'Enkele pragmatische aspecten van conversaties met schizofrene mensen', *Gramma 6/2*: 104–125.

—— (1987) 'On the problem of accessibility in conversations with schizophrenic people', in: R. Wodak and P. van de Craen (eds), *Neurotic and psychotic language behaviour*, Clevedon: Multilingual Matters Ltd, 304–332.

Bock, P. K. (1980) *Continuities in psychological anthropology. A historical introduction*, San Francisco: W. H. Freeman and Company.

Booth, W. C. (1983) 'Freedom of interpretation: Bakhtin and the challenge of feminist critisism', in: W. Mitchell (ed.), *The politics of interpretation*, 51–83.

Bosch, R. J. van den (1990) 'Schizofrenie en andere functionele stoornissen', in: W. Vandereycken, C. Hoogduin and P. Emmelkamp (eds), *Handboek psychopathologie, deel 1*, Houten/Antwerpen: Bohn Stafleu Van Loghum.

—— (1993) *Schizofrenie. Subjectieve ervaringen en cognitief onderzoek*. Houten: Bohn Stafleu Van Lochum.

Boyle, M. (1990) *Schizophrenia. A scientific delusion?* London: Routledge.

Brooks, P. (1984) *Reading for the plot: design and intention in narrative*, New York: A. A. Knopf.

Brown, R. (1973) 'Schizophrenia, language, and reality', *American Psychologist 28*: 395–403.

Caughey, J. L. (1984) *Imaginary social worlds. A cultural approach*, Lincoln/London: University of Nebraska Press.

Caw, P. (1974) 'Operational, representational, and explanatory models', *American Anthropologist 76/1*: 1–11.

Chaika, E. (1981) 'How shall a discourse be understood?', *Discourse Processes 4*: 71–88.

Chapman, L. and J. Chapman (1965) 'Interpretation of words in schizophrenia', *Journal of Personality and Social Psychology 1*: 135–146.

Church, K. (1995) *Forbidden narratives. Critical autobiography as social science*. London: Gordon and Breach.

Cook, J. C. (1971) 'Interpreting and decoding autistic communication', *Perspectives in Psychiatric Care 9*: 24–28.

Corin, E. E. (1990) 'Facts and meaning in psychiatry. An anthropological approach to the lifeworld of schizophrenics', *Culture, Medicine and Psychiatry 14/2*: 153–189.

Crapanzano, V. (1977) 'Preface', in: V. Crapanzano and V. Garrison (eds), *Case studies in spirit possession*. New York: Wiley and Sons.

Csordas, T. J. (1990) 'Embodiment as a paradigm for anthropology', *Ethos 18*: 5–47.

—— (1994) *Embodiment and experience. The existential ground of culture and self.* Cambridge: Cambridge University Press.

Cullberg, J. (1989) *Dynamik psykiatri*, Stockholm: Natur och Kultur.

D'Andrade, R. (1981) 'The cultural part of cognition', *Cognitive Science 5*: 179–195.

—— (1984) 'Cultural meaning systems', in: R. Shweder and R. Levine (eds), *Culture theory: essays on the social origin of mind, self, and emotion*, Chicago: University of Chicago Press, 88–123.

—— (1992) 'Schemas and motivation', in: R. D'Andrade and C. Strauss (eds), *Human motives and cultural models*, Cambridge: Cambridge University Press, 23–45.

D'Andrade, R. and C. Strauss (eds) (1992) *Human motives and cultural models*, Cambridge: Cambridge University Press.

Davis, K. (1988) *Power under the microscope: toward a grounded theory of gender relations in medical encounters*, Dordrecht/Providence, RI: Foris Publications.

Deane, W. N. (1963) 'On talking with the deluded schizophrenic patient in social therapy', *Journal of Indivdual Psychology 19*: 191–203.

Devereux, G. (1954) 'Normal and abnormal: the key problem of psychiatric anthropology', in: G. Devereux, *Some uses of anthropology: theoretical and applied*. Washington, DC: Washington Anthropological Society, 23–48.

—— (1980) *Basic problems of ethnopsychiatry*, Chicago: University of Chicago Press.

Devisch, R. (1993) *Weaving the threads of life. The Khita Gyn-Eco-Logical healing cult among the Yaka*, Chicago: University of Chicago Press.

DiGiacomo, S. (1987) 'Biomedicine as a cultural system. An anthropologist in the kingdom of the sick', in: H. Baer (ed.), *Encounters with biomedicine*. New York: Gordon and Breach, 315–347.

Douglas, M. (1966) *Purity and danger. An analysis of the concepts of pollution and taboo*, London: Routledge and Kegan Paul.

—— (1982) *Natural symbols*, New York: Pantheon Books.

DSM-III-R (1988) *Beknopte handleiding bij de diagnostische criteria van de DSM-III-R*, trans. G. Koster van Groos, Amsterdam: Swets and Zeitlinger. (American Psychiatric Association. 1987. *Quick reference to the diagnostic criteria from DSM-III-R*. Washington, DC: American Psychiatric Association).

Dumont, L. (1970) *Homo hierarchicus*, Chicago: University of Chicago Press.

Duranti, A. and C. Goodwin (eds) (1992) *Rethinking context. Language as an interactive phenomenon*, Cambridge: Cambridge University Press.

Estroff, S. (1981) *Making it crazy. An ethnography of psychiatric clients in an American community*, Berkeley: University of California Press.

—— (1993) 'Identity, disability, and schizophrenia: the problem of chronicity', in: S. Lindenbaum and M. Lock (eds), *Knowledge, power and practice*, Berkeley: University of California Press, 247–287.

Ewing, K. P. (1990) 'The illusion of wholeness: "culture", "self", and the experience of inconsistency', *Ethos 18/3*: 251–278.

Feder, L. (1980) *Madness in literature*, Princeton, NJ: Princeton University Press.

Foster, N. (1983) *The anti-aesthetic: essays on postmodern culture*, Port Townsend, WA: Bay Press.

Foucault, M. (1964) *La folie, l'absence d'œuvre*, Paris: La Table Ronde.

—— (1964) *The history of sexuality. Vol. I: An introduction*, Harmondsworth: Penguin.

—— (1966) *Les mots et les choses*, Paris: Gallimard.

—— (1972) *The archeology of knowledge*, New York: Pantheon Books.

Frank, A. (1994) 'Reclaiming an orphan genre: the first-person narrative of illness', *Literature and Medicine 13/1*: 1–21.

—— (1995) *The wounded storyteller: body, illness, and ethics*, Chicago: University of Chicago Press.

Freeman, T. (1973) *A psychoanalytic study of the psychosis*, New York: International Universities Press Inc.

Freud, S. (1913) *Totem und Tabu: Einige Übereinstimmungen im Seelenleben der Wilden und der Neurotiker*, Leipzig: Heller.
—— (1920) *Jenseits des Lustprinzips*. Studienausgabe III, 213–272.
—— (1924) Der Realitätsverlust bei Neurose und Psychose (1924), *Freud, Psychoanalytische Theorie Deel 3*. (1988)
Frosch, J. (1983) *The psychotic process*, New York: International Universities Press Inc.
Gaines, A. D. (1979) 'Definitions and diagnosis', *Culture, Medicine and Psychiatry 3/4*: 381–418.
—— (1992) *Ethnopsychiatry. The cultural construction of professional and folk psychiatries*, Albany: State University of New York Press.
Gaines, A. D. and P. E. Farmer (1986) 'Visible saints: social cynosures and dysphoria in the Mediterranean tradition', *Culture, Medicine and Psychiatry 10*: 295–330.
Gale, J. E. (1991) *Conversation analysis of therapeutic discourse: the pursuit of a therapeutic agenda*, Norwood, NJ: Ablex Publishing Corporation.
Garfinkel, H. (1967) *Studies in ethnomethodology*, Englewood Cliffs, NJ: Prentice Hall.
Gatewood, J. (1983) 'Loose talk: linguistic competence and recognition ability', *American Anthropologist 85/2*: 378–387.
Geertz, C. (1973) *The interpretation of cultures*, New York: Basic Books.
Gell, A. (1979) 'Reflections on a cut finger: taboo in the Umeda conception of the self', in: R. Hook (ed.), *Fantasy and symbol. Studies in anthropological interpretation*. New York: Academic Press, 133–149.
Gernaat, H. (1993) 'Het bellop van schizofrenie in Afrika', *Tijdschrift voor Psychiatrie 35/9*: 612–625.
Giel, R. (1984) 'Onze moeite met moeilijke mensen', *Tijdschrift voor Psychiatrie 26/4*: 244–262.
Giel, R., Y. Kitaw, F. Workneh and R. Mesfin (1974) 'Ticket to heaven: psychiatric illness in a religious community in Ethiopia', *Social Science and Medicine 8*: 549–556.
Gilmore, P. (1985) 'Silence and sulking: emotional displays in the classroom', in: D. Tannen and M. Saville-Troike (eds), *Perspectives on silence*, Norwood, NJ: Ablex, 139–165.
Girard, G. (1990) *Wat vanaf het begin der tijden verborgen was*, Kampen: Kok Agora (trans. J. Kleisen. Original: *Des choses cachées depuis la fondation du monde*. 1978. Paris: Grasset).
Girard, R. (1978) *To double business bound: essays on literature, mimesis and anthropology*, Baltimore, MD: Johns Hopkins University Press.
Goffman, E. (1959) *The presentation of self in every day life*, Garden City, NY: Doubleday.
—— (1961a) *Asylums: essays on the social situation of mental patients and other inmates*, Garden City, NY: Doubleday.
—— (1961b) *Encounters: two studies in the sociology of interactions*, Indianapolis: Bobbs-Merill.
—— (1963a) *Stigma. Notes on the management of spoiled identity*, Englewood Cliffs, NJ: Prentice Hall.
—— (1963b) *Behaviour in public places: notes on the social organization of gatherings*, New York: Free Press.
—— (1967) *Interaction ritual: essays in face-to-face behavior*, Garden City, NY: Doubleday.
—— (1971) *Strategic action*, Philadelphia: University of Pennsylvania Press.

—— (1974) *Frame analysis: an essay on the organization of experience*, New York: Harper and Row.

Goldschmidt, W. (1976) 'Absent eyes and idle hands: socialization for low affect among the Sebei', in: T. Schwartz (ed.), *Socialization as cultural communication*, Berkeley: University of California Press, 65–72.

Goldstein, M. J., D. J. Miklowitz, A. M. Strachan, J. A. Doane, K. H. Nuechterlein and D. Feingold (1989) 'Patterns of expressed emotion and patient coping styles that characterise the families of recent onset schizophrenics', *British Journal of Psychiatry* 155/supp.5: 107–111.

Good, B. (1994) *Medicine, rationality and experience. An anthropological perspective*, Cambridge: Cambridge University Press.

Good, B., H. Herrera, M. Delvecchio Good and J. Cooper (1985) 'Reflexivity, counter-transference and clinical ethnography: a case from a psychiatric cultural consultation clinic', in: R. Hahn and A. D. Gaines (eds), *Physicians of western medicine. Anthropological approaches to theory and practice*, Dordrecht: Reidel, 193–223.

Goolishian, H. and L. Winderman (1988) 'Constructivism, autopoiesis and problem determined systems', *Irish Journal of Psychology* 9/1 (special issue): 130–144.

Grice, H. (1975) 'Logic and conversation', in: P. Cole and J. Morgan (eds), *Syntax and semantics, Vol. 3, Speech acts*, New York: Academic Press.

Gumperz, J. J. (1982a) *Discourse strategies*, Cambridge: Cambridge University Press.

—— (1982b) *Language and social identity*, Cambridge: Cambridge University Press.

—— (1992) 'Contextualization and understanding', in: A. Duranti and C. Goodwin (eds), *Rethinking context. Language as an interactive phenomenon*, Cambridge: Cambridge University Press, 229–253.

Gunderson, J. G., A. F. Frank and H. M. Katz (1984) 'Effects of psychotherapy in schizophrenia, II. Comparative outcome of two forms of treatment', *Schizophrenia Bulletin* 10: 564–598.

Haaster, H. van (1991) *Wartaal. Een onderzoek naar methoden van competentieverhoging in de geestelijke gezondheidszorg*, Amsterdam: Thesis.

Habermas, J. (1988) *Nachmetaphysisches Denken: Philosophische Aufsätze*, Frankfurt am Main: Suhrkamp.

—— (1990) *Moral consciousness and communicative action*, Cambridge, MA: MIT Press.

Hall, E. T. (1973) *The silent language*, New York: Anchor Press.

Hart, O. van der (1981) 'Het gebruik van mythen en rituelen in psychotherapie', *Maandblad voor Geestelijke Volksgezondheid 6*: 529–545.

Harvey, P. D. (1983) 'Speech competence in manic and schizophrenic psychoses: the association between clinically rated thought disorder and cohesion and reference performance', *Journal of Abnormal Psychology 92/3*: 368–377.

Have, P. ten (1987) *Sequenties en formuleringen. Aspecten van de interactionele organisatie van huisarts-spreekuurgesprekken*, Amsterdam: Academisch Proefschrift Universiteit van Amsterdam.

—— (1991a) 'The doctor is silent: observations on episodes without vocal receipt during medical consultations', in: B. Conein, M. de Fornel and L. Quéré (eds), *Les formes de la conversation, Vol. 2*. Issy-les-Moulinaux: CNET.

—— (1991b) 'Medische ondervraging: tussentijdse overwegingen bij een lopend onderzoek', in: R. van Hout and E. Huls (eds), *Artikelen van de eerste sociolinguistische conferentie*, Delft: Eburon, 207–223.

Have, P. ten and M. Komter (1982) 'De angst voor de tape: over bezwaren tegen het gebruik van de bandrecorder voor onderzoek', in: C. Bouw, F. Bovenkerk, K. Bruin and L. Brunt (eds), *Hoe weet je dat? Wegen van sociaal onderzoek*, Amsterdam: Wetenschappelijke uitgeverij, 228–242.

Heylighen, F., E. Rosseel and F. Demeyere (eds) (1991) *Self-steering and cognition in complex systems*, New York: Gordon and Breach.

Hoenig, J. (1969) *The desegregation of the mentally ill*, London: Routledge and Kegan Paul.

—— (1983) 'The concept of schizophrenia', *The British Journal of Psychiatry 142*: 547–556.

Hoffman, L. (1988) 'A constructivist position for family therapy', *Irish Journal of Psychology 9/1* (special issue): 110–130.

Hoffman, R. E. (1986a) 'Tree structures, the work of listening, and schizophrenic discourse: a reply to Beveridge and Brown', *Brain and Language 27*: 385–392.

—— (1986b) 'Verbal hallucinations and language production processes in schizophrenia', *The Behavioral and Brain Sciences 9*: 503–548.

Holland, D. (1992) 'How cultural systems become desire: a case study of American romance', in: R. D'Andrade and C. Strauss (eds), *Human motives and cultural models*, Cambridge: Cambridge University Press, 61–89.

Holland, D. and N. Quinn (eds) (1987) *Cultural models in language and thought*, Cambridge: Cambridge University Press.

Holland, D. and D. Skinner (1987) 'Prestige and intimacy: the cultural models behind the American's talk about gender types', in: D. Holland and N. Quinn (eds), *Cultural models in language and thought*, Cambridge: Cambridge University Press.

Hoorde, H. van (1986) 'Statistriatrie', *Tijdschrift voor Psychiatrie 28/1*: 6–14.

Hotchkiss, A. and P. Harvey (1986) 'Linguistic analysis of speech disorder in psychosis', *Clinical Psychology Review 6*: 155–175.

Jablensky, A., N. Sartorius, G. Ernberg, M. Anker, A. Korten, J. E. Cooper, R. Day and A. Bertelsen (1992) 'Schizophrenia: manifestations, incidence and course in different cultures. A World Health Organization ten country study', *Psychological Medicine 20* (suppl.): 7–97.

Jacobsen, E. (1967) *Psychotic conflict and reality*, New York: International Universities Press.

Jansen, W. (1982) 'Mythe of macht. Langdurige zwangerschappen in Noord Afrika', *Tijdschrift voor vrouwenstudies 2*: 98–119.

Jenner, J. A. (1992) 'Het non-suicide-contract: een vormkeus', *Tijdschrift voor Psychiatrie 34/1*: 54–59.

Johnston, M. and P. Holzman (1979) *Assessing schizophrenic thinking*, San Francisco: Jossey Bass Publishers.

Jongerius, A., A. van Gool and R. Laport (1991) 'Ervaringen van familieleden rondom een psychiatrische opname: Verslag van een veldonderzoek', *Tijdschrift voor Psychiatrie 33/4*: 276–286.

Kaplan, B. (1964) *The inner world of mental illness*, New York: Harper and Row.

Katz, R. (1989) 'Healing and transformation: perspectives on development, education and community', in: C. Ward (ed.). *Altered states of consciousness and mental health*, London: Sage, 207–229.

Keesing, R. M. (1987) 'Models, "folk" and "cultural": paradigms regained', in: D. Holland and N. Quinn (eds), *Cultural models in language and thought*, Cambridge: Cambridge University Press, 369–395.

Kerkhof, A. (1985) *Suicide en geestelijke gezondheidszorg*, Lisse: Swetz and Zeitlinger.

Kernberg, O. (1975) *Borderline conditions and pathological narcissism*, New York: Jason Aronson.

Kirmeyer, L. (1993) 'Healing and the invention of metaphor: the effectiveness of symbols revisited', *Culture, Medicine, and Psychiatry 17/2*: 161–197.

Kleinman, A. (1988) *Rethinking psychiatry. From cultural category to personal experience*, New York: The Free Press.

—— (1995) *Writing at the margin. Discourse between anthropology and medicine*, Berkeley: University of California Press.

Kohut, H. (1971) *Narzissmus*, Frankfurt: Suhrkamp.

Kooy, M. (1992) *Met mij is niets aan de hand. Leven met een psychotische partner*, Haarlem: De Toorts.

Kosinsky, J. (1965) *The painted bird*, New York: Bantam.

Kramer, F. (1990) *Geschiedenis van de zorg voor geesteszieken*, Lochem: Uitgeversmaatschappij De Tijdstroom.

Krumeich, A. (1994) *The blessings of motherhood. Health, pregnancy and child care in Dominica*, Amsterdam: Het Spinhuis.

Kubie, L. S. (1953) 'The distortion of the symbolic process in neurosis and psychosis', *Journal of the American Psychoanalytic Association 1*: 59–86.

Kuiper, P. C. (1980) *Verborgen betekenissen. Psychoanalyse, fenomenologie, hermeneutiek*, Deventer: Van Loghum Slaterus.

Kuipers, J. C. (1989) ' "Medical discourse" in anthropological context: views of language and power', *Medical Anthropology Quarterly 3/2*: 99–123.

Kuipers, L., D. Sturgeon, R. Berkowitz and J. Leff (1983) 'Characteristics of expressed emotion: its relationship to speech and looking in schizophrenic patients and their relatives', *British Journal of Clinical Psychology 22*: 257–264.

Labov, W. and D. Fanshel (1977) *Therapeutic discourse: psychotherapy as conversation*, New York: Academic Press.

Lacan, J. (1966) *Écrits*. Paris: Éditions du Seuil.

Laing, R. D. (1971) *The politics of family, and other essays*, London: Tavistock Publications.

Lakoff, G. and M. Johnson (1980) *Metaphors we live by*, Chicago/London: University of Chicago Press.

Lakoff, R. (1982) 'Persuasive discourse and ordinary conversation, with examples from advertising, in: D. Tannen (ed.), *Analyzing discourse: text and talk*, Washington, DC: GU Press, 25–42.

LeCours, A. and M. Varnier-Clement (1976) 'Schizophasia and jargonaphasia: a comparative description with comments on Chaika's and Fromkin's respective looks at "schizophrenic" language', *Brain and Language 3*: 516–565.

Leech, G. (1983) *Principles of pragmatics*, London: Longman.

Leff, J. and C. Vaughn (1981) 'The role of maintenance therapy and relatives' expressed emotion in relapse of schizophrenia: a two-year follow-up', *British Journal of Psychiatry 139*: 102–104.

—— (1992) 'The international pilot study of schizophrenia: five-year follow-up findings', *Psychological Medicine 22*: 131–145.

Legemaate, J. (1991) 'Informed consent in de psychiatrie', *Tijdschrift voor Psychiatrie 33/7*: 496–499.

Lehtonen, J. and K. Sajavaara (1985) 'The silent Finn', in: D. Tannen and M. Saville-Troike (eds), *Perspectives on silence*, Norwood, NJ: Ablex, 193–205.

Lévi-Strauss, C. (1962) *Totemism*, Boston: Beacon Press.

—— (1996) *The savage mind*, Oxford: Oxford University Press.

Levy, R. I. (1984) 'Emotion, knowing, and culture', in: R. Shweder and R. A. LeVine (eds), *Culture theory. Essays on mind, self, and emotion*, Cambridge: Cambridge University Press, 214–238.

Light, D. (1980) *Becoming psychiatrists: the professional transformation of self*, New York: Norton.

Littlewood, R. (2000) 'Psychiatry's culture', in: V. Skultans and J. Cox (eds), *Anthropological approaches to psychological medicine. Crossing bridges*, London: Jessica Kingsley, 66–94.

Littlewood, R. and M. Lipsedge (1989) *Aliens and alienists: ethnic minorities and psychiatry*, London: Unwin Hyman.

Loois, H. (1964) 'Het hospitalisatiesyndroom', *Tijdschrift voor ziekenverpleging 22*.

Lutz, C. A. (1985) 'Depression and the translation of emotional worlds', in: A. Kleinman and B. Good (eds), *Culture and depression*, Berkeley: University of California Press, 63–101.

—— (1987) 'Goals, events, and understanding in Ifaluk emotion theory', in: D. Holland and N. Quinn (eds), *Cultural models in language and thought*, Cambridge: Cambridge University Press, pp. 290–313.

—— (1990) 'Engendered emotion: gender, power, and the rhetoric of emotional control in American discourse', in: C. Lutz and L. Abu-Lughod (eds), *Language and the politics of emotion*, Cambridge: Cambridge University Press, 69–92.

Lutz, C. A. and L. Abu-Lughod (eds) (1990) *Language and the politics of emotion*, Cambridge: Cambridge University Press.

McGlashan, T. H. (1984) 'The chessnut lodge follow-up 1 study', *Archives of General Psychiatry 41*: 586–601.

Maher, B. (1972) 'The language of schizophrenia: a review and interpretation', *British Journal of Psychiatry 120*: 3–17.

Maher, B., T. Manschreck and M. Rucklos (1980) 'Contextual constraint and the recall of verbal material in schizophrenia: the effect of thought disorder', *British Journal of Psychiatry 137*: 69–73.

Mahler, M. (1969) *Symbiose und Individuation*, Stuttgart: Klett.

Malinowski, B. (1922) 'Argonauts of Western Pacific: an account of native enterprise and adventure in the archipelagoes of Melanesian New Guinea', in: *Studies in economics and political science: Series of monographs by writers connected with the London School of Economics and Political Science*. London: Routledge.

Maltz, D. N. (1985) 'Joyful noise and reverent silence: the significance of noise in Pentecostal worship', in: D. Tannen and M. Saville-Troike (eds), *Perspectives on silence*, Norwood, NJ: Ablex, 113–139.

Martínez-Hernáez, A. (2000) *What's behind the symptom? On psychiatric observation and anthropological understanding*, New York: Gordon and Breach.

Mazeland, H. (1992) *Vraag/antwoord-sequenties*, Amsterdam: Stichting Neerlandistiek.

Miller, A. (1991) *Het drama van het begaafde kind. Een studie over narcisme*, Houten: Het Wereldvenster (trans. T. Davids. Original title 1979, *Das Drama des begabten Kindes und die Suche nach dem wahren Selbst*).

Mishler, E. (1984) *The discourse of medicine: dialectics of medical interviews*, Norwood, NJ: Ablex.

Moerman, M. (1988) *Talking culture. Ethnography and conversation analysis*, Philadelphia: University of Pennsylvania Press.

Mooy, A. (1988) *Taal en verlangen. Lacans theorie van de psychoanalyse*, Meppel: Boom.

Moyaert, P. (1982a) 'Taal, lichamelijkheid en affect in de schizofrenie', *Tijdschrift voor Psychiatrie 24/1*: 49–69.

—— (1982b) 'Taal, lichamelijkheid en affect in de schizofrenie (II)', *Tijdschrift voor Psychiatrie 24/11–12*: 696–707.

—— (1982c) 'Een betekenisproduktie zonder geschiedenis', in: H. Bakx, J. Bernlef, P. de Meijer, H. Tentije and J. Vogelaar (eds), *Gestoorde teksten, verstoorde teksten. Raster 24*: 135–153.

Murphy, R. (1987) *The body silent*, New York: Henry Holt.

Nichter, M. (1981) 'Idioms of distress: alternatives in the expression of psychosocial distress: a case study from South India', *Culture, Medicine and Psychiatry 5*: 379–408.

Obeyesekere, G. (1985) 'Buddhism, depression and the work of culture in Sri Lanka', in: A. Kleinman and B. Good (eds), *Culture and depression*, Berkeley: University of California Press.

—— (1990) *The work of culture. Symbolic transformation in psychoanalysis and anthropology*, Chicago: University of Chicago Press.

Ochs, E. (1992) 'Indexing gender', in: A. Duranti and C. Goodwin (eds), *Rethinking context. Language as an interactive phenomenon*, Cambridge: Cambridge University Press.

Oderwald, A. (1985) *Geneeskunde, kritiek en semiologie*, Leuven/Amersfoort: Acco.

Oey, H. (1990) 'Schrijven met het scheermes', *NRC*, 6 November.

Oosterhuis, H. (1993) 'Zonder inspirerend toekomstbeeld is het moeilijk leven', *De Volkskrant*, 27 January.

Perry, J. W. (1976) *Roots of renewal in myth and madness*, San Francisco: Jossey-Bass.

Podvoll, E. M. (1990) *The seduction of madness: revolutionary insights into the world of psychosis and a compassionate approach to recovery at home*, New York: Harper Collins.

Pols, J. (1984) *Mythe and macht. Over de kritische psychiatrie van Thomas S. Szasz*, Nijmegen: Sun.

Pool, R. (1989) *There must have been something: interpretations of illness and misfortune in a Cameroon village*, PhD thesis, Amsterdam: University of Amsterdam.

Porter, R. (1987) *A social history of madness: stories of the insane*, London: Weidenfeld and Nicholson.

Price, L. (1987) 'Ecuadorian illness stories: cultural knowledge in natural discourse', in: D. Holland and N. Quinn (eds), *Cultural models in language and thought*, Cambridge: Cambridge University Press, 313–343.

Quinn, N. (1987) 'Convergent evidence for a cultural model of American marriage', in: D. Holland and N. Quinn (eds), *Cultural models in language and thought*, Cambridge: Cambridge University Press.

—— (1992) 'The motivational force of self-understanding: evidence from wives' inner conflicts', in: R. D'Andrade and C. Strauss (eds), *Human motives and cultural models*, Cambridge: Cambridge University Press, 90–127.

Rabelais, F. (1980) *Gargantua en Pantagruel*, Amsterdam: de Arbeiderspers. Vert. J. A. Sandfort.

Rabinow, P. and W. Sullivan (eds) (1979) *Interpretive social science*. Berkeley: University of California Press.

Rappaport, R. (1978) 'Adaptation and the structure of ritual', in: N. Blurton-Jones and V. Reynolds (eds), *Human behavior and adaptation, Vol. 18*, New York: Halsted Press.

Rehbein, J. (1977) *Komplexes Handeln*, Stuttgart: Metzler.

Rhodes, L. (1991) *Emptying beds. The work of an emergency psychiatric unit*, Berkeley: University of Califonia Press.

Richters, A. (1988) 'Psychiatrische classificering en geestelijke gezondheid. Een feministisch-antropologische kritiek', in: J. Rolies (ed.), *De gezonde burger. Gezondheid als norm*, Nijmegen: Sun, 141–175.

—— (1991) *De medisch antropoloog als verteller en vertaler*, Academisch Proefschrift, Delft: Eburon.

Ricoeur, P. (1969) *The symbolism of evil*, Boston: Beacon.

Rochester, S. and J. Martin (1979) *Crazy talk. A study of the discourse of schizophrenic people*, New York: Plenum Press.

Romme, M. A. J. (1967) *Doel en middel: Een bijdrage tot de medische economie door middel van een sociaal geneeskundige exploratie van de selectie voor opname van psychiatrische patiënten*. Proefschrift Universiteit van Amsterdam.

Romme, M. A. J. and A. Escher (eds) (1990) *Stemmen horen accepteren*, Maastricht: Rijksuniversiteit Limburg.

Rosenwald, G. C. and R. L. Ochberg (eds) (1992) *Storied lives. The cultural politics of self-understanding*, New Haven, CT: Yale University Press.

Rosseel, E. (1990) 'New cybernetics and the social sciences', in: F. Heylighen, E. Rosseel and F. Demeyere (eds), *Self-steering and cognition in complex systems*, New York: Gordon and Breach, 17–33.

Rümke, H. C. (1948) *Studies en voordrachten over de psychiatrie*, Amsterdam, 1–16.

Sachs, H. and E. Schlegoff (1979) 'Two preferences in the organization of reference to persons in conversation and their interaction', in: G. Psathas (ed.), *Everyday language: studies in ethnomethodology*, New York: Erlbaum, 15–21.

Sacks, H., E. A. Schlegoff and G. Jefferson (1974) 'A symplest systematics for the organization of turn-taking for conversation', *Language 50*: 696–735.

Sadger, I. (1929) 'Ein Beitrag zum Problem des Selbstmord', *Z. psychoanal. Päd 3*: 389.

Salzinger, K., S. Portnoy, D. Pisoni and R. Feldman (1970) 'The immediacy hypothesis and response-produced stimuli in schizophrenic speech', *Journal of Abnormal Psychology 76*: 258–264.

Saunders, G. R. (1985) 'Silence and noise as emotion management styles: an Italian case', in: D. Tannen and M. Saville-Troike (eds), *Perspectives on silence*, Norwood, NJ: Ablex, 165–185.

Saville-Troike, M. (1985) 'The place of silence in an integrated theory of communication', in: D. Tannen and M. Saville-Troike (eds), *Perspectives on silence*, Norwood, NJ: Ablex, 3–21.

Scarry, E. (1985) *The body in pain. The making and unmaking of the world*, Oxford: Oxford University Press.

Schiffrin, D. (1987) *Discourse markers*, Cambridge: Cambridge University Press.

Schilder, P. (1933) 'Neuroses and psychoses', in: L. Bender (ed.), *On neurosis, Paul Schilder*, New York: International Universities Press Inc, 1–16.

Schlegoff, E. (1968) 'Sequencing in conversational openings', *American Anthropologist 70*: 1075–1095.

—— (1979) 'The relevance of repair to syntax-for-conversation', in: T. Givón (ed.), *Syntax and semantics: discourse and syntax*, New York: Academic Press, 261–299.

—— (1982) 'Discourse as an interactional achievement: some uses of "uh huh" and other things that come between sentences', in: D. Tannen (ed.), *Analyzing discourse: text and talk*, Washington, DC: Georgetown University Press, 71–93.

Schlegoff, E. A., G. Jefferson and H. Sachs (1977) 'The preference for self correction in the organization of repair in conversation', *Language 53*: 361–382.

Schutz, A. (1971) 'On multiple realities', in: A. Schutz, *Collected papers, Vol. 1: The problem of social reality*, The Hague: Martinus Nijhoff.

Sciortino, R. M. E. (1992) *Care-takers of cure. A study of health centre nurses in rural Central Java*, Amsterdam: Academisch Proefschrift.

Scollon, R. (1985) 'The machine stops: silence in the metaphor of malfunction', in: D. Tannen and M. Saville-Troike (eds), *Perspectives on silence*, Norwood, NJ: Ablex, 21–31.

Scott, J. (1985) *Weapons of the weak. Everyday forms of resistance*, New York: Yale University Press.

Searles, H. F. (1961) 'Schizophrenic communication', *Psychoanalysis and the Psychoanalytic Review 128*: 3–50.

Shafer, R. (1984) 'The pursuit of failure and the idealization of unhappiness', *American Psychologist 39*: 398–405.

Sherzer, J. (1987) 'A diversity of voices: men's and women's speech in ethnographic perspective', in: S. Philips, S. Steele and C. Tanz (eds), *Language, gender and sex in a comparative perspective*, Cambridge: Cambridge University Press.

Shweder, R. A. (1991) *Thinking through cultures. Expeditions in cultural psychology*, Cambridge, MA: Harvard University Press.

Shweder, R. A. and E. Bourne (1984) 'Does the concept of the person vary cross-culturally?', in: R. A. Shweder and R. Levine (eds), *Culture theory. Essays on mind, self and emotion*. Cambridge: Cambridge University Press, 158–200.

Shweder, R. A. and R. Levine (eds) (1984) *Culture theory. Essays on mind, self and emotion*, Cambridge: Cambridge University Press.

Skultans, V. (1991) 'Anthropology and psychiatry: the uneasy alliance', *Transcultural Psychiatric Research Review 28/1*: 5–25.

Smith, E. (1970) 'Associative and editing processes in schizophrenic communication', *Journal of Abnormal Psychology 75*: 182–186.

Solomon, R. (1984) 'Getting angry: the Jamesian theory of emotion in anthropology', in: R. Shweder and R. Levine (eds), *Culture theory. Essays on mind, self, and emotion*, Cambridge: Cambridge University Press, 238–257.

Sperber, D. (1975) *Rethinking symbolism*, Cambridge: Cambridge University Press.

Sperber, D. and D. Wilson (1986) *Relevance. Communication and cognition*. Oxford: Basil Blackwell.

Stein, H. F. (1991) *American medicine as culture*, Boulder, CO: Westview Press.

Strauss, C. (1992) 'What makes Tony run? Schemas as motives reconsidered', in: R. D'Andrade and C. Strauss (eds), *Human motives and cultural models*, Cambridge: Cambridge University Press, 191–224.

Sudnow, D. (1967) *Passing on: the social organization of dying*, Englewood Cliffs, NJ: Prentice-Hall.

Sullivan, H. S. (1974) *Schizophrenia as a human process*, New York: Norton.

Swaan, A. de (1979) *De opkomst van het psychotherapeutisch bedrijf*, Utrecht: Het Spectrum.

Synnott, A. (1993) *The body social. Symbolism, self and society*, London: Routledge.
Szasz, T. (1976) *Schizophrenia: the sacred symbol of psychiatry*, New York: Basic Books.
—— (1994) *Cruel compassion: psychiatric control of society's unwanted*, New York: Wiley.
Tannen, D. (1990) *You just don't understand: women and men in conversation*, New York: Morrow.
Taussig, M. T. (1980) 'Reification and the consciousness of the patient', *Social Science and Medicine 148*: 3–13.
Trimbos, K. (1957) *Antipsychiatrie, een overzicht*, Deventer: Van Loghum Slaterus.
Turnbull, C. M. (1972) *The mountain people*, London: Pan Books.
Turner, V. (1974) *Dramas, fields and metaphors. Symbolic action in human society*, Ithaca, NY and London: Cornell University Press.
—— (1975) *Revelation and divination in Ndembu ritual*, Ithaca, NY and London: Cornell University Press.
Tyler, S. (1978) *The said and the unsaid. Mind, meaning, and culture*, New York: Academic Press.
Van Dongen, E. (1989) *Die deur is de wereld. Communicatie en betekenisgeving in een therapeutische gemeenschap*, doctoral dissertation, Utrecht: Universiteit van Utrecht.
—— (1990) 'Middelen van onderdrukking en verzet: de sociale betekenis van medicijnen in een psychiatrische afdeling', *Medische Antropologie 2/1*: 39–50.
—— (1991a) 'Werkelijkheid in waanzin: sociale aspecten in het spreken van psychotische patiënten', *Medische Antropologie 3/1*: 67–85.
—— (1991b) 'Oorlog en zakendoen. Over het gebruik van metaforen in teambesprekingen in een psychiatrisch instituut', *Tijdschrift voor Psychiatrie 33/2*: 138–145.
—— (1993a) 'Recensie van Van Haasters "Wartaal"', *Antropologische Verkenningen 12/2*: 80–81.
—— (1993b) 'Moderne gek wordt weer op narrenschip geplaatst', *De Volkskrant, Forum*, 9 April.
—— (1993c) '"Ik zit in de werkelijkheid te praten en jij in een fantasiewereld". Conversaties van psychotische mensen met hulpverleners', *Antropologische Verkenningen 12/2*: 1–24.
—— (1993d) 'Knecht van de duivel, dienaar van God. Zelfdiagnose en rituelen van een schizofreen', *Medische Antropologie 5/2*: 227–239
—— (1998) '"I wish a happy end." Hope in the lives of chronic schizophrenic patients', *Anthropology and Medicine 5/1*: 169–193.
—— (2002) *Walking stories. An oddnography of mad people's work with culture*, Amsterdam: Rozenberg Publishers.
Vos, M. S. and H. van Berkestijn (1993) 'De geschiedenis van de opleiding tot psychiater in Nederland', *Tijdschrift voor Psychiatrie 1*: 18–33.
Walker, A. (1985) 'The two faces of silence: the effect of witness hesitancy on lawyers' impressions', in: D. Tannen and M. Saville-Troike (eds), *Perspectives on silence*, Norwood, NJ: Ablex, 55–77.
Wallace, A. (1956) 'Revitalization movements: some theoretical considerations for their comparative study', *American Anthropologist 58*: 264–281.
Ward, C. A. (1989) *Altered states of consciousness and mental health*, London: Sage.
White, G. M. (1992) 'Ethnopsychology', in: T. Schwartz, G. M. White and C. A. Lutz (eds), *New directions in psychological anthropology*, Cambridge: Cambridge University Press, 21–47.

Winnicott, D. W. (1965) *The maturational processes and the facilitating environment: studies in the theory of emotional development*, London: Hogarth.

World Health Organization (WHO) (1978) *Mental disorders: glossary and guide to their classification in accordance with the ninth revision of the international classification of diseases*, Geneva: WHO.

—— (1992) *The ICD-10 classification of mental and behavioral disorders. Clinical descriptions and diagnostic guidelines*, Geneva: WHO.

Young, A. (1988) 'Reading DSM-III on PTSD: an anthropological account of a core text in American psychiatry', paper for Anthropologies of Medicine, Hamburg.

—— (1995) *The harmony of illusions. Inventing post-traumatic stress disorders*, Princeton, NJ: Princeton University Press.

Index

abnormality 37, 41, 48, 146, 220; dual
life-worlds of psychotic people 151–2,
154, 157, 164; social/cultural
conceptions 13, 14, 24, 27, 224
Abu-Lughod, L. 102
acceptance, of illness 48, 49, 60, 227
access 97
acting out 61
aggression 31, 51, 61, 65, 66, 180, 181,
183, 199, 215, 222, 223
alcoholism 31
alienation 28, 34, 35, 60, 185–97, 221
alignment (Goffman) 79
ambulant social care 14, 33, 238n3
Andreasen, N. 235n15
anger 30, 107, 178
anthropological psychiatry 4
anthropology: and psychosis 20–7, 230,
233n2; research methodology 7–10, 12,
205
anti-psychiatry 4, 14, 233n2
anxiety 132, 177, 178, 179, 180
apathy 210, 241n14
archetypal images 20
Assen, G. 230
autonomy 29, 51, 52, 65, 223, 226, 230
avoidance rituals (Goffman) 106
avoidance strategy 73, 90, 100, 110, 111,
127
Ayurvedic medicine 220

Bakhtin, M. M. 154, 215
Bateson, G. 44, 229
begging 161–6
behavior 2, 21, 35, 39–40, 43–4, 54,
152, 221, 228; concealing psychotic
world 29–30, 31, 73; disorderly and

inappropriate 50–1, 53–4, 118, 120,
135–7, 218, 219; regulation in LTR 60,
65; revealing psychotic world 31, 114,
115, 118
Berger, P. L. 57, 67
Berkesteijn, H. van 234n7
Bijsterveld, D. van 235–6n20
biomedical model 14, 15, 18, 24, 218–19
Bock, P. K. 236n26
body 25, 198, 229; touch and terror
205–14, 215, 216, 229; and the world
210–14; in the world 214–17; world
within 207–10
Booth, W. C. 215
Bosch, R. J. van den 19
boundaries 4
boundary crossing 3, 13, 30–1, 51, 53–4;
revealing psychotic world 113, 115–18,
120–4
Boyle, M. 12
bricolage 5, 25, 26, 149, 150, 154, 156,
174, 184–5, 221, 222, 232
Brooks, P. 199

care to measure 47, 50
catastrophes 211, 212
Caughey, J. L. 228
centrality/divinity 174–80, 181, 183, 184,
196, 197, 199, 213, 228
ceremonial profanities (Goffman) 114,
136–7, 215
Chaika, E. 235–6n20
chaos 37, 50–1, 54, 55, 56, 57, 70, 110,
171, 193–4, 219, 223
Chaucer, Geoffrey 214
chronic care *see* LTR
clown role 13, 75, 137, 214–15

www.ingramcontent.com/pod-product-compliance
Ingram Content Group UK Ltd.
Pitfield, Milton Keynes, MK11 3LW, UK
UKHW020357010325
455677UK00021B/505